# THE YELLOW HOUSE

## Sarah M. Broom

corsair

CORSAIR

First published in the US in 2019 by Grove Atlantic
First published in Great Britain in 2020 by Corsair

1 3 5 7 9 10 8 6 4 2

*for three women, with love and heart*

*Amelia "Lolo"*

*Auntie Elaine*

*Ivory Mae*

# Contents

# MAP

*draw me a map of what you see*
*then I will draw a map of what you never see*
*and guess me whose map will be bigger than whose?*

Kei Miller

*To learn how to read any map is to be indoctrinated*
*into that mapmaker's culture.*

Peter Turchi

From high up, fifteen thousand feet above, where the aerial photographs are taken, 4121 Wilson Avenue, the address I know best, is a minuscule point, a scab of green. In satellite images shot from higher still, my former street dissolves into the toe of Louisiana's boot. From this vantage point, our address, now mite size, would appear to sit in the Gulf of Mexico. Distance lends perspective, but it can also shade, misinterpret. From these great heights, my brother Carl would not be seen.

Carl, who is also my brother Rabbit, sits his days and nights away at 4121 Wilson Avenue at least five times a week after working his maintenance job at NASA or when he is not fishing or near to the water where he loves to be. Four thousand fifteen days past the Water, beyond all news cycles known to man, still sits a skinny man in shorts, white socks pulled up to his kneecaps, one gold picture frame around his front tooth.

Sometimes you can find Carl alone on our lot, poised on an ice chest, searching the view, as if for a sign, as if for a wonder. Or else, seated at a pecan-colored dining table with intricately carved legs, holding court. The table where Carl sometimes sits is on the spot where our living room used to be but where instead of floor there is green grass trying to grow.

See Carl gesturing with a long arm, if he feels like it, wearing dark shades even if it is night. See Rabbit with his legs crossed at the ankle, a long-legged man, knotted up.

I can see him there now, in my mind's eye, silent and holding a beer. Babysitting ruins. But that is not his language or sentiment; he would never betray the Yellow House like that.

Carl often finds company on Wilson Avenue where he keeps watch. Friends will arrive and pop their trunks, revealing coolers containing spirits on ice. "Help yourself, baby," they will say. If someone has to pee, they do it in what used to be our den. Or they use the bright-blue porta potty sitting at the back of the yard, where the shed once was. Now, this plastic, vertical bathroom is the only structure on the lot. Written on its front in white block letters on black background: CITY OF NEW ORLEANS.

I have stacked twelve or thirteen history-telling books about New Orleans. *Beautiful Crescent; New Orleans, Yesterday and Today; New Orleans as It Was; New Orleans: The Place and the People; Fabulous New Orleans; New Orleans: A Guide to America's Most Interesting City.* So on and so forth. I have thumbed through each of these, past voluminous sections about the French Quarter, the Garden District, and St. Charles Avenue, in search of the area of the city where I grew up, New Orleans East. Mentions are rare and spare, afterthoughts. There are no guided tours to this part of the city, except for the disaster bus tours that became an industry after Hurricane Katrina, carting visitors around, pointing out the great destruction of neighborhoods that were never known or set foot in before the Water, except by their residents.

Imagine that the streets are dead quiet, and you lived on those dead quiet streets, and there is nothing left of anything you once owned. Those rare survivors who are still present on the scene, working in those skeletal byways, are dressed in blue disposable jumpsuits and wearing face masks to avoid being burned by the black mold that is everywhere in their homes, climbing up the walls, forming slippery abstract figures underfoot. While this is going on and you are wondering whether you will find remains of anything that you ever loved, tourists are passing by in an air-conditioned bus snapping images of your personal destruction. There is something affirming, I can see, in the acknowledgment by the tourists of the horrendous destructive act, but it still might feel like invasion. And anyway, I do not believe the tour buses ever made it to the street where I grew up.

In one of these piled books that describes the suburbs, New Orleans East is not included, but Jefferson Parish, which lies outside city bounds, and several cemeteries are. Cemeteries, as far as I know, cannot be counted as actual neighborhoods even though local lore describes aboveground tombs as houses of the dead.

On a detailed city map once given to me by Avis Rent a Car, the French Quarter has been shaded in light turquoise, magnified in a box at the bottom of the page. New Orleans East is cut off, a point beyond, a blank space on someone's mental map. This is perhaps a practical matter. New Orleans East is fifty times the size of the French Quarter, one-fourth of the city's developed surface. Properly mapped, it might swallow the page whole.

What the Avis map does not tell you is that to travel the seven miles from the French Quarter to the Yellow House in which I grew up, you would take Interstate 10 heading east. When this portion of the interstate opened in 1968, hundreds of great oaks along Claiborne Avenue, the black shopping district for my mother and grandmother, had been chopped down, their roots evicted. One hundred fifty-five houses were demolished to make way.

Driving the interstate, you will know that you are on track when you see signs indicating VIEUX CARRÉ FINAL EXIT, but do not get off. Stay on.

After another four miles, you will arrive at the bridge we call the High Rise for the dramatic arc it makes over the Industrial Canal that connects the Mississippi River to Lake Pontchartrain but exiles eastern New Orleans from the rest of the city. Being at the top of the High Rise feels like resting on the verge of discovery, but the descent is cruel and steep.

Exit suddenly at Chef Menteur, a four-lane highway built on an ancient high ridge once traversed by Native American tribes but that now carries cars all the way to Florida or Texas. Chef Menteur bifurcates the short, industrialized end of Wilson Avenue, where I grew up, from the longer residential end of mostly brick houses and of my former elementary school, originally named Jefferson Davis after the Confederate president before becoming Ernest Morial after the first black mayor of New Orleans. It is nameless now—a field of green grass bounded by a chain-link fence.

Even as I write this, I am troubled again by what it meant for us—me and my eleven siblings—to have to cross Chef Menteur Highway, which was then and is now a sea of prostitution with cars pulling over, sometimes partway onto the sidewalk, creeping alongside you even if you were only a child on an errand; these were mostly men in cars, making deals.

Cars could drag you down Chef Menteur without realizing it, as one dragged my sister Karen when she was eight years old. Drivers in speeding cars self-destructed on this highway. Alvin, my childhood friend, would die in this way. Someone could grab and abduct you while you stood there on Chef Menteur's neutral ground, as we call medians. Or see you standing there when you did not want to be seen, as I would not, many years into young womanhood, when I avoided showing people the place where I lived. When I think of Chef Menteur Highway and of being cut off—from the other side of the street, from the city center, plain cut off—I think of all of this.

Chef Menteur was named after either a Choctaw Indian chief or a governor who lied too much. The name, translated from French, means "chief liar." This is the poetry of New Orleans names. That city hall sits on a street named lost. Perdido.

Once you have exited onto Chef Menteur, drive one mile in the far-right lane. Along the way you will pass a Chevron gas station, an auto parts store, and blank billboards advertising nothing at all. You will find yourself in what has been described in articles and books appearing in the eighties and nineties as the "true land of no return," afflicted with "overgrown yards, outdated billboards," where "weary 1960s-era commercial architecture commingle with cyclone-fenced lots . . . and mundane 1970s residential architecture." Where "a general malaise hangs over."

You will pass run-down apartment complexes on your left and on your right, in areas that used to be called the Grove, the Goose, and the Gap, where growing up, my brothers made allegiances and enemies and where a bullet grazed my brother Darryl's face in the middle of a school dance. You will pass an emptied-out building that used to be a bank where Mom and I visited the drive-through and where the teller passed lollipops with the deposit slip. You will go by Causey's Country Kitchen, the soul food restaurant where, after the Water, a luxury bus from the parking lot lodged itself into the lunch counter.

Closer to our street, you will see Natal's Supermarket, which is really only a corner store, where Mom sent me as a kid to buy "liver cheese" for one dollar a pound. Years later, a graduate student at Berkeley, I would discover that the liver cheese we paid practically nothing for was dressed up, called pâté, and cost nine dollars a pound.

At the light where Wilson Avenue intersects Chef, turn right at the foundation that once held a tire shop that used to be a laundromat where my older siblings survived Hurricane Betsy in 1965.

After you make that right turn onto the short end of Wilson Avenue, look left and you will see an empty lot where the gas station used to be and where Mr. Spanata from Italy built his family's compound. Gone now. Next door to that is the cottage where Ms. Schmidt from uptown lived before my siblings Michael and Karen and Byron rented it, at different times, but where no one lives now.

Next door to that (all the houses on the short end except for one were on the left side of the street) is a concrete slab representing the house where the Davis family lived before getting fed up with the short end of Wilson and moving elsewhere.

Then you will come upon Ms. Octavia's cream-colored shotgun house that now belongs to her granddaughter Rachelle—the only remaining legal inhabitant of the street—before finally arriving at what used to be our Yellow House.

My mother, Ivory Mae, bought this house in 1961 when she was nineteen years old. It was her first and only house. Within its walls, my mother made her world. Twelve children passed through its doors: descendants of Ivory Mae Broom and her first husband, Edward Webb; of Ivory Mae Broom and Simon Broom; and of Simon Broom and his first wife, Carrie Broom. We are Simon Jr., Deborah, Valeria, Eddie, Michael, Darryl, Carl, Karen, Troy, Byron, Lynette, and Sarah. We span the generations, born to every decade, beginning in the forties. I arrived ten hours before the eighties.

When you are babiest in a family with eleven older points of view, eleven disparate rallying cries, eleven demanding and pay-attention-to-me voices—all variations of the communal story—developing your own becomes a matter of survival. There can be, in this scenario, no neutral ground.

Yet feelings of transgression linger, the conviction that by writing down the history of the people who have come before me—who, in a way, compose me—I have upended the natural order of things.

When I call my eldest brother, Simon, at his home in North Carolina to explain all the things I want to know and why, he expresses worry that by writing this all down here, I will disrupt, unravel, and tear down everything the Broom family has ever built. He would like, now, to live in the future and forget about the past. "There is a lot we have subconsciously agreed that we don't want to know," he tells me. When he asks about my project, I am imprecise, lofty, saying I am writing about "architecture and belonging and space."

"It is a problem when you are talking too much," he says. I take his sentence down in my notebook at the moment he says it, just as he says it. I have not added a single word. Nor have I taken anything away.

In New Orleans, we tell direction by where we are in relation to the Mississippi River, in relation to water. Our house was bounded by water. The Mississippi snaked three miles to the back of us. Less than a mile away, west and south, were the Industrial Canal and its interlinking Intracoastal Waterway. Lake Pontchartrain sat two miles north. To the far east lay the Rigolets, a strait connecting Lake Pontchartrain to Lake Borgne, a brackish lagoon that opens into the Gulf of Mexico. We were surrounded by boats, barges, and trains; ingresses and egresses—a stone's throw from the Old Road, which is what we called Old Gentilly Road. My father, Simon Broom, took the Old Road to his job at NASA. Later, my brother Carl took the Old Road to his job at NASA. Same road, same maintenance job, different men. But the road is impassable now because at a certain point, illegal tire and trash dumps block the way. The train tracks perched above the Old Road were laid in the 1870s for the Louisville and Nashville Railroad, trains that passed almost nightly in my growing up. Their clacking and roar were the sounds outside my window as I tried to sleep. The Old Road could, if clear, lead you to the Michoud neighborhood, where Vietnamese immigrants settled after the Vietnam War; or to Resthaven cemetery, where my best childhood friend, Alvin, is buried; or to NASA's manufacturing plant, where rocket boosters were built for the Apollo space mission but where Hollywood fantasies are conjured now, its unused acres frequently leased as movie sets.

By bringing you here, to the Yellow House, I have gone against my learnings. *You know this house not all that comfortable for other people,* my mother was always saying.

Before it was the Yellow House, the only house I knew, it was a green house, the house my eleven siblings knew. The facts of the world before me inform, give shape and context to my own life. The Yellow House was witness to our lives. When it fell down, something in me burst. My mother is always saying, *Begin as you want to end.* But my beginning precedes me. Absences allow us one power over them: They do not speak a word. We say of them what we want. Still, they hover, pointing fingers at our backs. No place to go now but into deep ground.

# MOVEMENT I

## The World Before Me

*The things we have forgotten are housed.*
*Our soul is an abode and by remembering houses and rooms,*
*we learn to abide within ourselves.*

Gaston Bachelard

# I

## *Amelia "Lolo"*

*I*n the world before me, the world into which I was born and the world to which I belong, my grandmother, my mother's mother, Amelia, was born in 1915 or 1916 to John Gant and Rosanna Perry, a shadow of a woman about whom only scratchings are known. Even the spelling of Rosanna's name is uncertain. She appears briefly in Lafourche Parish census records for 1910 and 1920. These papers tell us that my great-grandmother lived in Raceland, Louisiana, could not read or write, and that she had been widowed. Next to my great-grandmother Rosanna's name, no form of work was ever indicated. Those are the facts as they were recorded, but this is the story as the generations tell it.

Rosanna Perry had these five children: Edna, Joseph, Freddie, my grandmother Amelia, and Lillie Mae. Doctors had warned Rosanna that another child would kill her; still, Lillie Mae was born in August 1921 when Amelia was five or six years old. It has always been said that my great-grandmother Rosanna Perry died in childbirth when she was thirty-four, but those who might know are not alive to confirm, deny, or offer alternative theories, and burial records cannot be found. Whatever the facts, Rosanna disappeared.

Of Rosanna's children, the only one ever to reside under the same roof with her was the son Joseph. Where her other four children went after being born, why they went, and with whom they lived is uncertain. And so even if Rosanna did not die giving birth to Lillie Mae, my grandmother Amelia still would not have had a mother.

Grandmother was born on Ormond Plantation, named after an Irish castle, next to which the West Indies colonial–style Louisiana replication would appear bedraggled and dim. Ormond sits haughtily still, it doesn't care, along Louisiana's River Road, seventy miles of two lanes hugging tight to the curves of the Mississippi River, its waters hidden behind levees that look like molehills. The "fabled Great Mississippi River Road," present-day brochures call it. Its "showy houses, gay piazzas, trim gardens, and numerous slave-villages, all clean and neat," read the description during its pre–Civil War heyday when tons of "white gold" sugarcane were grown and processed in Louisiana, building generational wealth and power for white plantation owners.

What modern marketers never tout is how in 1811 the largest slave revolt in American history, an army of five hundred or so, wound its way along the River Road for two days, strategically headed toward New Orleans to take over the city, stopping only to light plantations afire after loading up on weaponry. They made it far, considering—twenty of forty-one miles—before a local white militia halted them. Some slaves escaped; others were shot on the spot. Of the unlucky ones put on trial, most had their heads severed and placed on poles atop the River Road's levees— forty miles of heads, the grisly trophies of petrified whites.

Today, the "pillared splendor" (as a recent brochure describes) of the River Road's plantations is flanked and outmatched by petrochemical refineries, their silver nostrils blowing toxic smoke.

Long before the near-to-end when my grandmother would forget her life's story, she claimed July 1916 as her birth date even though it was officially recorded a year or two after the fact. Fixed details were important to stories, Amelia knew, even if you couldn't prove them.

She was named after her father, John Gant's, mother, Emelia, whom she would never meet. Grandmother's namesake presided over a large family who had spent all of their lives in St. Charles Parish, where Ormond Plantation is, in a town now called St. Rose but was then called Elkinsville after freed slave Palmer Elkins, who in the 1880s made for himself and his family a self-sufficient community composed of four dirt streets, named in the order in which they appeared: First, Second, Third, and Fourth. The Gants were tall, brooding men well known in the community. Samuel Gant, brother to Amelia's father, was pastor of Mount Zion Baptist, Grandmother's church in her later years, where her funeral service would be held and where her son Joseph still serves as deacon.

Sometime in Amelia's childhood, no one is sure exactly when, she left St. Rose where she was born for New Orleans, a thirty-minute drive away, to live with her eldest sister. Edna had married Henry Carter, whom everyone called Uncle Goody. Edna was a Jehovah's Witness, the young Amelia her right hand, toting *Watchtower* bulletins around city streets on long soul-saving sprees that netted few returns. Amelia never converted; she had the kind of mind to resist.

Edna and Uncle Goody lived uptown on Philip Street in a community of women where everyone called themselves something other than their given name, it seemed, where familial relationships were often based on need rather than blood. What you decided to call yourself, these women seemed to say, was genealogy too.

The disappeared Rosanna Perry had two sisters who were part of this community. People called her eldest sister Mama. Mama also answered to Aunt Shugah (Shew-gah), a supposedly Creolized version of Sugar except it is actually only a restating of the English word, the stress moved elsewhere. Aunt Shugah's actual name was Bertha Riens. She was also sister to Tontie Swede, short for Sweetie. Aunt Shugah was the biological mother of a woman who only ever called herself TeTe, with whom Amelia shared a sisterhood even though they were cousins.

These women, who lived in close proximity, composed a home. They were the real place—more real than the City of New Orleans—where

Amelia resided. In this world, Amelia became Lolo, another version of her name entirely, the origins of which no one can pinpoint. Everyone called her Lolo, no one uttered her given name again, not even her eventual children, which exacted on the one hand a distance between child and parent and on the other an unnatural closeness and knowing.

Lolo's life contains silent leaps with little tangible evidence to consult. But then flecks of story appear: Grandmother was a young girl living with her sister Edna, then suddenly she was fourteen years old and living in a boardinghouse on Tchoupitoulas Street in the Irish Channel neighborhood of New Orleans.

　　Along with a teenage Lolo in the boardinghouse lived John Vaughan and his wife, Sarah McCutcheon, the woman Lolo would come to call Nanan and regard as her mother and whom Lolo's children—Joseph, Elaine, and Ivory—would call Grandmother. She was Sarah Randolph by birth and Sarah McCutcheon by marriage; she was not a blood mother to Lolo, but she acted with the rights and liberties of one. Sometimes, when Sarah McCutcheon was upset she'd say, "I'm Aunt Carolina's daughter," but no one had any idea who Aunt Carolina was. And no one dared ask. It seemed an astounding riddle.

　　Two stories get told about Sarah McCutcheon: that she raised Lolo and that she once owned a restaurant that closed after a man she loved ran off with all her money. But before that, Sarah Randolph married Emile McCutcheon and they lived briefly together in St. Charles Parish. This must be how Sarah McCutcheon came to know Lolo's father, John Gant; or how she came to know Lolo's mother, Rosanna Perry.

　　Lolo learned from Sarah McCutcheon how to find the numinous in the everyday. It was from her that Grandmother learned to dress the body and dress a house like you would the body. How she saw firsthand that cooking was a protected ritual, a séance really. *Grandma McCutcheon had this big potbelly stove, black cast iron. It was the best food I've ever eaten, period. Meatballs with tomato gravy, stewed chicken, stew meat with potatoes. She'd make her own biscuits from scratch. She'd make root beer and put it in the bottles. She'd get these tomatoes, you didn't even know about no lettuce. She sliced these tomatoes so thin, put them in a bowl with vinegar and sugar. You'd be drinking the juice.* That's my mother, Ivory Mae, speaking for herself.

Cooking had to be done *right* because food carried around in it all kinds of evil and all kinds of good just waiting to be wrought. This was why, for instance, before you ate a cucumber you rubbed the two ends of it together *to get the fever out.* And why you always cooked the slime all the way out of the okra before you served it. Why? You didn't ask, because inquiry from children or young people toward an elder was not allowed. You didn't make eye contact with adults either. You spoke to other children if you were a child. These were protections.

But even if you could ask why, Sarah McCutcheon would likely say, "Because they said." "They" were omniscient and omnipresent, requiring no explanation.

Each meal was a creation, derived from scratch, the smell and taste unified. Sarah McCutcheon painstakingly taught Lolo this. Lolo would teach her three children, too. Whatever seasoning my mother and her brother and sister chopped for food had to be so fine it would not be visible in the finished dish. Chunky meant unrefined, that care had not been taken, that the thing was done in haste. If it did not look appetizing, Sarah McCutcheon taught Lolo—and Lolo taught her own children—it could not be good to eat, and this small germ of an idea that appearance determines taste settled deep, especially in my mother, Ivory Mae, who to this day does not eat what does not appear *right.*

At fourteen, Grandmother had not been to school within the past year, according to 1930's census documents. She had dropped out after fifth grade but could read and write. And she knew, above all, how to work, which is always the beginning of fashioning a self.

Lolo worked for what she wanted, but what she set her sights on was always changing. She was practical, known to tell an aspiring but not-quite-there person, "You got champagne taste with beer money." The

matriarch of one family she cleaned for was always giving Lolo her old
china, her elaborate heavy curtains. These beautiful, sometimes fragile
things had to be handled a certain way. They were the kinds of objects
that slowed you down, could take some of the crass out of you. This
family nurtured but did not ignite Lolo's love for beautiful things. That
had come from Sarah McCutcheon, long before.

Lolo placed men in the category of beautiful things. Lionel Soule
was one. A married man, a devout Catholic whose wife was unable to
have children, he fathered Lolo's three—Joseph, Elaine, and Ivory—but
was present in name alone, bestowing upon Elaine and Ivory a last name,
Soule, which in the right company spoke something about them. Lionel
Soule was descended from free people of color; his antecedents included
a French slaveowner, Valentin Saulet, who served as a lieutenant in the
colonial French administration during the city's founding days. Having
a French or Spanish ancestor confirmed your nativeness in a city colonized
by the French for forty-five years, ruled by the Spanish for another forty,
then owned again by the French for twenty days before they sold it to
America in 1803, a city where existed as early as 1722 a buffer class, neither
African and slave nor white and free, but people of color who often owned

property—houses, yes, but sometimes also slaves, at a time in America when the combination of "free" and "person of color" was a less-than-rare concept. This group—often self-identified as Creole; claiming a mixture of French, Spanish, and Native American ancestry; passing for white if they could and if they chose—had been granted access to the kinds of work held only by white people: in the arts (painting, opera, sculpture), or as metalworkers, carpenters, doctors, and lawyers.

This was partly why my Uncle Joe, though Lionel's son, was confused and disappointed about having been given his mother's maiden name, Gant. He claims he thought he was Joseph Soule up until he was a grown man in the navy, when the sergeant called out Joseph Gant, the name on his birth certificate, causing him to look around "like a stonecold fool," he says now. When he asked his mother why he carried his grandfather's last name she said, "You lucky you had a name."

Lolo was dark skinned and fine with big thick legs that men loved to grab hold of. There is a single image of a young Lolo—her hair slicked back with curled-under bangs running the width of her forehead—taken at Magnolia Studio, the only black-owned photo studio in the city. It had the best-dressed waiting room. To advertise, they hung along the outside and inside walls images of "folks small and great." If you wanted to know whether a person you'd met on the street was somebody, you checked for their image on the walls of Magnolia Studio.

In her photo, Lolo wears horn-rimmed cat-eye glasses and a pastel-blue dress with white accents on the collar and on the pockets. Her shoes are dazzling red—the photographer painted them so—her ankles thick in the pumps. She stands tall, one arm on top of a pillar serving as prop, her hand partly open, the other on her right hip. She has what my mother calls dancing eyes, what I call laughing eyes. Instead of smiling, she just knows.

Lionel Soule glimpsed his two eldest, Joseph and Elaine, only a few times in rushed transactions when my grandmother appeared at his dock job to collect folded-up money from his palm. Auntie Elaine remembers this one detail: "With every word you could hear his fake teeth going click, click, click." In her earliest years, my mother thought the following about her father: *I didn't know I had no daddy. I thought I just came here. I swear. I thought he was dead. I assume if he ain't around, he must be dead.* Which explains why when the one time her father, Lionel, came to visit, my mother ran and hid herself behind a door. Rather than wait for her or persuade her to come out, Lionel Soule left and never came back. *Ain't that the pitifullest thing you ever heard?*

# II

# *Joseph, Elaine, and Ivory*

$\mathcal{G}$randmother named my mother Ivory after the color of elephant tusk. Those who are still alive to tell stories say Grandmother, who was twenty-five when Ivory Mae was born, became infatuated with elephants during frequent lunch breaks at the Audubon Zoo, which was within walking distance of a mansion on St. Charles Avenue where she once worked.

Uncle Goody called the child not by her coloration, Ivory, but by her birth year: '41, the end of the Great Depression—the residue of which still mucked Uncle Goody's life. Ivory's nickname had the weight of a history Uncle Goody could not shake, which Ivory Mae understood made her highly significant, to Uncle Goody at least. "Where Old Forty-One?" he would always say.

*Forty-One! The year of my birthday was what he called me. Here come Old Forty-One. I used to like it. I used to get so happy.*

It paid to be his chosen. Uncle Goody worked on the Louisville and Nashville Railroad cleaning boxcars and lining them with wood. Sometimes he oiled the railcar brakes. At home, he presented another self, making molasses candy that stretched long like taffy. When Ivory

Mae was around, she was always the first to taste. *That was the first time I knew that men knew how to make candy.*

Joseph, Elaine, and Ivory: When people said one name, they almost always said the other two. Joseph was three years older than Elaine, and Elaine was two years older than Ivory. The trio formed a small intimate band closed for membership.

Everyone knew that Joseph, Elaine, and Ivory belonged to Lolo, not by coloration, which could throw off the undiscerning (they bore their father's color), but by their manner and how they dressed. Of the three children, Elaine was darkest, and she was the color of pecan candy—a milky tan. They were starched children, their lives regimented, Lolo's attempt to create for them a childhood she had not had. This was why in every place she rented, she painted the walls first, as if doing so granted them permanence, which was the thing she craved. She bought brand-new wood furniture that looked to have been passed down through generations—Joseph, Elaine, and Ivory sustaining the aura of antiquity with their daily polishings. She shopped in the best stores, always collecting beautiful things and storing them away to be used later. But these untouched passions, boxes upon stacked boxes, succumbed to fire one night while the family stood on the sidewalk watching one of Lolo's remade houses on Philip Street in the Irish Channel burn to the ground.

Of her history, Lolo seemed to know only her mother's and father's names and the names of those who raised her. She favored the moment, knew how remembering the past could elicit despair. For a long time, my mother says, Grandmother kept retelling the story of how she prayed unceasingly to see her mother, Rosanna Perry, in dreams. The vision took forever to manifest and when it did during sleep one night, the woman who appeared was a dead mother surrounded by a brood of zombified cousins. Grandmother, frightened by these corpses, was forced to rebuke the evil dead spirit, telling it to go away from her and never to return. All of this heightened because she could not rightfully identify the spirit in her dream, having never glimpsed her mother in life or in photograph.

The past played tricks, Lolo knew. The present was a created thing.

Maybe this was what led her to try her fate in Chicago around 1942, leaving six-year-old Joseph, three-year-old Elaine, and two-year-old Ivory behind with Aunt Shugah and her daughter, TeTe.

After Lionel Soule came a man called Son who drove cabs for the V-8 company, the only car service black people in New Orleans could call. Son left for Chicago in a rush. It is said that Grandmother flew to him there for a weeklong visit that became a yearlong stay. Lolo took a job in the bakery where Son worked. She planned to save, set up a decent life in a remade Chicago apartment, and send for her kids; but her leave-taking must have revived feelings of her own mother's abandonment, her children now in the hands of the same group of women who raised her.

Lolo's eldest boy, Joseph, tested the women. "I could get spankings, but as soon as the hurt stop I'm doing something else they didn't think I had no business doing," he says. "That was just part of my personality." Elaine cried whenever her mouth wasn't chewing on something. "I want Lolo," she moaned over and over again. "Give me Lolo."

From Chicago, Grandmother heard reports that Joseph, Elaine, and Ivory weren't well fed. Out of all the things to go wrong, this one thing seemed untenable. "I promised when I got to be a man I wasn't gone eat no more weenies and spaghetti," Uncle Joe told me. "TeTe wasn't no good cook and that's what we used to eat every day."

And so Lolo came back.

No one likes to dwell on her going away, for it speaks too loudly and reveals too much. It could be said that she almost escaped this particular story. I imagine her in Chicago wearing a great fur-collared overcoat, fighting freezing cold, her fingers and ears tingling then going numb. Chicago was the possibility of a life shorn of her fragmented past, the chance to make a new story from start to finish, but leaving her children was also the repeat of an ancient pattern.

Back in New Orleans, she cleaned during the day so she could afford night classes at Coinson's School of Practical Nurses, where she was best remembered for her uniforms: frozen-white bleached dresses and matching nurse's cap with freshly polished shoes and stockings that were a clashing veil against her dark skin. It was a white you were afraid to touch. She was determined to finish, and she did, working eventually at Charity Hospital downtown and in private homes everywhere around the city, sometimes for employers whose houses she had once cleaned.

Sometime after Chicago, Grandmother began to whisper under her breath how even if she didn't have a pot to piss in, she wasn't ever leaving her children again. My mother heard her say this. And, too, she started talking to her community of women confidantes about how she was actually mother to six children, how there was a set of twins and another lone child who died before Joseph was born. These stories of Lolo's were overheard, "caught" by her children like wisps, then held inside for them to tell much later.

By the time Ivory Mae was seven years old, Grandmother was firmly planted in a double house on South Roman Street uptown, between Second and Third Streets. She had married a longshoreman thirteen years her senior whom the children called Mr. Elvin and who is described by most people as some version of what Mom remembers: *He used to talk to the television. Easygoing guy. More like a little common man. He went along with the program. He liked to drink.*

The 2500 block of Roman where they lived was hemmed in by two bars and a small grocery store that seemed to hold the block down like paperweights. Whites ran the grocery stores, blacks the barrooms, unless it was a "real classy joint," says Uncle Joe. But this was New Orleans. Black and poor lived in eyesight of rich and white or white-looking. The projects, for instance, stood blocks away from St. Charles Avenue's mansions; a different social world always lay just around the corner. Also just around the block from Lolo's house, on Claiborne Avenue, was the Rex Den, a massive warehouse where Mardi Gras floats were made. Some blocks down the street, on Jackson Avenue, lived Aunt Shugah's daughter, TeTe, on whose porch it was tradition to watch Zulu and Rex krewes—social clubs with fake kings and queens and real social hierarchies—parade by on Carnival morning.

In 1947, Elaine and Ivory Mae posed at Magnolia Studio for their only remaining childhood photograph. They were dressed like twins, in identical white dresses with pouffy sleeves, real flowers pinned on their chests. Each wore black patent leather Mary Jane shoes with ruffled white socks. Elaine was already mean mouthed, her hair in long plaits that reached the middle of her back. Ivory stands awkwardly beside her, leaning away, her weight on the side of her outer foot. But Auntie holds firm to her baby sister's waist, using her height as heft. This would be the last time in their lives when Elaine, who never rose above five feet, three inches, would be taller than her baby sister who grew to five feet, eight inches. In the photograph, Mom's small plait sticks up in front, and her mouth is wide open in a dazed face. She is tugging at the bottom of her dress, possibly trying to cover a visible patch of skin that shines just above her knee.

By this time in their lives, Joseph, Elaine, and Ivory were *like lil maids,* waking up and making their beds first thing, sweeping and dusting, *the house would be shining. We were brought up with cleanliness.* All of Lolo's children knew how to clean, including the boy. "Guess who be out there windin' them clothes through that wringer? Your big uncle," Uncle Joe told me. When two of Lolo's friends whom the children called

Aunt Ruth and Aunt Agnes arrived at Roman Street for the annual Mardi Gras and Nursing Club balls, Joseph, Elaine, and Ivory pressed their gowns and laid them out on the bed for the women to slip into after they had taken their baths. When they returned from their parties, they found lamplit rooms, their slippers by turned-down beds, their nightclothes already laid out for them.

After school, while Lolo attended nursing classes, Joseph, Elaine, and Ivory grocery-shopped from a list their mother had made, the three of them toting bags down the street. Elaine always finished her chores early while Ivory lounged, watching her sister and the clock until time wore down, close to when their mother would appear, at which point she would run around the house frantically. *I had to be made to do things.*

Even at Hoffman Junior High School, Ivory Mae resisted working in the garden because only the girls were required to do so. *Look like I was always in a beating way.* Ivory Mae was sassy mouthed. "She'll answer back if it kills her," Grandmother was always saying. Elaine was the tomboy, playing marbles, climbing trees, breaking her collarbone and leg. "I was a whip." She could fight the boys, too, defending her baby sister who she thought "let people walk all over her." When Elaine was not fighting, she was shy. "Elaine had more of a quiet personality than Ivory," Uncle Joe said. "But when she came out of that quiet it was like terror. Ivory and I both had them flip mouths and thing. That helped bring us into either being liked or hated according to what side you was on. Elaine was quiet and didn't say nothing, but Elaine would do so much fighting you didn't need to say nothing." Still, Elaine and Ivory were always chosen for major parts in spring plays at Hoffman, whether or not they could sing or dance. They were light skinned, "pretty colored," teachers would say. Elaine was chosen for Queen of McDonogh 36 when she was in second grade. *Elaine had all that hair, which never was good, but they had combed it and it was all sticking up. She wore a lil tiara, looking mean as hell.* Elaine also wore an aloofness that could disappear you. You could sometimes feel, speaking to her, that she was physically there but had walled herself up somewhere inside.

Joseph was spoiled by women from the start. His grandmother Sarah McCutcheon was the first to buy him a two-wheel bike. He preferred to spend his time at her house in the Irish Channel, which proved a more adventurous life for a young boy. Sarah McCutcheon lived in front of town on St. James between Tchoupitoulas and Religious Street, just across from the rice mill, a stone's throw from the railroad tracks near to the Mississippi River. Joseph was responsible for finding wood for the stove and for the fireplace, and this would lead him to the railroad tracks where he'd salvage discarded wood once used to line the boxcars that transported goods all across the country. Sometimes, if he showed up at the wharf when the ships were unloading, a longshoreman might bust a bag of sugar or rice or coffee or bananas and Uncle Joe would hold them in his shirt to carry back to Sarah McCutcheon on St. James Street.

Woodson Elementary, McDonogh 36, Hoffman Junior High, and Booker T. Washington—Joseph's, Elaine's, and Ivory's schools—were segregated for all of their school years and long after 1954's *Brown v. Board of Education*, the results of which were not seen in New Orleans until November 1960 when three six-year-olds, Tessie Provost, Leona Tate, and Gail Etienne, dressed in full skirts and patent leather shoes, with massive white bows atop their heads, arrived at an all-white McDonogh 19, where they would remain the only three students in school that entire year, taught in classrooms with brown paper taped to windows, blocking sun and jeers from white parents raging outside. The same day in November, first grader Ruby Bridges, a lone black girl surrounded by three US marshals, integrated William Frantz Elementary, spending half a school year as the *only* student. A decade later, on the eve of the 1970s, integration in New Orleans high schools would still cause riots. Four decades later, it would remain factually incorrect to describe New Orleans schools as fully integrated.

*Lolo always told us we could be whatever we wanted to be. When we were growing up, we never thought of white people as superior to us. We always thought we were equal to them or better.*

But Joseph, Elaine, and Ivory had only to walk to the curb outside their Roman Street house to see Taylor Park and its sign: NO NIGGERS, NO CHINESE AND NO DOGS. It was a strange sight, the mostly empty, fenced-in park in a black neighborhood. If the neighborhood children wanted a park to run around in or a pool for swimming, they had to travel to Freret Street's Shakespeare Park, several miles away. "It seemed most of the black people in New Orleans had to go over there," Uncle Joe said. Getting to Shakespeare Park required a ride on segregated buses.

But there was an added complication in New Orleans, a city fixated on and obsessed with gradations of skin color. My mother, Ivory Mae, understood from a young age the value in her light skin and freckles and in the texture of her wavy hair, which she called *good*. The favoritism came through in the double-standard ways of all prejudice, in the way people lit up when they saw Ivory but did not come alive so much for Elaine, who wondered why she was a few shades darker than Joseph and Ivory and with thicker hair that she herself described as "a pain to comb."

As a child, my mother internalized this colorism, the effects of which sometimes showed in shocking ways.

One day Ivory, Elaine, and Grandmother's sister Lillie Mae were sitting together on the Roman Street stoop watching people. Mom was eight years old. A schoolmate, whom Mom called Black Andrew, walked by. He was headed to Johnny's Grocery store. This was not unusual. Andrew passed two, three, sometimes four times a day, whenever he raised a nickel or a couple of pennies for candy. When he went by he stared, sometimes winking at Ivory Mae, who glared back from the porch. She was always taunting: *Black Andrew, hey lil black boy.* The neighborhood children on their respective porches urged her on without needing to. *That lil black boy ain't none of my boyfriend* she remembers telling them.

*He never did look like he was clean. I mean he was really a little black boy, nappy and everything.* She meant that he was dark skinned, the color of her own mother, the color of her mother's sister Lillie Mae, who was sitting right beside her.

"You have cheeks to call that boy black?" said Lillie Mae. "Look at your ma. What color is she?"

*My mama not black,* small Ivory Mae had said then.

*She wasn't black to me. She was my mama and my mama wasn't black. Looked to me like they was trying to make my mama like the black people I didn't like.*

"I guess we saw it sort of like the white men saw it," says Uncle Joe now, trying to explain his baby sister. "As people being lower than us."

Joseph roamed, but his sisters played in sight of adults, except for weekends when they were given a quarter, which could go far at the ten-cent stores on Claiborne Avenue. *We would buy our barrettes. I used to always pick nice colors. We were always neat kids. We used to look like we were more kept than the other kids that would be around us, like little rich kids. When we were little bitty children, five years old or maybe seven, we ain't wore nothin' but Stride Rite. Lolo believed you put good shoes on your feet.*

"Hold your heads up," Grandmother was always saying. If they didn't have a penny in their pocket no one had to know that. "It's how you carry yourself," she would say. They were to hold something of themselves in reserve, to never ever give it all away, to value each other more than anyone else, and to stay out of other people's houses where anything could happen. *We were sheltered. We couldn't go by people house. I never had a whole lot of friends. People stood to themselves. We were just Elaine, Ivory, and Joseph and a few people who came along.*

The children wore the color white on special occasions: for picture taking, church services at the Divine Mission of God on Sundays, and then every May, on John McDonogh Day.

John McDonogh was a wealthy slave owner who in 1850 bequeathed half of his estate to New Orleans public schools, insisting that his money be used for "the establishment and support of free schools wherein the poor and the poor only and of both sexes and classes and castes of color shall have admittance."

This "patron saint of New Orleans public schools," as city officials sometimes called him, had other requirements too—that the Bible be used as the main textbook and also "one small request . . . one little favor to ask, and it shall be the last . . . that it may be permitted, annually, to the children of the free schools situated nearest to the place of my interment, to plant and water a few flowers around my grave."

Students who attended schools named after McDonogh visited his grave site yearly, some of them taking a ferry across the river to where he was buried alongside his slaves at McDonoghville Plantation. Even after 1860, when his family had his remains exhumed and moved to his native Baltimore, schoolchildren continued to gather at his emptied grave to honor him. They did so until 1898 when a statue was erected in New Orleans's Lafayette Square, facing Gallier Hall, which was then city hall. McDonogh's bronze head looked straight ahead while a chiseled boy scaled the monument, reaching with one hand to lay a garland in perpetual honor at the base of McDonogh's bust. A sculptured girl with cascading hair stood at the base of the monument, holding the boy's free hand, looking up.

On McDonogh Day, all the children of the more than thirty McDonogh schools wore their best white clothes to the segregated event. Black and white students arrived by separate buses. The black children waited in the sun while the white children completed their procession to honor John McDonogh. *We would be standing up there for hours and hours sweating inside our pretty white dresses.*

A school band played as the white children gathered around McDonogh's statue to sing McDonogh's song:

> *O' wake the trumpet of renown*
> *Far echoing a hero's name*
> *McDonogh: let the trumpet blow*
> *And with the garland twine his brow*
> *Extol him with your voices now*
> *Praise to him; all praise to him!*

Mayor deLesseps Story "Chep" Morrison awarded the key to the city to one sixth grader from each white school; then the black students had their turn. By the time they arrived at the middle of McDonogh's song, several black children would have fainted from the noontime heat bearing down, dirtying up their white. Those still standing sang on, holding wilted flowers for John McDonogh's replica. Those passed-out students would have missed the bestowing of the key on one sixth grader from each black school.

It was not surprising then that in 1954 black students, principals, and teachers protested John McDonogh Day for years of what local civil rights leaders called "countless unpleasantries of humiliation and shame." Only thirty-four of the thirty-two thousand black students citywide appeared before the statue that year. Ivory Mae, who was then thirteen, and her siblings were not among them.

After that, Joseph, Elaine, and Ivory wore their white only to church. Sarah McCutcheon introduced Lolo and her young children to the Divine Mission of God. Its sanctuary was a double shotgun house uptown on Soniat Street that was church on one side, house on the other. *The minute you walked in there, you could imagine being in a part of heaven. There was a little porch you went up on and then into the church. Nothing else would exist.* Services were held in daytime; you left them at night.

The mission had no more than twenty-five congregants, all of whom believed their leader, Dr. Joseph Martin, was a prophet, the kind who could speak to the rain and tell it to stop. On several occasions he did so, several people claim, holding back thunderstorms so his church members could make it to their cars without getting soaked. He was said to turn back terrible hurricanes and calm the winds. His prophecies exceeded the meteorological. He told of the little people who would come across the ocean in droves, which he later claimed were the Vietnamese refugees who started arriving in 1975.

Congregants called themselves Holy Catholic. The church drew from Catholic rituals but was not listed in any directory, nor were the congregants ever visited by the archbishop. Strict Catholics who visited, like Joe Gant's friend Harold, said congregants were ridiculing Catholic traditions, practicing hoodoo. "It was an individualized thing," Joe Gant said.

Inside the church, four days a week, otherwise ordinary people transformed themselves. The women kept their white cloaks in a wooden armoire in the church; the men wore long white robes with wide sleeves and kingly crowns made of felt. Some people wore headbands patched with golden stars. The children of congregants marched down the aisles like future prophets, holding royal blue banners that rose high up above their heads.

The entire congregation was the choir. *Everybody singing together sounded like the trumpets. We used to all get up and march a circle around the church.*

> *Oh Daniel he was a good man*
> *Lord, he prayed three times a day*
> *Oh the angels opened up the windah,*
>     *just to hear what Daniel had to say*
> *For I thank God I'm in his care*

In a lifted moment, singing this song or another one like it, Mom was first saved at the Mission. One minute she was singing about feeling the fire burning then jumping up wildly the next. Elaine went over and held her sister around the waist as if she were a tree. "Don't hold her, let her go," people were yelling. Elaine did let go, after a while, and Ivory Mae kept on at her salvation. After this, Ivory Mae began to develop a keen sense that she was *God's kid*. That's what she would call herself, in a possessive way, as if she were an only child. This annoyed Elaine. Ivory Mae now addressed God directly in regular prayers. *Father God*, she began, and he became for her (and would forever stay) the birth father she never had.

Every April twelfth on the Mission's anniversary, each member spoke their "determinations," what they intended to do for God and who they intended to be in the coming year. These speeches ran three or four pages, which led dedication services to extend far past midnight. *I used to always sing this lil light of mine, I'm gonna let it shine. I used to say my desire is to be a nurse. I used to say that because Lolo was a nurse and I wanted to be like her.*

Joseph wanted to be like his mother, too, but mostly in presentation, which he sometimes affected to the detriment and exclusion of other useful qualities. He was the only boy at Hoffman's eighth-grade graduation who wore a tailor-made suit. It was gray with a collar and lapels hand stitched in a darker gray thread that made "a beautiful show," Uncle Joe says. Everyone had to wear a suit, but most were store-bought. Those who couldn't afford one still graduated, but they didn't march with the class. Joseph's suit from Harry Hyman's shop on Rampart Street looked so rare that even teachers were complimenting him. "That was one of the high points of my life," he says now, at seventy-six years old. He was six feet, four inches and narrow (and still is, wearing the same size clothes now that he did then). His hair waved up with water, which the girls liked.

That eighth-grade graduation suit and the attention it drew marked the start of Joe Gant's lifelong love of clothes. He could dress better than the girls. Joseph's obsession with preserving the creases in the pants he spent hours ironing, made him act strange sometimes. "I used to get dressed to go out and I wouldn't ever sit down." When he grew to driving age, he eased into his car reluctantly, the underside of his long legs barely grazing the seat, which forced him to drive through town straight backed, like a man in a perpetual state of alarm. "Some people think clothes do something for them, I thought I did something for clothes," he told me. "I was cocky, in other words."

Joseph spent his earnings from summer jobs on a wardrobe for high school that included tailor-made slacks and nylon underwear from Paris, which he bought from Rubenstein Brothers on Canal Street. Blacks couldn't try clothes on then. Joseph went in knowing his size: 42 long or extra long, depending on the style; 36 sleeve; 16-and-a-half-inch neck. He also bought the ties all boys were required to wear at Booker T. Washington High School. If you forgot the tie, you wore one of the old ones collected in every classroom for those who couldn't afford it. "I didn't wear any of that shit. I had my own tie. It did a lot for your manlihood and thing," he said. "Something about the tie gave me a sense of importance, a sense of being extra-special like."

Joseph wore tailored suits, but Elaine and Ivory made their outfits. Sewing was making a self, and this Ivory Mae especially loved. Even in middle school sewing classes, she had an eye for the movement of clothes on a body and could decide the right special touch, always improvising patterns with a surprising detail that set her apart.

Young women learned fashion from each other, mostly on the streets, but also at Ebony Fashion Fairs held yearly at the Municipal Auditorium where the women attendees dressed so hard that they outshone and lost regard for the models parading onstage, who wore unattainable things. Ivory Mae was never much for the outlandish, anyway. Her style was deceptively simple, her clothes flattering the right curves. Dresses you might wear for special occasions she wore every day. In this way she and Joseph were alike. They dressed to be seen, which is how it came to be that they built up a reputation for floor showing, as Uncle Joe calls it. "Yeah, we knew we looked good." They danced wherever there was a floor—a bar or a ball. The sidewalk, sometimes. "We used to go in clubs and start dancing from the door. For a poor man I used to dress my can off," he says. "That's what used to get me in so much trouble and thing with the ladies."

He and his baby sister, Ivory, would swing it out, jitterbugging and carrying on. Ivory was always fun and always light on her feet. She was especially gifted at being led and men generally loved this quality in her. Sometimes Ivory would enter a club where she was to meet Joseph already dancing a number, the two of them working up to each other, the drama of which could cause a commotion. "Once we touched each other," Uncle Joe says, "it was on. People be dancing, they get off the floor and let us dance, knowing we gone clown. People who didn't know us thought we were some kind of celebrity, making all them different turns and thing. I'd turn her with my hand. Sometime I'd have my back to her and catch her hand and spin her round two, three times, maybe do a lil split or something like that, you know, common stuff."

They were wild about improvisation, enacting their ideal freedom, which was precisely why Grandmother never wanted to dance with her son Joseph. "Boy, dance straight," she would always say. "You clown too much."

No one clowned more than another boy in the neighborhood who always stole the show. His name was Edward, but those who knew him only ever called him by his last name: Webb.

# III

## Webb

$\mathcal{M}$ost people just couldn't see no matter how hard they turned it how Webb and Ivory Mae got tied together. They were not even boyfriend and girlfriend, but back in those days no one ever seemed it anyway. Quiet often meant sneaky, but as far as people knew Ivory Mae was a faithful student at Booker T. Washington High, the kind teachers always cast their vision upon; she was going to be somebody.

About Webb, little of an academic nature could be said. "If he had a following he could have been a comedian," Uncle Joe, who was several grades ahead of him, says now. Webb sometimes stammered when he spoke, but this only encouraged his style, made him the type of person everyone knew if not liked. Webb had the build of a quarterback, which he was. *He wasn't no main player, but he was there, he had on a uniform.*

Webb and Ivory Mae grew up together, barely a street apart. Webb was the third of Mildred Ray Hobley's children, the only boy, brother to Minnie, Dawnie, and Marie. His sisters called him Lil Brother. He was one year older than Ivory Mae and knew her from the time she wore white ruffle socks in hard-soled training shoes. They could have passed for brother and sister in terms of complexion and high-flying personality, but look: Mildred had dreams for all of her four children. Webb marrying Ivory Mae was not one of them.

He was crazy about her though. Could not get enough of just looking in her face. And his cousin Roosevelt was sweet on Elaine, the tomboy. For the most part, Ivory Mae couldn't stand Webb; he got on her nerves, bad. To her, he was a trying-to-be trickster, always thinking he was funnier than he was. There she would be on the porch, pretending aloofness when he would come loping over, *pigeon-toed-like, he'd do all kind of dances on the sidewalk.* He had a small dog that he knew Ivory Mae despised. His idea of being playful was to throw the dog at her, tell the dog *Get her, get her, get her,* which would make Ivory mad at first but then happy, secretly, later. They had between them the kind of intimacy born of growing up near another person and thus taking them for granted. Later on, once they were boyfriend and girlfriend, they sat on the porch kissing in plain sight.

Tenth grade was over and it was summertime, which meant you hung out more, tried to figure out what else to do besides look. Now Ivory Mae wanted to know what came next, after the kissing. *Webb and I were just fooling around, like friends, you know, teaching and learning. We were going to school and learning about the birds and the bees and then I was pregnant. It was really just one time that we were intimate. It wasn't no big love affair.*

In those days, children did not speak openly to their parents. "Get out from grown folks' business," you were told. *Whatever we found out, we found out on our own.* In hindsight, there were the platitudes, like keep your dress down and your legs closed, but it was not clear what this meant, whether this was about sitting on a bus while wearing a dress or sex. The latter would not have automatically crossed Ivory Mae's mind, but she was impulsive when she wanted, drawn to instant gratification, the kind to listen later.

After Ms. Anna Mae, a family friend from the apartments back behind their house, took Ivory Mae to Charity Hospital where the doctor confirmed her pregnancy, Grandmother marched over to Mildred's house and worked out the details.

If Lolo was disappointed, she did not say.

In September 1958, when Ivory Mae would have begun eleventh grade and Webb his senior year, they were married instead, standing in the living room of Te Te's house on Jackson Avenue, surrounded by Elaine and Roosevelt, Mildred and Lolo, and Webb's sisters. Webb had traded in his football jersey for a groom's dark suit and tie. *He had his nice lil shoes on. I was decked out like a lil bride. We was doing it up.* Ivory had borrowed a white wedding dress and veil from her brother Joseph's married girlfriend, Doretha. She wore brand-new white shoes. Her attire was appropriate for the time, but when she looks back at it: *I really didn't need to have no wedding gown. I could have worn something I already had. No wonder Webb's people ain't like me.*

But Mrs. Mildred was not the sort of woman to dash a young girl's feelings. She meant to have a strong say in the marriages of her children, but this one time things had gone awry. She had already forbidden her three girls from even looking in the direction of Joe Gant. Even as a boy, he didn't always own his actions. Instead of saying, for example, that he moved in with a woman, he would say the woman came to him and "got his clothes a piece at a time and brought it to they own house. Now that's gospel."

These were the no-good, have-nothing ways Mildred's children were to avoid. "I didn't have enough money for them," Joe Gant says. "She didn't want her daughters talking to nobody in the neighborhood who she thought wasn't going nowhere. Your mama wasn't in they class either."

Her light skin and hair, things that Ivory Mae thought made her special, meant nothing to Mildred and her family who had the same features. Ivory wasn't judged to be going anywhere from the looks of it, and now here was evidence. She had ruined things for Webb, and this notion, sprinkled especially by his sisters, settled in the family, corrupting even the sweetest impulses of the young couple who tried to play the part, now that the baby was coming.

The couple spoke their vows. Webb slipped onto Ivory Mae's finger rings his mother had been given by her own mother. An engagement band and the wedding ring both went on at the same time.

*It wasn't no party after. Cake and ice cream and everybody went about they business. We went out somewhere to some lil club or some kind of craziness, our lil black clubs around Washington Avenue.* There they might have seen Ernie K-Doe perform, long before he had a name, before he built the Mother-in-Law Lounge, his permed hair made mythic. No, this was back when he still performed in tennis shoes, which were considered improper for a singing man, before he could afford leather. *When he finally got a record, people said he could buy him some shoes now.*

They courted *after* the wedding. Movies and dancing at the Blue Door and Tony's down on St. Peter, outside the French Quarter, across Rampart, where black people could go. The Pimlico Club where another high school dropout, a girl named Irma Thomas, sang. That was when music was *normal and natural* as Mom calls it, *just coming from within you.* Back in the clubs, Mom looking sharp with the other girls her age—she still wasn't showing—they posed for photographs standing around a pinball machine. *Of course we were silly, giggling.*

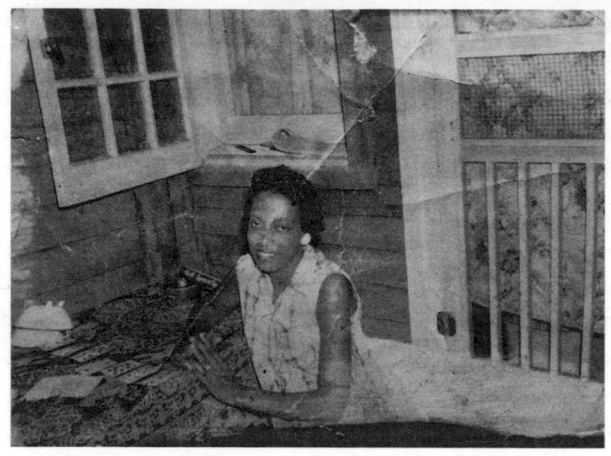

Instead of school, Ivory Mae walked around the corner to her good friend Rosie Lee Jackson's house. Rosie Lee was the one girl she knew who had already gotten pregnant, already gotten married, already had a baby.

*I think that's why I like cabbage so much now, cause she look like she was always cooking cabbage. I used to climb on her bed after I ate and sleep.*

Ivory missed school. She was always running into former classmates. No one could believe it: Ivory Mae, of all people. Lying on Rosie Lee's bed, Mom nursed small desires while her belly grew. She planned to return to Booker T. Washington after the baby arrived; she knew other girls who had done this.

Webb spent his days chasing work or working construction jobs with his stepfather, Nathan Hobley, a brick mason who laid French Quarter courtyards and with whom he barely got along. Webb had a hard time being serious. Nathan Hobley would hold mock job interviews at the kitchen table, Webb sitting across from him, failing.

As a married couple, Webb and Ivory Mae had a room in Nathan and Mildred's house in New Orleans East, on Darby Street, an out-of-the way, semi-industrial section off Old Gentilly Road. Nathan was an astute businessman, pioneer minded, owning several houses in the East before it was common for black people to do so. But being in Mildred's house made Ivory Mae feel hemmed in. *It was a place I really didn't have anywhere to go.* The house was nice enough. It sat back off the street, but it was in the country as Ivory Mae saw it. None of her friends lived there. She was always calling somebody to bring her back to *town,* by which she meant the city, to Dryades Street in Central City, where Grandmother and Mr. Elvin had moved to another rented house. She was small with a tiny belly up until the last few months when she swelled suddenly with Eddie, who was a huge child, nearly nine pounds, with a square head shaped just like his father's.

*When I brought him home nobody thought he was a baby, looked like he could have been a month old.* Eddie was a serious infant, inquisitive. He was a wide child and terribly hungry from his first day on earth. My mother attempted to breastfeed him but so ravenous was he that she gave up. *He look like he never had enough. You could hear him sucking from a mile away.* His insatiable thirst ruined it for all eight of the children who would come after. The memory of his sucking and gnawing created such torment that Ivory Mae could not bring herself to breastfeed again.

Just after Eddie was born, Booker T. Washington High School changed its policy. Mothers were no longer accepted. Ivory Mae could, the school suggested, finish at a special school for delinquents, *for messed-up kids,* but she couldn't see being set apart in this, the wrong way. She pleaded with the principal to please make an exception and take her back, but she was a poor example for the other girls now. Nothing about her looks and charm could change that, he said. She had entered womanhood, her first dream of finishing high school and going to college dissolved.

In May, a few months after Eddie was born, Webb enlisted in the army. He was sent to South Carolina's Fort Jackson for basic training and then to Fort Hood, Texas, where he was stationed. When he left New Orleans, Mom was pregnant again with a boy she would name Michael.

She was pregnant when she and Webb married and pregnant when he died.

The circumstances of Webb's death, a shortened version of which was reported to Ivory Mae the morning of November 1, 1960, were summarized this way in the investigator's statement:

> On 31 October 1960, approximately 2320 hours, Pfc Edward J. Webb . . . Company C, 6th Infantry, 1st Armored Division, Fort Hood, Texas, was walking west on the right side of highway 190, in the city limits of Killeen, Texas, with two other members of his unit. While walking in the right lane of a four-lane road, WEBB was struck, from the rear, by a vehicle driven by Sp4 Ervil J. HUGHES . . . who fled the scene without making his identity known. WEBB was pronounced Dead on Arrival at the US Army Hospital as a result of the injuries sustained in this accident.

Everyone knew that Webb could have a temper. Even in his hometown with people that he knew. His own stepfather hired and fired him from construction jobs repeatedly, because he couldn't take directions. And he liked to drink. People could see him getting into a row at a bar in the back parts of Fort Hood because sometimes, in his fearlessness, he didn't know when to stop. He might have pushed the wrong man too far. Back home, theories swirled about Webb's death. The army provided almost no detail. Most of his family and friends insisted that it was racially motivated, had to be, I mean, just look at the bare facts: black man run over while walking home, no explanation whatsoever, no fuss, no arrests.

The epicrisis, a more narrative summation appended to Webb's autopsy report, reveals slightly more detail:

> It is understood by word of mouth that this young colored Enlisted Man was walking in the middle of the pavement on Route 190 in

Killeen and was under the influence of alcohol. This behavior ter-
minated in a car hitting and felling him to the ground. His colleagues
at the side of the road were confused by the accident and did not
seek either to remove him from the roadway and/or to stop traffic
running over him. Instead, they tried to wave down cars to obtain
assistance. Then, a car ran over the body of Webb as he lay in the
road ... Alcohol appears to have either released a suicidal trait in
the deceased or to have made him unaware of the dangers of walking
in the path of traffic.

A map drawn in a later court case that charged the hit-and-run driver
with negligent homicide indicates that it was a dry, moonlit night with
broken clouds. Webb's left shoe was knocked off of him when he was
catapulted many feet into the air before dropping down onto concrete
pavement that was, according to this map, in "excellent condition." The
driver was never convicted.

His official cause of death is listed as "cerebral concussion and sub-
arachnoid hemorrhage." Webb was eighteen years, ten months, and seven
days old, two months away from his birthday on Christmas Day.

On the death certificate, listed both as "next of kin or next friend"
and "wife" is Ivory Soule Webb, address 4116 Darby Street, New Orleans.

Lying there in the casket, Webb looked three times his age. His skin was
darker than Mom had remembered, his head swollen due to the circumstances of his dying. She stood there looking at her husband of two years,
but really he was her childhood friend of forever. They had lived together
as husband and wife in the same house for less than a year before his
enlistment. What was there between them now? There were the love
letters about sweet childish things: how one day his woman would make
his house a home, generalities mostly, and two children now between
them, another on the way.

Michael had been born in April 1960, six months before his father
died. Sometime between Michael's birth and Webb's death, Ivory became

pregnant for a third time. By the time Darryl was born, six months after Webb's burial, another father was already standing in the first one's place. This would seem to haunt Darryl all of his life. From early on, he would call himself the black sheep of the family. No one wanted to touch the circumstances of Darryl's birth in order to fashion a narrative. People were talking, saying that Ivory Mae was running around in the months preceding Webb's death, that she was seen with another, much darker man, Simon Broom. Everything was all jumbled up; people couldn't agree on the facts. Darryl, sensitive and sharply attuned, bore everyone else's uncertainties as his own. The rumor that Darryl was conceived three months or so before Webb's death while Simon and Ivory Mae—both married—were courting held Darryl in a no-place with no single story of his beginnings, a condition made worse by family members who, out of malice or their own hurt, told him over and again how he was misidentified and thus misplaced. "Just look at you boy. You ain't no Webb," Darryl remembers being told by some family member. My mother, the only one to know the truth, shrugged it all off when asked many years later. *What's done is done. Gone. Over and done with.*

She would, in fact, always insist that there was no difference among any of us children—that our having been raised by her made null any paternal or maternal differences.

About Eddie, Webb's eldest, there was no such question; he bore a different burden. A year old when Webb died, he was his father's image— big head and all. Whenever Webb's mother, Mildred, looked at him she'd say, "Lil Brother never be dead now."

# IV

## Simon Broom

Four years later, in the spring of 1964, Sarah McCutcheon died.

That summer, Mother married Father in the backyard of 4803 Wilson Avenue in New Orleans East.

Carl, Ivory Mae's first child with Simon, was not yet a year old. During the wedding he sat perched on Mom's right hip, his foot kicking against her pregnant belly, knowing nothing of the scene taking place right in front of his eyes. Karen, Mom's fifth child, would be born that fall and come home to this rented three-bedroom brick house.

Reverend Ross, who worked with Simon Broom at NASA, officiated. The nice neighbor living in the other half of the double house, who was also the landlord, had made for the reception white-bread finger sandwiches with the brown edges cut off the way Mom liked them.

Auntie Elaine, my mother's sister, who was grown up now and had started wearing her signature flaming red hair, stood there as witness. *It wasn't a big deal. It wasn't no event.* That seems a long time ago now, and Mom closes down passageways to memory when something doesn't make sense or when the thing or person no longer exists, which is possibly the same thing.

It was never just the two of them, Ivory and Simon, not even at the begin-ning of their story. They each came to the relationship with children and with spouses. According to Mom, she first saw Dad in the late fifties at his cousin's hole-in-the-wall bar somewhere in the vicinity of Roman Street, where he had come to play a card game. Auntie says they first met at her marriage to Webb's cousin Roosevelt. One of Dad's brothers said they met at a restaurant where he and Simon were working as busboys. Wherever it was, they first laid eyes on each other while Ivory was still married to Webb, before she had any idea how that would end. Simon had a wife, too, but they were separated, he told Ivory *in so many words.* He was, in still other words, skirting the truth. Anyway, this was not about practicalities yet but about what flourished between them, those delirious feelings.

Simon Broom was six feet, two inches and dark skinned with *keen features, the handsomest man I ever seen.* Opposite Webb in looks and style, he physically overwhelmed her. Projecting an ease that Ivory Mae loved, he seemed a man in possession of himself, if not things. Nineteen years her elder, he had massive hands, gray-stained from years of work, which meant, Ivory Mae reasoned, that he could fix whatever in his and her world was broken. Plus, his diction. *He had a proud talk. Like the Kennedy brothers. When he spoke, I felt like I just needed to be listening.* His booming voice seduced Ivory, scared some, and led others to want to fight.

One thing was certain: Simon had not simply happened to her, as had Webb. Simon Broom felt like a choice. She took him on.

He was born to Beaulah Richard and Willie Broom in Raceland, Loui-siana. Beaulah was a Creole-speaking, pipe-smoking woman. They built their own farm in Raceland on a nameless edge of town near a street now called Broom. Simon was the third youngest of eleven children, only three of whom were girls. By the time thirty-eight-year-old Simon met Ivory

Mae when she was nineteen, he had already lived several lives. He had spent his childhood working on the family farm. School, held in the local black church, consisted of several classes taught simultaneously in one large room with no walls. Most days were chaos, but Simon finished fourth grade.

When he was sixteen, cousins brought him to New Orleans, an hour—a whole universe—away from Raceland. People say family friends taught him how to act citified then, and that is how he came to speak proper, learn to dress sharp, and have the high-class bearing that my mother fell for. But this sounds like a story city people tell other city people about country people. In 1943, at nineteen years old, Simon claimed he was two years older in order to join the navy, as had most of his brothers before him. When he enlisted, Ivory Mae was still toddling around Sarah McCutcheon's house in the Irish Channel, making dolls out of Coke bottles. He served in the Asiatic-Pacific Theater, in what in America is called the Philippine Liberation and elsewhere the Battle of Manila, the brutal fight that helped end World War II. He earned five stars fighting on behalf of a country that listed his name on a roll-call docket as: Simon Broom (n), the (n) for negro or negroid or nigger.

After the war, Simon Broom was handed a check for $167.36 and set free to make a life for himself. Asked, on discharge papers, about his ideal job, he wrote: "Assistant Manager (half owner) of moving van." Years after his military release, when Ivory Mae was seven years old, Simon married Carrie Howard, whose large family had come from Hahnville and New Sarpy, tiny towns thirty miles from New Orleans. In 1949, when Carrie and Simon's first child, Simon Broom Jr., was born in Charity Hospital, Simon the father was already working as a longshoreman. Carrie worked, too, first as a secretary at the naval base and then as a clerk at the Orleans Parish School Board. She was not the type to suffer fools. She was an organist in church, believed deeply in education, and bore for Simon two more children, named Deborah and Valeria, to whom she preached her convictions.

When Simon and Ivory Mae met all those years later, his age and experience were precisely what drew her. When Simon danced close to Ivory and she looked up at him, her hips rowing the air, he told her about how he had never—as a middle-aged man—had a woman so much younger, not in his lifetime, almost but not yet. He knew how to put the right words together.

But Simon *wasn't no dating type of man. He wasn't no going to the movies kind of man*, either. He mostly worked. His mantra was "I'll sleep when I'm dead." Like his father, Willie, he played the trombone or sometimes the banjo or the tuba in Doc Paulin's Brass Band, and he would often take Ivory Mae along with him, the two of them alone together, for once without the children, riding to gigs in his near-to-broken-down car, the instruments between them.

Simon's eldest boy would never live with his father and stepmother the way his sisters would. After his mother, Carrie, died in the summer of 1963—two weeks before Carl was born—Simon Jr. stayed in the same high school, living with his grandmother Beaulah Richard in rural Raceland, surrounded by the cousins and classmates he knew. He'd won a scholarship to Johnson C. Smith College. Simon Broom Sr. put him on a Greyhound bus to Charlotte, North Carolina. He has been there ever since.

Simon and Carrie Howard Broom's daughters, Deborah and Valeria, ten and eight years old, were still reeling from their mother's sudden death when they moved into the rented brick house on Wilson after the wedding. Valeria seemed numb, but Deborah, who was older, fought out her rejection of this new arrangement. She was direct and loudmouthed, striving to upend, it could seem, this imposed, unnatural order of things. She asked questions. She spoke her wants and wishes.

She had already seen what silence brought. The entire summer when they were away in Raceland at Grandmother Beaulah's house, surrounded by kin, their mother was back in the city, battling leukemia, dying. "I didn't know what the heck was going on because nobody was telling us details," Deborah says.

Deborah first learned about her new family while living with Grandmother Beaulah in Raceland shortly after her mother died. A neighbor was combing Deborah's hair; she was on her way to be baptized. "She started rolling out this scenario. These are gonna be your brothers," the woman said to her, describing Eddie, Michael, Darryl, and Carl.

"No they not," Deborah returned. "I don't even know these people." She considered it a while longer, then asked again: "Who *are* these people?" "But it wasn't up to me," she says now.

Eventually, the girls were taken to meet the strangers. Deborah screamed and hollered, " 'Where is my mom?' I kept saying I don't want to go meet these people. That first year after my mom died, I went crazy. I was in a shell-shocked state almost."

On a winter morning, Simon Broom drove Deborah and Valeria from Raceland to meet Ivory Mae and her four children for the first time. Simon left them there until sometime before night. He was the kind of man who always had another place where he urgently needed to be.

When the sisters arrived, they saw Eddie, Michael, and Darryl, "three beady-eyed boys," says Valeria, staring back at them. And Ivory Mae, their father's new woman, thin everywhere except for in the stomach (she was pregnant with Karen) and light skinned. The new woman, as Deborah and Valeria saw her, walked quietly around with little expression; they remember her as mostly silent with exploring, sometimes critical eyes. She looked and behaved nothing like their mother, Carrie, who was tall with a booming talking voice and a deep tenor singing one. "I'm Miss Ivory," Mom said to Deborah and Valeria. They would call her Miss Ivory for the rest of their lives.

The girls later moved into that rented brick house on Wilson. Four-year-old Eddie, firstborn of Ivory Mae's biological children, was suddenly younger than his new sisters. Deborah, who had been a middle child, was now the second eldest and Valeria the third, ranking above Eddie, who, before the girls arrived, had been the serious older brother to Michael and Darryl. Eddie was practical and special feeling, surrounded by doting aunts—Webb's sisters—and Mrs. Mildred who needed him to stay alive the way his dead father had not. Eddie would fight to keep hold of his original position as eldest of Mom's children for the rest of his life, seeing the new rearrangement as an unlawful jerking away of his familial standing.

# V

## Short End, Long Street

$\mathcal{I}$n March 1961—three years before the families merged and five months after Webb's death—this advertisement for 4121 Wilson appeared in the *Times-Picayune* newspaper:

Sale by Civil Sheriff
SINGLE ONE-STORY
FRAME DWELLING

A CERTAIN LOT OF GROUND . . . situated in the THIRD DISTRICT of this City of New Orleans, in what is known as "ORANGEDALE SUBDIVISION," said subdivision being located on Gentilly Road at second crossing of the L & N R.R. on the lake or north side of said road . . . Lot #7 . . . bounded by WILSON AVENUE, GENTILLY ROAD, LOMBARD STREET . . . measures 25 feet front . . . by a depth between equal and parallel lines of 160 feet. TERMS: CASH.

When this advertisement ran, the area that would later be called New Orleans East was largely cypress swamp, its ground too soft to support trees or the weight of three humans. It was overrun with nutria and muskrat, prime hunting ground.

From the beginning, no one could agree on what to call the place. But namelessness is a form of naming. It was a vast swath of land, more than 40,000 acres. Some people called it Gentilly East, others plain Gentilly. Show-offs called it Chantilly, supposedly after French-speaking city founders. It was called the area "east of the Industrial Canal," "Orleans East," or just "eastern New Orleans." Some people called it by their neighborhood names, what used to be: Orangedale or Citrus. Pines Village, Little Woods, or Plum Orchard. My generation would call it the East.

Big Texas money bought a single name that stuck: its vast cypress swamps were acquired by a single firm, New Orleans East Inc., formed by Texas millionaires Toddic Lee Wynne and Clint "Midas Touch" Murchison, one of whom owned the Dallas Cowboys, both of whom owned oil companies. Everything, they felt, could be drained. "Like the early explorers, New Orleans now gazes out over its remaining underdeveloped acreage to the east," Ray Samuel, a local advertising man hired by New Orleans East Inc., wrote in a promotional pamphlet. "Here lies the opportunity for the city's further expansion, toward the complete realization of its destiny." That was the dream.

New Orleans East suddenly became one of the most "unusual real estate stories of this country, the largest single holding by any one person or company within corporate limits of a major city," Ray Samuel claimed. Rather than differentiate among the thirty-two thousand acres purchased by New Orleans East Inc. and those eastern neighborhoods that existed long before the company's arrival (like Pines Village and Plum Orchard), people began calling the entire area by the one broad corporate name: New Orleans East.

Back in 1959, when New Orleans East Inc.'s plans were first under way, the development was expected to "surpass anything that has been done in the past. The huge tract will ultimately have everything, including 175,000 or more residents," a brochure claimed. Developers boldly foresaw a million residents by 1970. This seemed possible. New Orleans was booming, feeling extremely prosperous and proud in the days following Mayor deLesseps "Chep" Morrison's election in 1946. Chep billed himself a reformer before that was political deadspeak. *Time* magazine proclaimed him "King of the Crescent City," for all the bridge, road paving, and building projects he pushed through, including city hall, which in 1957 was deemed "one of the finest and most beautiful municipal buildings in the world." "Glass-and-class," Chep called the new city hall, which was built on top of Louis Armstrong's childhood neighborhood. "Slum cancer," was how Chep referred to those working-class communities of wooden cottages and shotgun houses that were bulldozed to make way for "glass-and-class." These infrastructure projects launched Chep, who some loved simply because he had a New Orleans–sounding name, onto a world stage. He was the city's first national mayor.

By 1960, the population of New Orleans had grown to 627,525, which made it the fifteenth-largest American city. Politicians, businessmen, developers, and planners projected that it would only climb from there, fueled by advances in the oil and gas industry, a revitalized (more mechanized) port that would ensure the city's world-class port status, the economy boosted over the long term by the soaring success of the nascent aerospace industry. "The National Aeronautical and Space Administration's Michoud plant in the eastern part of the city hums with feverish and costly activity," the newspaper stories went. That was the story coming out of city hall, the small-print narrative on the full-page advertisements that appeared in glossy local magazines. Except none of these projections would ever come true. New Orleans would not hold steady, not in the least. The city's population reached its apex in 1960. But no one knew that then.

The newspapers fell hard for New Orleans East. Here was a story with possibility for high drama involving men and money and wetlands, dreaming and draining, and emergence and fate. Not so different from the founding tale of New Orleans itself: unlikely impossible city rising from swamplands, waging guerrilla war against the natural order of things, against yellow fever and all manner of pestilence, most of the city below sea level, surrounded by water on all sides, sinking, unfathomable, precarious—and now look at it!

NEW ORLEANS EAST BIGGEST THING IN YEARS, read the headline in the *Times-Picayune.*

CITY WITHIN A CITY RISING IN THE SOUTH, proclaimed the *New York Times.*

That New Orleans East was now a "new frontier," ripe for development, was bemoaned by columnist McFadden Duffy in the *Times-Picayune*: "This tract was once the personal property of daring French colonists, the productive plantation and game preserve of New Orleans' forefathers. The shotgun blast, the snap of the trap, the whizz of the reel will be heard no more. The 'call of the wild' moves elsewhere, once more crowded out by progress."

It was called a "Model City . . . taking form within an old and glamorous one" that if successful would have made New Orleans "the brightest spot in the South, the envy of every land-shy community in America."

And then, too, it was the space age. Men were blasting off; the country electrified by the Apollo missions and the thought of explorations to come. Few Americans knew that the rocket boosters for the first stage of the Saturn launch from Cape Canaveral, Florida, were constructed in NASA's New Orleans East facilities, in the Michoud neighborhood, where my father, Simon Broom, worked and his son Carl would later work.

The 131-metric-ton stage one boosters built in the East were, one could say, the most important aspect of the rocket for they carried the fuel and oxygen needed for combustion, producing 7.5 million pounds of thrust; launching the rocket into space; and at thirty-eight miles up, self-destructing, burning up in the earth's atmosphere, allowing the now-lightened rocket to continue its mission to the far reaches, the boosters sacrificed for the greater good.

NASA became the main draw that New Orleans East Inc. used to lure other industry. Folgers Coffee was one of the first businesses to come and one of the only ones to stay.

"Boosted into the space age by the Saturn rocket, the dream of New Orleans East shows signs of accelerated movement into reality," wrote a local reporter in 1962. "The dream is staggering—to transform a flat, low wilderness into a city, the size of Baton Rouge, within the city of New Orleans."

In those dreaming days when the city was helping launch men to the moon, in those heady times before white flight, civil rights, the oil bust, subsidence, before tourism would become the main economic engine and codependent, Ray Samuel pronounced: "If ever the future can be studied from the past, New Orleans, augmented by its last remaining section, is surely destined for a tomorrow that neither the facile pen of the journalist nor the measured phrases of a lawyer can express. Posterity will certainly look upon it one day and say, 'What hath God wrought.'"

But when the advertisement for the Yellow House appeared in the Auctions section of the newspaper in 1961 alongside other properties seized due to tax liens or defaulted mortgages or marriages gone bad, my mother wasn't thinking about the hype.

She was a widow, eight months pregnant and renting an apartment on Upperline Street. Webb's stepfather, Nathan Hobley, had begun to visit, impressing upon her the value of owning a home. He drove her around to look at houses, mostly in New Orleans East, which in 1961 was overwhelmingly white. Mom saw herself living in the city, not the distant arm of it, but Hobley encouraged her to pioneer eastward, as he and Webb's mother, Mildred, already had and as others would undoubtedly do. But what did being a pioneer actually *feel* like? And how would you know if you were one? You knew, for starters, when you were the only black family on the street.

Hobley preferred the houses on the longer side of Wilson Avenue, away from Chef Menteur's traffic, the railroad tracks, and the Mississippi River, closer to the schools and the supermarkets. But this one in the ad he had torn from the newspaper was on the short side of Wilson. It was a modest wooden shotgun house painted light green, with a screened-in porch. The structure needed work, but something about it drew Ivory Mae in. The land was almost wild, with grass between the houses—*I can't stand no close-together houses*—where kids could run and play, where the only cars on the street were meant to be there, a rural village right in the middle of building up. Her attraction to the narrow pale structure was nothing resembling love; it was more like dreaming.

She would take it.

Hobley made an offer on Ivory Mae's behalf. The house cost $3,200. It would take a few years to renovate, but Mom would oversee the work from the rented brick house across Chef on the long end of Wilson, the house where she married Simon Broom. Mom paid for her house with money from Webb's life insurance policy. She was nineteen years old, the first in her immediate family to own a house, a dream toward which her own mother, Lolo, still bent all of her strivings.

In 1964, three years after Ivory Mae bought her home, it was ready; the merged family's move there from the rented brick house was not far. If need be, items could be pushed down Wilson Avenue on wheels, past the houses on both sides, until the stoplight where Chef Menteur Highway whizzed its travel motion and where sat the Red Barn with its country-and-western music blaring, then over to the short end of the long street and down maybe fifty feet to 4121.

From the start, the house was sinking in the back. *It needed to be built back up.*

For fifty dollars a load, dump trucks arrived with gravel and rocks and stones. No one was exempt from the work. Mom pushed wheelbarrows back and forth from the front to the back over a temporary bridge made from boards that Simon laid down, her feet and legs muddied. Boy neighbors who saw her said she was a beauty out there, working so hard, inspiring everyone else.

"It was cold," neighbor Walter Davis remembers. "Her nose was running. She would roll up with that barrow, unload that barrow, going back and forth there. My dad and them said, 'Get out there and go help.'" They lent a hand, but she stayed there working, too.

After the family had moved in, Simon Broom planted two cedar trees at the front near to the ditch between the yard and an unpaved Wilson Avenue. The trees, the same height as six-year-old Eddie, were spaced so that you walked between them onto a long dirt pathway leading to the front door. Simon cemented the path, then painted it an ugly taupe more beautiful after it faded.

Ivory Mae made a camellia- and magnolia-filled garden that ran from the front of the house along the side. She planted mimosas—rain trees, they called them, for how they grew pretty pink flowers that fell in such scattered bulk you could sweep them all day and not be done. She planted gladiolas, the way she had seen her mother, Lolo, do. And pink geraniums.

The land did not refuse her advances. She kept going. She laid out a row of shrubbery that ran the entire length of the house, 160 feet. Facing the street, underneath the big front window, she planted cactus trees, as if setting a trap.

Ivory and Simon hung narrow black metal numbers on the front of the house in a crooked vertical line:

4

1

2

1

The screened-in porch existed only briefly, long enough for a few nights out there sipping Old Grand-Dad. Mr. Taylor, an electrician and one of Simon's best friends, was there a lot, smoking his cigars. He was a short wrinkle-faced man, a white version of Sammy Davis Jr. in navy-blue Dickies. Mom would be holding a cigarette, taking puffs from time to time, not even inhaling, the thing burning down to a nub in her hand.

The porch was converted into an extension of the living room, with beautiful French windows that opened out. Mom hung heavy satin curtains that she'd sewn, curtains that she changed out in the winter and spring when the house was remade.

*It was beautiful because that was my first house that I actually owned. Everything was new then. The house was my beginnings. I made it new with Simon's help and my own skills. Brand-new furniture, the one time everything was new. And brand-new carpet. Bright yellow carpet of all things. Why in the hell were people with a thousand children getting yellow carpet. They would be pretty, but it would be a lot of work trying to keep them up.* When the rugs dirtied, Simon rented a carpet cleaner from K&B drugstore off Chef Menteur.

Mom had already started collecting French provincial–style pieces from Barnett's, *a place that sold real nice furnitures. You put so much money down and you would pay maybe fifty or sixty dollars a month. Every time I paid that off I'd get something else.* The couch was wide with yellow brocade fabric with hints of gold and *the prettiest legs.* Its two matching slipper chairs sat in each corner of the room. *And just like my mother I had that big gold mirror that sit right as soon as you walk in the door.*

You walked in and saw you reflected back.

Karen's baby bed was set up in the living room on the perch, a slightly raised and thus stagelike area where the screened-in porch used to be. Karen, like every child who was born to Ivory and Simon, slept in the baby bed until she was so big the bed broke down. Ivory Mae felt her and Simon's bed in the room next door could become dangerous. *We*

*could smother them, you know, if they was sleeping and you were having
sex and all.*

When people tell you their stories, they can say whatever they want.

When Ivory and Simon were both feeling good, after bourbon and a small
party usually, Ivory Mae spoke about buying the yard in between the two
houses, the strip of land that still belonged to Della Davis, who paid taxes
on it from California. Mom dreamed of converting her narrow house into
a double with a porch and a center hall.

*I always dreamt I would have this house that was so pretty. It was
gonna have a nice front yard, a big backyard. Three bedrooms. A sewing
room. I always pictured a front room that had a window with a little seat
running across it. I could see myself just sitting up on the couch with my
foot up. I was gonna have these pillows at my back. I'm reading a book,
just sitting there looking at the rain, at anything. It wasn't a big ole house,
just a nice house.*

In those years, it seemed Simon was always adding on: to the house
and to the family. Not yet with kids, but with dogs. Mostly collies. Beauty
was coal black but missing a tail; there were Jack and Butch, *dogs that
looked at you like they was old men.* For them, a silver chain-link fence
went up, alongside the house in the space between 4121 and Ms. Octavia's
house next door.

No one ever saw Simon Broom cry until the first time one of his dogs
died. *He'd weep like one of them children had died. Big grown man all tore
up and crying like a baby. I'd have to get him right again.* The dogs were
buried in the backyard, out by the septic tanks, close to the back property
line; on the other side of the fence were cottages full of people living.

Their immediate neighbors, Octavia and Alvin Javis, had one daughter, Karen, whom they obsessed over and thus ruined. Karen bore three
children: Herman, Rachelle, and Alvin.

Octavia Javis was sister to Samuel Davis Sr., who lived in the house
next door to them, two houses down from Ivory Mae's new house. When

Samuel Davis and his family moved to Wilson Avenue in the summer of 1963 from a one-bedroom apartment complex with the kitchen and bathroom in the hallway, he and his wife, Mae Margaret Fulbright, already had seven children. Samuel's house was a solid square with slate siding and two doors on the side. It was one big room, formerly part of a military hospital that had been moved to Wilson, but much larger than what they'd had before.

The Davises were also neighbors to Ms. Schmidt, a tall, thin gray-haired white woman who wore thick white cotton socks all the time, for her diabetes. "Ms. Schmidt was uptown," Sam Davis Jr. says. "Her home was uptown. Next to us, she had money."

Her house, a white two-bedroom cottage with a hallway, was separated from the rest of the street by a tall wooden fence that marked a land of no return, especially for boys playing ball. "She took every ball we ever had," my brother Michael says.

"She was just mean to be mean," says Joyce, Sam's sister. "You'd go up on that porch and knock on that door. 'Get off my porch! What you knocking on my door for?' Now once in a while you might catch her in a semi-good mood. That's when she'd finally give you that ball back."

She had two pecan trees, one that sat back by the garage, another closer to the street. She didn't mind the children picking the short, fat pecans that fell near the garage, "You had to work to eat those," Sam Davis remembers. But the ones on the tree closest to the front were the kind you wanted, long and thin and off-limits.

Ms. Schmidt had a garage double the size of her cottage, where she parked her beige early model Ford. As soon as her car turned onto the street from Chef Menteur, she was nearly at her drive. Her universe, therefore, did not consist of much except her house and Mr. Spanata's land, a complex of persimmon groves on two narrow plots, and several houses that faced inward, a small village arranged to mimic his native home in Italy.

Whereas the persimmons in Ms. Octavia's backyard were tiny, Mr. Spanata's were the size of apples.

"He was from the old, old country and didn't want to change," says Walter Davis. "He grew persimmons that I ain't never seen nobody else have. You could take and eat as many as you wanted."

From Chef Menteur Highway, the houses ran down toward Old Gentilly Road in this order: Spanata, Schmidt, Davis, Javis, and Broom.

The short end of Wilson stayed still in a way, anchored as it was by the houses on one side of the street. The houses and the families who belonged to them composed the short end of Wilson's identity, which weathered with time, changed suddenly, then completely fell in on itself, like much else. But back then, it held steady while the other side of the street changed wildly. When Ivory and Simon moved in, the land across the street from the houses was Oak Haven trailer park, owned by J. T. LaNasa, a scheming local businessman.

The children from the houses would, as sport, stand curbside watching trailer homes roll in on the backs of giant eighteen-wheeler trucks whose girth and grunting rattled the street. "Who these people gone be?" Michael would ask Eddie, who was a year older. "I wonder if they got some children."

The families—all of them white—arrived after the trailer homes had been settled on their narrow plots, the Astroturf already laid down, the families pulling up in cars with the hood two times longer than the body, dragging the ground, packed with their belongings. The license plates rarely read "Louisiana." The new neighbors and their rolling homes presented a stark contrast to the fixedness of the houses, the existence of the trailers confirming an elsewhere, the fact that the American dream was a moving target that had to be chased down.

At first Oak Haven existed only across the street from the houses, but because business at Michoud's assembly plant—one of the largest in the world, housing NASA, Boeing, and Chrysler—was booming, Oak Haven expanded to the side of Ivory Mae's house, extending to where

Old Gentilly Road and Wilson met, helped along by LaNasa's newspaper offer of "first month's rent free if you qualify."

The land where the houses stood was always on the verge of being bought up.

So-and-so wanted to buy the sinking land that the houses sat on, but the owners resisted. Wanted the land in order to expand Chef Menteur and then to expand the Louisville and Nashville Railroad line. J. T. LaNasa wanted to expand his trailer park business. The houses were inefficient, LaNasa always said, taking up too much space, to say they weren't all that special. LaNasa, a short, stout man who lived with his family on Gentilly Boulevard across the Industrial Canal, would pull up in his brand-new pickup truck to tend to trailer park business, then stop by the front of the houses on his way out. His offers were laughable. To his mind, it was inevitable: the five houses would be overcome. He returned again and again bearing paltry offers, dangled in such a way that if you weren't careful you might mistake them for compliments.

That September of the move, in 1964, the Beatles came to town.

A motorcade of black stretch limos ferried them out of the airport. The procession made its way down Chef Menteur, past Wilson Avenue. The interstate was a year from finished, making Chef Menteur the only route through the East. The Beatles made a chaotic arrival to the Congress Inn, four miles from Wilson, a squat, one-story motel on Chef Menteur Highway that advertised itself as "100 units . . . with complete lounge and dining facilities," evidence of New Orleans East Inc.'s building "extravaganza."

The Congress Inn was nothing special. But it was a place where fewer fans might converge and if it was damaged, no one would care. This motel would not suffer as might the Roosevelt Hotel downtown, which had begged Beatles management to cancel the group's reservation there.

Gathered at the Congress Inn when the limos pulled up were screaming, fainting girls and ambulances to take them away. The Beatles flew out from the cars into Room 100, where the windows had been boarded up as if a hurricane were coming. Mayor Victor Schiro arrived that afternoon and proclaimed that one had in fact come. The Beatles were, he said, an "English storm." He said, too, that they played music "on a cousinship with jazz, the jumping, danceable historic art form which New Orleans has contributed to world culture," before presenting each member of the group with a key to the city and designating that day, September 16, 1964, Beatles Day.

While Beatlemania erupted just down the road, barely a person on the short end of Wilson Avenue knew it. Around the same time fainting girls were carried off in ambulances, Napoleon Fulbright was jumping down from a freight train that moved along the Louisville and Nashville Railroad tracks at the edge of Wilson, his guitar flung over his shoulder. The older Davis children were running down the block toward the tracks to meet their uncle, Mae Margaret Davis's brother, joined along the way by Michael, Eddie, Darryl, and a tottering Carl, all of them yelling "NAPOLEON!"

"We'd be so happy when he came," Michael says.

"CALDONIA! CALDONIA! What makes your big head so hard!" Napoleon Fulbright, who also went by the name Moti, sang his favorite tune that night, lit by campfire in the Davises' yard, his shadow flitting around the dark block. Napoleon was a man caught in a loop: either crying and singing or singing and crying, arriving in a town or leaving for elsewhere.

He was a hobo and a wino if you were judging by looks, a master carpenter and railroad man by trade. During his stays, he picked up work around town, taught Walter and Sam carpentry, and did renovations around his sister Mae Margaret's house. She'd want a hall here, a wall there.

He cried, the stories go, because he'd gotten involved in the occult and had tried to put a hex on someone, but that backfired, didn't go where it was supposed to, making Napoleon a man forever unseated. From that point on, it is said, he couldn't abide any one place for too long.

The mobile homes outnumbered the houses on the short end of Wilson, but the houses pulled rank. Ours was directly across from Oak Haven's horseshoe drive, paved with broken clamshells that stabbed bare feet. My brothers, led by Michael, played a game of running their bicycles as fast as they could through the U-shaped drive, white tenants yelling out, "Nigger" as they went. The word seemed extended, floating like a blimp; you could still hear it as you flew out of there and back across the street to the side where you belonged.

The houses were ordered inside and out by the standards of the times and so were the children. The adults wore titles in front their names—Miss, Mrs., Mr., Sir, Ma'am. No one knows what would have happened if you failed to address an adult in that way, because it never happened. Children belonged to each other but not to themselves. The street seemed to know when someone deserved chastisement and any parent could oblige. When one did, everything held quiet for a time.

From the time they were small boys, Michael and Darryl went around cursing. When this memory is revived today everyone laughs because, of course. When Simon Broom could no longer stand it, he decided Michael, as the older of the two, needed a spanking.

Go cut a switch.

Michael returned dangling a substandard twig.

"*Mr.* Simon went out there and cut a branch off a tree and beat that negro with it," Sam Davis Jr. recalls now. "What tripped me out, it wasn't that he got beat with a switch, this dude got beat with a branch."

Everyone knew, too, the ferocity of Mr. Samuel, Sam and Walter's dad. He had a reputation for slowly cueing up his punishments. He'd lean the weight of himself to one side of the doorsill and start to talking about what the Bible said.

"Honor your father and mother . . ." Mr. Samuel always began.

"I hate to do this to you, son. I really do.

"So that your days may be long . . .

"But after what you did. It just can't be avoided.

"So that all may be well with you . . ."

It took him a long time to come round to the action. "When Dad whupped, he whupped the whole house, he whupped everything in the house," says his son Walter Davis now.

The older children lorded over the younger. Sam and Walter Davis were the elder by three and four years over Eddie and Michael.

Sam often designed entire summer days, marching the Davis and Broom boys in single file like young army recruits all the way down the Old Road where Mount Pilgrim Church was, chanting military cadences as they went. Naturally, anyone who got out of line would be disciplined.

Along the way, the smaller boys fished for crawfish in the ditches along Old Gentilly Road where, if you weren't careful, one of your car tires might find itself. They'd drop nets into the ditch and pull up buckets and buckets of crawfish for boiling.

Michael and Darryl would often break off along with JoJo, the Davises' youngest boy, to climb over the railroad tracks into the woods where they wandered for hours, fishing and falling into bodies of water formed in the last rains. On the way back, they picked blueberries along the train tracks.

There were ditches everywhere you looked. "It was like we were the rural part of New Orleans," Walter Davis said. One fall, at the start of third grade, his teacher at his black elementary school, McDonogh 40, asked how many students had left town. One kid had gone to Los Angeles, another to Chicago. Walter raised his hand and said he'd traveled to Gentilly, referring to his family's move to Wilson Avenue. "Boy, I said if anybody left town," the teacher said.

"I'm sitting there thinking, 'We didn't leave town?'" says Walter now. "That's when I found out that the East was part of New Orleans."

The women stayed home while the men and boys worked, except for Mae Margaret, who worked small jobs without her husband, Samuel Davis, knowing, beating it back to home before him, ruffling her hair and slipping into a frock. Mr. Samuel worked close to the Industrial Canal at American Marine Shipyard, which in 1967 built the largest aluminum oceangoing commercial ship in world history. Two hundred twenty-six feet at a cost of $1.6 million, but still, Samuel Davis never earned enough to own a car. When he died it was on the job, pumping out a barge.

Simon Broom had begun his work at NASA for the contractor Mason-Rust as a groundskeeper and maintenance man, which meant he tended the plant's 832 acres, painting, grass cutting, and repairing whatever needed it. His niece Geneva, the daughter of his sister Corrine, worked at NASA, too, but in a lab. He could see her through the narrow window in the lab door wearing a white hazmat suit.

The older boys mimicked the men and found work on the short end of the street or in its vicinity.

Walter and Sam had as some of their hustles cutting grass, landscape design, and washing the trailers in Oak Haven, many of which, unlike the houses, had air-conditioning so that "when you opened the door that cold air would run out of there." Walter knew because he'd gotten familiar; his employers would offer him Coca-Cola in six-ounce glass bottles. In time, he'd also clean the trailers' insides, which is how he worked a vacuum for the first time. One tenant offered him corned beef with chowchow relish. He was thinking he had it going on and that life couldn't get better.

Sam Davis was on the way to Spee-D Super Market on Chef Menteur one day when a Gypsy family who were living across the highway on Chef next to a greenhouse stopped him. "They asked me to get something from the store for them. That was gonna be a nickel or a dime. I said, 'Yeah, I'll get it.' They said, 'You wanna make some more?' They had me cut the grass. Said, 'You wanna make some more money?' I said, 'Yeah!' They had a chicken out there in the yard, they had a goose out there in the yard, they had a lamb out there in the yard. Look, everything that was in the yard died that day. They wanted me to kill it. Said, 'Grab the chicken, kill the chicken.' I tried. I was running around after that chicken. I did want to catch the chicken. I could not catch that chicken. Old lady ran over there, I don't know how she got that chicken, grabbed that bad boy, swung it up, broke its neck, came down with it, took a hatchet, chop. This is all one move, martial arts stuff. I said, 'I want my money.' Well here's how they paid me. All that stuff was walkin' round out there in the yard, they gave me a big ole plate of all that stuff. That's how they paid a brother. I went home. I was mad. I gave that plate to my mom. She didn't have no problem with all that stuff dyin'. She was from the country. Mama tore that up."

This story sounds outrageous but around the same time an advertisement appeared in the *Times-Picayune*'s Lost section: "ANYONE knowing the whereabouts of either Gypsy or Spanish people with a large tan-and-white collie, please call WH 5-3775."

The first year they lived in the not-yet-yellow house, Simon and Ivory Mae threw parties in the backyard for every holiday or birthday, or any other excuse. The liquor was stocked and stored in the shed at the back of the property. Simon would spend the entire morning cutting the grass, setting up tables and chairs. His friends from NASA would come and so would members of the various social and pleasure clubs to which he and Ivory belonged. All of the neighbors knew to appear.

Ivory Mae loved entertaining. She prepared the food herself: stuffed eggs, potato salad, and fried catfish. Sometimes, she pulled vegetables from her small garden. They had begun growing tomatoes and okra on the land.

Friday was a recurring holiday, too: Mom would either take the bus to meet Simon at Schwegmann's Super Market across the Danziger Bridge on Gentilly Road, or he'd come to the house to retrieve her. They dressed nice to go to the store because chances are you'd run into people you knew. Inside, they'd start off holding hands, Simon's entire salary balled up in his pocket. One full basket led easily to two. Simon knew everyone—if he didn't know them he would soon—and was always stopped in the aisle having conversations. *The ice cream and thing be melting in the cart he so busy talking.*

Simon Broom built a wooden bridge wide enough for the car tires to roll over the ditch into the land close to the side door of the house where the children would run out and unload the bags.

From time to time, Simon set up a projector in the backyard, turning Fridays into movie night for anyone who wanted to come watch Hollywood fantasies—horrors like *The Last Man on Earth*, which the children loved, and *Mary Poppins*—the side of the house becoming, for a night, the greatest movie screen.

# VI

## *Betsy*

"Look," says Eddie. "It was like a movie, OK?" He was six then.

"It was pitch-black, nighttime," says Deborah, who was eleven.

Nineteen sixty-five. Tail end of a notably mild hurricane season. It rained so hard the yards between the houses flooded—standing water for three days—but that was normal. This mid-September storm was erratic, busybodied; it seemed not to be able to make up its mind on where to go. "Wandering Hurricane Betsy, large and tempestuous," the newspapers said.

The house was full of babies. Karen was not yet one; that birthday was two weeks away. Carl had just turned two. Michael was five. Darryl, four. Valeria, eight.

Simon had been called by NASA to join the emergency crew piling sandbags, but that was just in case. He expected to get right back. And anyway, Uncle Joe was staying at the house then. He was in between loves. No one knew the details, but some woman had put him out, or he had left some woman. Neither scenario was unusual for him.

"We all went to bed," says Deborah.

Last she knew, the hurricane had turned, was headed to coastal Florida.

"All of a sudden I hear: 'Get out the bed. Now, now, now.'"
It was midnight.
"We put our feet down on the floor."
Water.
The house turned frantic.
Miss Ivory said, "Get the baby bag." Karen was the baby.

Later, it was said that the water rose twenty feet in fifteen minutes.

There was no attic to climb up into, no way to sit above it all to wait it out. When Uncle Joe opened the front door, water bum-rushed him. Deborah panicked: "We gon die, we gon die."

"She started screaming at the top of her lungs like a person going crazy," says Uncle Joe.

"She went into hysterics," says Eddie. "And look, they couldn't stop her."

"Yeah, cause it was black. It was . . ." says Deborah.

"She wouldn't move," says Eddie. "She was stuck."

"So I slapped the piss out of her," says Uncle Joe now. "Shut up," he remembers saying. "This ain't no damn movie."

The water was waist-deep on the two adults. They waded through snakes and downed wires toward the high ground of Chef Menteur Highway, which was, for once, carless, to shelter in Mr. LaNasa's high-sitting trailer park business at the corner.

Carl rode Uncle Joe's back, Deborah his side, holding tight to the baby bag. Mom had Karen and Valeria, one on either hip.

Eddie, Michael, and Darryl swam like fish.

"I was a tiny boy," says Michael. "Water was so high. I'm swimming, I'm swimming. The dogs, too. The water was moving through here like we was in a river."

*He's right. The water was sweeping us down the street.*

The water had in fact swept in like a river, its course and fury made possible by many things, most of them man-made. Poorly constructed levees, for one.

And two: navigation canals touted as great economic engines that would raise the profile of a weakened Port of New Orleans by creating more efficient water routes that would, it was hoped, draw more commercial traffic. The Industrial Canal, dredged in 1923, physically separating New Orleans East from the rest of the city in order to link the Mississippi River to Lake Pontchartrain, was the first. Then in 1942, the Intracoastal Waterway was expanded through eastern New Orleans to connect with the Industrial Canal. But in 1958, construction began on one, more damaging than the rest: seventy federally funded miles of watery channel linking the Gulf of Mexico to the heart of New Orleans, shortening ocean vessels' travel distance by sixty-three miles. It would officially be named the Mississippi River Gulf Outlet, but everyone would call it MR-GO.

As with much of New Orleans East's development, in the early days of MR-GO only its positives were touted. In 1956, Louisiana governor Earl K. Long praised the "inestimable value to (1) the immediate area through which it passes, (2) the state of Louisiana and the city and port of New Orleans, (3) and the entire Mississippi Valley." When construction began in 1958, the marshes lit up in a dynamite explosion that BOOM, BOOM, BOOMED, debris flying three hundred feet in the air, raining fragments and mud on the heads of scurrying city officials, "many of whom looked for cover that was nowhere to be found," the local paper reported. Mayor Chep Morrison called it "one of the miracles of our time that will have the effect of bringing another Mississippi River to New Orleans." He could not know just how true his prophecy would turn out to be.

Soon after it was built, the environmental catastrophe MR-GO wrought would become evident. Ghost cypress tree trunks stood up everywhere in the water like witnesses, evidence of vanquished cypress forests. The now unrestrained salt water that flowed in from the Gulf would damage surrounding wetlands and lagoons, and erode the natural storm surge barrier protecting low-lying places like New Orleans East. This is what happened during Hurricane Betsy: one-hundred-plus-mile-per-hour winds blew in from the east, pushing swollen Gulf waters across Lake Borgne, a vast lagoon surrounded by marshes and open to the Gulf. Water entered the funnel formed by the Intracoastal Waterway and MR-GO. Within this network of man-made canals, the storm surge reached ten feet and topped the levees surrounding it, breaching some. This is how water came to be rushing in at the front door when Uncle Joe opened it; and how water came to flood more than 160,000 homes, rising to eaves height in some. At the same time, Lake Pontchartrain's surge entered the Industrial Canal and ruptured adjacent levees, including those in the Lower Ninth Ward, topographically higher than the East, but equally vulnerable for how close it is to the canal.

It was a flood so devastating that Walter Davis said, "I was thinking, 'Man, I can tell my grandkids about this.' That's how awesome Betsy was." So awesome was Betsy that her name was retired from the tropical cyclone naming list. Governor John McKeithen vowed on television and on the radio, in front of everybody, that "nothing like this will ever happen again."

President Lyndon B. Johnson flew into the Lower Ninth Ward the next day—the area, even then, was a drowned and abandoned symbol of water's destructive power when facilitated by human error—declaring the city and surrounding areas a disaster zone and eventually pledging an $85 million protection plan that would rebuild levees and shore up flood protection systems, which would, in August 2005, forty years after Betsy, fail.

Those who dared look close knew this would be so, just as they knew that many of the new houses built in the East, owing to slipshod construction, were already having major subsidence problems; this sinking would only worsen. They knew that sometimes after hard rains sewage from canals rose in people's toilets and tubs like the devil's bath, that the dream would not, could not hold, because the foundation was bad.

In the days after Betsy, people tallied their losses. The damage exceeded $1.2 billion, a record for the time. There was mud everywhere. Drowned rats and dead cats floated. National Guard trucks drove around. Some people were arrested for looting.

People in the deluged areas recalled hearing dynamite, an eruption in the middle of their scrambling. "The levees were blown on purpose," my brother Michael says. Levees had been blown before by the federal government, during the Great Mississippi Flood of 1927 to divert water away from more "valuable" neighborhoods. In New Orleans East, the marshes had been blown to dredge MR-GO. Everyone in the area heard. They knew the sound of dynamite. Thus Michael's story was not entirely in the realm of fantasy. This story, that the levees were blown, the poorest used as sacrificial lambs, would survive and be revived through the generations.

The city's vulnerability to widespread flooding and the images of stranded poor people shocked the nation. HUNDREDS MAROONED ON ROOFS AS SWOLLEN WATERS RIP LEVEE. HURRICANE BETSY LEAVES NEW ORLEANS WITH 16-FOOT FLOOD, the *Chicago Tribune*'s front page blared. And: 70,000 LEFT HOMELESS AS WATER RISES.

"Why weren't the people of inundated areas evacuated?" asked Dr. Edward Teller, a Berkeley atomic scientist, during a speech in New Orleans before the Mid-Continent Oil and Gas Association, weeks after the storm. "Your city had hours of warning," he went on. "Why wasn't it anticipated that the levee of the Industrial Canal might break . . . that the Mississippi River Gulf Outlet might overflow?" City officials resisted his plain questions, attacking his integrity instead: "The uprooting of people is not as simple as Dr. Teller wants it to be . . . to evacuate a million people into the wilderness in the middle of the night would have resulted in more casualties." But, Teller said, people had only twenty minutes to evacuate between the time they knew water was rushing in and the time it had risen over their heads.

"Who is this Teller who comes in here making unauthorized, ridiculous, and irresponsible statements?" asked newly elected mayor Victor

Schiro, using his status as a native New Orleanian to deride the foreigner as an outsider, short of understanding, an interloper who could not possibly know.

"He's talking completely out of his field now," said Louisiana Governor John McKeithen. "Why, he has probably never been to Louisiana before. He flew in here Tuesday night and damned us all and then flew back to Los Angeles the same night," he said before quoting President Lyndon B. Johnson, who he claimed called Teller a "scientific nut."

More than seventy-five people died in Betsy. Most drowned. Or they died of heart attacks while waiting to drown. Fishing boats were overturned, people whipped to death by winds. Or their houses collapsed on top of them. A few people died while being evacuated, literally while walking from their house to the rescue boat.

Even though expanses of New Orleans East Inc.'s property lay underwater, development surged on. Everyone vowed to rebuild higher, better. The feeling caught. New apartment houses went up everywhere on Chef Menteur Highway and elsewhere in the East, just as the interstate highway was expanded and the North Claiborne Overpass erected, decimating much of the cultural and economic life of historic black neighborhoods. It was still boom time; oil was cheap. NASA in Michoud had sustained superficial damage in Betsy—broken glass, peeled-off roofs—but the space vehicles were untouched, and the program eventually expanded, with work on the Saturn V (to this day the largest, most powerful rocket in NASA history) under way for rocketing into space thirty-two months later. Liftoff.

MR-GO would become an expensive failure, eventually costing taxpayers $20,000 per boat that passed through. Rarely used, it would not usher in its projected revenue and jobs. But, post-Betsy, the levees would be shored up by the government just as Lyndon Johnson promised. New Orleans East Inc. and other eastern developers would use this fact in their advertisements to lure more and more people to the area. And in 1968, Congress would spur this repopulation along by creating the National Flood Insurance Program, which allowed people to buy flood insurance at low rates, even and especially in dangerous flood zones.

# VII

## *The Crown*

*A*fter the floodwaters receded, the Broom clan got to work removing carpets and waterlogged furniture, turning the house upside down, letting it air-dry. Nothing could be saved. Ivory Mae and her children stood on the curb watching the house, just as her mother had stood with her after their house had burned down. She was too young to understand loss then, but she knew now.

For weeks, the family stayed with Lolo on Dryades Street, applying for every possible voucher, the children getting typhoid and diphtheria shots, while Simon saw in the ruins a chance to build up. He recruited his brother-in-law Ernest Coleman and Ernest's son Lil Pa, skilled builders. Uncle Joe, who had become a detail-obsessed carpenter, helped, too. Mr. Taylor, the electrician from NASA, rewired the house, but badly. They poured a slab of concrete in the back and set about expanding upward, mistrusting the ground. This is how the shotgun house with two bedrooms became a camelback shotgun house with a second bathroom, a den, and an upstairs bedroom rearing toward the sky in the back, a crown that did not run the length of the house. If you looked at it from the side, it drew a boxy, backward lying-down L.

Simon salvaged much of the wood that was used from teardowns of perfectly fine buildings around the city, a tendency that Mom hated. Maintaining a house, she felt, was just like cooking: detail mattered. *Everything Simon did it would last for a minute. Even if he painted you would see some places where he missed it. He was a jack-of-all-trades and master of none.* Simon thought perfect work like Uncle Joe's took too long, which butted against Mom's constitution as Lolo's child. But she did not always say so. She had evolved from saying everything that came to mind to feeling everything and abiding it. When she spoke up, she and Simon fought mightily over how the house was rebuilt. Do it yourself then, he would say, furious. She couldn't, even if she might try. When the addition was close to finished, Dad thought he could save money. After the men had installed temporary stairs, he vowed to finish them alone to show Ivory Mae that he could. But he never would.

The family grew into all the spaces of the house: all rooms were multipurpose; all were lived in, the family's traces everywhere. Everything was used; nothing existed solely for show.

Every step you took in it was an important point on its map. And the house, fancier looking than before, drew people to it. This was why Uncle Joe always returned during his low times. And why there were always raucous parties; big booties squeezed into the den of the house; highballs aplenty; arms striving for the new ceiling, timed to musical beats; people milling about in the yard, telling stories, lying, and smoking.

Ivory and Simon made their bedroom in the nose of the house, closest to the street, their room separated from Valeria, Deborah, and Karen's—the girls' room—by the kitchen. It was the closest thing to privacy. They installed wicker accordion doors that did not lock. Michael was always barging in at the wrong moment. "Get out of here boy," Ivory Mae was always saying.

The girls lived in the back, as if to hold the house down. The boys made their place in the newly built crown. The upstairs window looked down upon the narrow space of yard between our and Ms. Octavia's house that now sat higher, on bricks, post-Betsy. Simon or Ivory Mae never ascended those temporary steps to upstairs, granting the boys a right to privacy that no one else had. Upstairs, Eddie, Michael, Darryl, and Carl made for themselves a private kingdom with boy rules and boy systems.

If the house was Mom's beginnings, if the house was her world, she had to find within it a seat. She set her sewing machine on a table underneath the windowsill in the kitchen just feet away from her bedroom. The window looked out onto Ms. Octavia's house and the lawn in between. Specifically, her window faced Ms. Octavia's bathroom window. That would have been her view, except she sat too low to see anything.

When Mom was sitting in her chair, crocheting or making clothes or curtains, the small bathroom original to the house stared at her back.

Carl Broom hated that small bathroom, said it seemed eerie from the start.

"Certain kind of window in there, when you look through you could see a cross way up in heaven, some kind of reflection," he says now. "I was scared of that son of a bitch."

By the time he left it, he would have sprayed all the walls of that bathroom with piss from trying to finish so quick.

The windowpane had a numinous quality that drew congregants from the Divine Mission of God who came to the house on Wilson, as if on pilgrimage, to see what Carl was nervous about. They stood three or four at a time in the small bathroom, fitting themselves in among the towels and cleaning supplies, supplicants lined along the bathtub where Eddie, Michael, and Darryl took a bath every night. "Three kids to a tub," says Darryl, "just like Adam and Eve before they knew they was naked." Dr. Martin proclaimed the window a sign from God, a blessing that had befallen 4121.

But then the blessed sign began appearing in other houses too, becoming a small phenomenon, a miracle for ordinary people owning a certain brand of windowpane, a human interest story on nightly newscasts.

There was something in the material of the glass, it was eventually decided, that sunlight drew out. The manufacturers had used a new material. They were sorry for the hype and for Carl's fear. You could call a certain 1-800 number for a replacement. *It just disappeared after they said that.* Thus retaining its magic.

Mom's seat was also near (every place was near another place in the shotgun house) the refrigerator, which was at first a humming monstrosity and later a grunting monstrosity with a lock to ward off the boys' growing hungers. Her seat was steps beyond the side door where the familiars knocked. If neighbors needed to borrow sugar or rice or salt, they went away satisfied, the goods wrapped in a paper towel.

From her seat, she made the clothes, every single piece that everyone in the house except Simon wore. This custom continued until the boys were teenagers and too embarrassed to wear pajamas made from the same bolt of fabric. The girls were teenagers and embarrassed, too, but they never had their way.

Sitting in this seat, she made new curtains for every room to match the coming in of seasons. She made curtains for the cars, too, for the white van and for the blue van that replaced it, the one she and Simon drove for many years before passing it on to the boys, who replaced the back seats with a twin bed, making a motel room on wheels that could be used for dates, Ivory Mae's curtains pulled shut.

Later, I would peer from this kitchen window and watch the van rocking with the motion of my brothers and their dates, but that is running ahead. The boys are still children. And I am not yet born.

Those vans, the white one and then the blue, were driven around town to Schwegmann's Super Market, to school graduations, to Zulu balls during Carnival time. Those vans were driven to meetings of the Pontchartrain Park Social Aid and Pleasure Club to which Ivory and Simon belonged. They were driven to Atlanta *following behind the Saints who lost every time.* Simon—a Freemason—made the social calendar; Mom made appearances.

The curtains made the van pretty, but Mom wished for a smaller, sportier car. New. This desire ran deep, but a two-seater would not match her current life. Mom longed for what now came to feel impractical, what wishes are made of. She loved, above all, beautiful things. Simon cared about affordability. His going-to-work car, a Buick Skylark, did not even go in reverse. Rather than spend the money to fix the car once and for all, he simply had the boys come and push it out from the driveway.

As Simon and Ivory settled into life in the rebuilt house, time moved in the usual distinct increments (morning, afternoon, evening; weekends and weekdays), but after a while, everything new turned old and they stopped seeing time as composed of moments. The years blurred.

Two years later and the temporary stairs were still temporary. During the building-up years, no new children were born, as if the house itself were the baby being raised. But then Deborah noticed the gray maternity dress hanging above the kitchen doorsill. The oldest three—Deborah, Valeria, and Eddie—moaned. Not another one. A new baby affected the girls' lives especially; they were the babysitters and the assistant housekeepers, picking up after the older boys and the younger children: Michael was seven, a year older than Darryl. Karen was three to Carl's four. Eddie thought things had gone too far: "I was wondering when the hell it was going to stop," he said. "I thought they was just going to the hospital and picking up kids." One more girl would have evened the score, but Troy was born on Thanksgiving Day 1967, which meant Uncle Joe made the holiday meal, memorable for not being Ivory Mae's cooking. People took this Thanksgiving anomaly out on Troy for years. But he was the first child to come home to the reborn house.

He was a quiet baby and would be a quiet man. Too quiet, Mom sometimes thought. He could go deadly still in his bassinet on the living room perch. Mom would come rushing, lifting and shaking him vigorously like a can of frozen orange juice. She later thought this shaking might have ruined him. Or else it was the cigarette smoke she blew into the soft spots of all of her babies' heads thinking that would cure the colic. She learned mothering by doing and by Lolo. *I didn't have friends. Mostly it was y'all, my children. And my mom. I called her every day, three or four times a day.* Often, she thought of these conversations while walking Eddie, Michael, and Darryl to private school at St. Paul the Apostle on Chef Menteur Highway. Their tuition was paid for by Webb's mother, Mildred, who never wavered in her promise to support her dead son's children. They wore starched white shirts and starched khakis pressed by Deborah and Valeria, who went to the only black public school in the area at the time, McDonogh 40. Valeria complained daily about her hair: "Miss Ivory put it in a million little plaits, a million barrettes sticking out everywhere." But what she hated was passing by St. Mary's Academy where the light-skinned girls flaunted their coloration, long hair, and class. Valeria was a seeing child; she noticed the way Eddie and Michael's aunts and grandmother treated them like small kings. "They ate up Eddie and Michael. We watched. We just . . . we just couldn't understand. Until later, when we were older."

Jefferson Davis Elementary on the long end of Wilson was still segregated, which was why in a letter to Mayor Victor Schiro, a tax consultant referred to the East as "safe" from school integration. As in: "Of course Lakeview, Aurora Gardens, East New Orleans . . . and part of Gentilly is still 'safe' but what about other parts of New Orleans?" Another letter writer made the case this way: "By integrating the schools of New Orleans there is a potential loss of sixty million dollars yearly in purchasing power, plus the loss of much revenue which have to be made up from some source. Will the negroes foot the bill with their welfare checks?????"

Eddie, who was nearly ten, scored badly in all his subjects at St. Paul, including physical education. After learning his father's story, Eddie felt that he was biding his time, waiting to die at eighteen just as Webb did.

Michael was an academic star. His class assignments were always perfect. He finished them earlier than the other children, then, out of boredom, taunted the kids who still worked. Darryl's behavior was the polar opposite. On report cards, teachers called him "everyone's favorite." "Darryl is just a wonderful example of what an ideal student should be! He's loved by all his teachers, and he seems to just do the *right* thing most of the time. It has been my pleasure to teach him; I anticipate a fine future for Darryl," one teacher wrote.

Around the time school let out and the four-o'clocks bloomed, Mom would be at the stove finishing a meal that tasted as good as it looked. Simon would have arrived home by now from his work at NASA, coming down Old Gentilly Road and turning right onto the short end of Wilson, his car the first in a long procession that took the same shortcut to avoid traffic on Chef Menteur Highway. When Simon pulled into the drive, the other men following him yelled out of their car windows, "Simon, you son of a bitch, working so close to home." The men kept on across congested Chef Menteur to their lives. Simon went inside for maybe a minute, then was back out in the yard, which was the room of the house he loved best. Sometimes, for no reason, after the kids were asleep, Ivory and Simon danced on the grass between the houses, Mom looking up at him, her arms stretched to hold on to his neck, her head buried in the middle of his chest. He still couldn't believe the sight of her. *His pretty little wife.* He felt powerless against her.

On nights such as this they sometimes found themselves sitting on the edge of their bed, Simon sometimes with his head in his hands—either he had a headache or he was thinking something through. No one can know now. He was always a young-acting old man; she seemed always a grown young woman.

Mom would say, *I love you, Simon.*

*I said I love you Simon.*

When he stayed silent, she pressed. *You don't love me back?*

"You're my beautiful, pretty little wife," he would always say. It was not enough, no, but nothing ever was.

One time, in 1969, two years after Troy, Simon turned to Ivory Mae and said, "We don't need to be having all of these children."

*You're right,* she had said.

And then?

Byron Keith was born.

Her children's births were not the main way Ivory Mae measured time passing. She recalled the particulars of births only if they were wrenching enough. The children born from her body were all one big delivery to her mind, mostly indistinguishable, the results nearly always the same. But Byron was born in springtime, unforgettable because her mother, Lolo, my grandmother, had bought her first house in St. Rose, minutes from Ormond Plantation where she was born. Preston Hollow was a U-shaped subdivision built for black people atop former oil fields, surrounded by petroleum processing plants, but this detail was not in the official sales pitch. The house on Mockingbird Lane was the fulfillment of a dream, a place where Grandmother's family could routinely gather, a place where she could unpack her beautiful things and give them a permanent geography. But her husband, Mr. Elvin, was against it, preferring city living. Lolo bought the house anyway. "He went to work a renter and came home a homeowner," says Uncle Joe. It is said that Grandmother gave him an ultimatum, declaring her love first, then telling him she was moving to St. Rose with or without him. So which was it?

With, his actions said. With.

Byron took his position as the baby boy of the male kingdom, but quietly. Michael was forever taunting him, sometimes dangerously. Once, he tried to hang Byron (like a shirt or a pair of pants) from Mom's clothesline in the backyard. Joyce Davis, the neighbor, saw it go down and tells a heroic story about how she was standing two houses over in her back door when she saw Michael lifting Byron onto a trash can, how at eight months pregnant she ran and climbed the fence into our yard to stop Michael, who she thought was playing but who kept at his work on Byron even after she called for him to "stop that boy, stop it now." He was tying a rope around Byron's neck and looking ready to remove the trash can. "If it were not for me," she says now, "Byron would not be here on this earth." But the Davises are prone to hyperbole. Joyce's mother, Mae Margaret, was said to have rescued Simon Broom, who was stuck underneath a car that had been poorly jacked up. Mae Margaret was sitting on her porch, the story goes, saw the car fall on Simon, and bounded over to singlehandedly lift it, releasing him from death's grasp.

Simon's life—which Mae Margaret had allegedly saved—consisted mostly of work. On weekends, he banged violently on the faux-wood paneling leading to the boys' room in the crown, his voice booming: "Come down." Any time past 5 a.m. he considered oversleeping. The boys—Eddie, Michael, Darryl, Carl, a too-small Troy, then later Byron—scurried and pouted on the way to whatever job he had found for them to do. "When every other kid in the world was sleeping," Eddie complains, they were already crisscrossing the city. "We either painted something, tore something down, or did pest control." In the evenings, they sometimes catered parties. Other times, they assisted Mr. Taylor on electrical jobs.

"The white Mr. Taylor," Carl says, "was Daddy's white best friend, but he also had a black best friend. His name was Mr. Taylor, too. We used to go around his shop and clean up." The black Mr. Taylor owned a barroom in back of a barbershop. Simon bartered his and the boys' services for haircuts. Every Friday night, the boys arrived to empty the black Mr. Taylor's trash barrels onto the back of Simon's old black Ford, which announced its arrival everywhere it went. On their drives, Simon related his philosophy on how everything should be done well, how what they started they needed to finish, wisdom he didn't always follow.

The boys sometimes went to Saints games before the Superdome was built, back when they were held at Tulane Stadium—but to work—entering the stadium against the wave of fans filing out. Eddie found this deeply embarrassing, but Michael made fun of it, throwing Carl into the massive dumpster and rolling him down the ramp that led indoors.

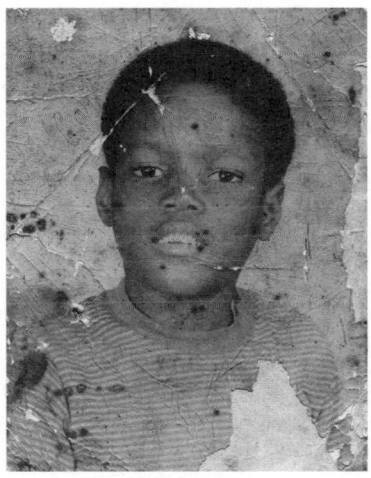

Carl was Simon number two except he could be wild in his appearance, his hair uneven and patchy, his skin dry as if he had fled the moisturizing sessions that came after Mom's bathing.

"I used to always get Daddy's trumpet ready for him," says Carl. "Just wipe it off for him and try to play it. He'd say, 'Boy, give it here, let me show you how to play that thing.'"

Of all the children, Michael could be counted on to make Simon mad. "I used to taunt him and mess with him. I thought I was so smart. I'd say, 'Time to cut the grass. Gr-*ass*.'" Doing things like taking his shotgun and sawing it off. "That really pissed him off." But when they had the yearly job painting "a big old house right off City Park" that took several weekends, Michael was a fearless helpmate, a tiny but capable boy who would climb to the highest part of the house and, perched there precariously, paint. "I ain't know that I could fall down and break my goddamn neck." Byron saw the boys doing their work and even though he was too little for much he begged to do his work, too.

Simon rarely seemed content with leisure. Except for when he was playing golf in Pontchartrain Park with a used set of golf clubs that "he used to hock every time we needed money," says Eddie. The other time was on Mardi Gras day when he wore his gorilla mask or dressed like a hobo with torn clothes and a briefcase with rags hanging out, the case filled with the alcohol that put him *three shades in the wind*. He would drop Ivory Mae and the children off at Grandmother's sister Lillie Mae's house for Carnival, retrieving them at the end of the day. Mom, who did not know how to drive, prayed for safety the entire way home, her children in the back seat.

In the house at night, Mom often dreamt vivid scenarios where her sister, Elaine, and her brother, Joseph, were in mortal danger and she flew above them wanting to rescue them, except she couldn't figure out how to land.

She was still "God's kid," she knew, but she sometimes felt not so different from the household fixtures, those immovable, bound things hanging on the walls that could not speak: golden angels and flying cherubs with cutouts underneath their wings for candles and dry flowers. A wall mirror half the size of the wall. To look at yourself in. Things with which to make a home. Delivered by messenger's hand to the front door of 4121 Wilson, after she had chosen them from the Home Interiors catalog.

She was not a fearful person, except when it came to crawling things with tails. When she was home alone with the kids, without another adult in the house, and saw a lizard, she called Ms. Octavia to come over and search up and down until she found the thing. Mom might stand back by the door to the bedroom and point and yell about how the thing was somewhere in the closet, crawling on and between the hanging clothes. Ms. Octavia would bury her head in among the clothes Ivory had made, bang her hand against Simon's golf club bag to scare the lizard up, and not stop until she rooted him out, dangling him between her thumb and index finger, dropping him outside in the yard.

The adults on the street stayed out of each other's houses for the most part, unless there was good cause: Mom would go inside Ms. Octavia's house when her husband, Alvin, died and Ms. Octavia would return the favor.

Big changes, the ones that reset the compass of a place, never appear so at the outset. Only time lets you see the accumulation of things. At the start of the seventies, the following stacked: An advertisement appeared in the *Times-Picayune* with the headline LOUISIANA PURCHASE 1971. "The biggest land deal of 1803 was the Louisiana Purchase," it read. "The biggest land opportunity in 1971 is New Orleans East." More than a decade had passed since the dream of New Orleans East Inc. had first been launched. Since then, Clint Murchison had died and Toddie Lee Wynne, feeling defeated, withdrew from the venture after his riverfront hotel deal fell through.

Nothing about the dream of New Orleans East Inc. had come to pass. The area contained 8,000 residents in 1971; 242,000 fewer than its original goal.

In 1972, the Apollo missions ended, reconfiguring things at NASA's Michoud plant, which had, most notably, built the first-stage Saturn V rocket that launched astronauts to the moon. Though the plant added $25 million to the local economy and Simon kept his job, the 12,000 employees, counted in 1965, dwindled to 2,500.

Residents in Pines Village, one of the earliest eastern neighborhoods, minutes from Ivory Mae and Simon's house, were threatening lawsuits against the city's Sewerage and Water Board for "mental anguish and anxiety suffered during floods and all heavy rainstorms." The city, they claimed, approved developers' plans even though they knew elevation was too low for sufficient drainage, a problem exacerbated by new communities that further taxed the substandard drainage systems, "negligence . . . that is injurious to our health and safety," one prophetic-seeming letter writer said. "What happens in this area will make New Orleans prosperous and strong financially or else it will cause the city to strangulate itself," he wrote. "Undeveloped it is a chain around the city's neck. . . . This area to the east is not a mirage. It will not go away if you ignore it. It will stay and haunt you if you do not start thinking of it as a part of the city."

In its design—more apartments and trailer parks than houses; more streetlights than trees and parks; more paved roads than walkways—certain parts of the East were best driven through. Landscapes communicate feeling. Walking, you can grab on to the texture of a place, get up close to the human beings who make it, but driving makes distance, grows fear.

The Red Barn on the corner of Chef and Wilson that before blasted Nancy Sinatra's "These Boots Are Made for Walkin'" became the Ebony Barn with Lee Dorsey's "Working in the Coal Mine" coming off the stereos, serving a new clientele. Around this same time, construction began on a public housing project, a scattered site some city planners called it, on Chef Menteur Highway just next door to the Ebony Barn. Its proper name was Pecan Grove, but on the streets it was just the Grove. Before it was all the way finished, the children on the short end sold Ms. Schmidt's fallen pecans to the construction workers. Ms. Schmidt couldn't have cared less; she was leaving the East soon anyway. The Grove would house 221 apartments in a reddish-brown brick, two-story compound. According to the newspapers, it was an "experiment" meant to bring residents from several different downtown housing projects closer to New Orleans East, which soon-to-be residents would call the country. From the start of the complex's going up, Simon Broom said it would infest everything around. He pointed to Press Park, where Ivory Mae's sister, Elaine, lived, another scattered site, more westward. Press Park had been built on top of the Agriculture Street Landfill, ninety-five acres and seventeen feet of cancer-causing waste.

By the late 1970s, the racial composition of the East had flipped. Within twenty years, the area had gone from mostly empty to mostly white (investment) to mostly black (divestment).

The street transformed, too. In 1972, Samuel Davis Jr., eldest son to Mr. Samuel, married and left the short end of Wilson. He was the first child raised on the street to do so.

My sister Deborah was second to go. She had graduated from Abramson High School in 1972, and was expecting to go to college, as her father had promised her mother before she died, but now Simon Broom had different ideas. He couldn't afford it, he said. He thought she should get a job and help support the growing family. Deborah would not do that, she told her father. Even though she was eighteen years old at the time, she was spanked. No, she was beaten by Simon Sr. with a sugarcane and then afterward, because she was raised to be obedient to elders, Deborah ironed his work shirt for the next day, ironed it the best she ever had, packed her bags, and waited for her mom's sisters to arrive and take her away with them. Despite him, she enrolled in college at Southern University of New Orleans days after leaving home.

Shortly after that, Karen was run over by a car on Chef Menteur Highway while trying to get to third grade.

Karen and Carl were one year, one grade, apart. Sometimes, the two of them walked alone to Jefferson Davis Elementary on the long end of Wilson. They were told to hold hands and cross together; they had done it often enough to take it for granted. Carl must have run ahead. Karen was a silent child, which was just the thing to get you forgotten.

Either the car ran up on the neutral ground while they waited for the light to change or else Karen was running against the light. No one wants to recall the details and no one wants to lie. However the way, a car dragged eight-year-old Karen by the tail of her dress, pulling her past several businesses down the highway, past Jack's Motel and Arbor Bowling Lanes. Eventually, the driver realized what he had done, that a child was caught on the fender of his car. At which point, he stopped to release her. Then tore away.

Now Karen was lying shoeless alongside Chef Menteur. Carl left her to run down Wilson to get Ivory Mae, who was inside the house doing something forgettable but who ran outside wearing clothes because when you have small children you always dress with the start of the day. But she was barefoot, outside running to Karen who was lying in the middle of Chief Liar road, cars whizzing by, not noticing her at all. *You could see all the way to her arm and leg meat straight through to the bone.* Karen, lying there in shock, said, "Mah, can I still go to school?"

In one of the cars that happened to be speeding down Chef when the ambulance arrived was Mrs. Mildred, Webb's mother. She stopped and thrust a coin purse into Ivory Mae's hand. Here, take this, she had said. In case you need it. My mother didn't resist.

Karen was rushed to Charity Hospital, downtown, where the doctors insisted that Mom should have brought the skin that had been torn off Karen's arms and legs; it could have been used, put back in its place. *If we had thought to look for the piece they could have sewed it back on.* Instead the surgeons cut skin from elsewhere on Karen to make the skin grafts.

They prophesied, the doctors did, that Karen would never play again. Her arms and legs would never be in motion; too much of the muscle had been damaged. But Ms. Sarah, the deceased Dr. Martin's daughter who now ran the Divine Mission of God, called their projections human folly, the work of feeble minds, and said it would not be so. This word, what Ms. Sarah said, was what Ivory Mae believed.

Karen would use her arms again. She would move them as though nothing had ever happened. The only evidence of the hit-and-run to remain was the skin itself, which had raised up to form islets on her arms and legs that she would forever hide underneath long sleeves and pants, which she wore everywhere, and still does, even in summertime.

Michael and Eddie and Darryl had by now been moved from St. Paul's private school to Jefferson Davis. Eddie wanted to go to another school and the adults complied. The tuition for the three could go toward something else, they must have reasoned. But this shift was traumatic. It changed Michael forever. Jefferson Davis had only recently tried to integrate. There were few black children in the school. Michael, Eddie, Darryl, and Karen were four of them.

In 1970, the mostly white teachers still called students niggers. Things like this still happened: Michael, ten and in fifth grade, scored a perfect grade on a math test. "They put a big ole zero on the thing," he said. "And so I'm checkin' it, going . . . I don't know what's wrong. It wasn't nothing but adding and subtracting. So I'm saying, this supposed to be right. I said something must be wrong with my brain that this look right to me. . . . They gave me a zero, so it have to be wrong? But everything was right." The white girl sitting in front of him—teacher's pet—turned around to look. "I was embarrassed for her to see my paper. I kept on checkin' it. I couldn't believe it. She said, loud-like, 'Gimme that paper, nigger'" and snatched the test from Michael's hand.

"I had my pencil in my hand, so I just jumped up and stabbed her a couple times with the pencil."

Mom and Dad were summoned to the superintendent's office downtown to discuss Michael. He was given an IQ test and scored off the charts, was deemed one of the smartest children in the school system, but he was suspended and punished for his actions. In the meeting, Michael kept insisting that the teacher show evidence—his perfect math test—but no one ever produced it.

"After that I just felt like, well, shit, I had everything right and they marked it wrong, so even if I'm right they still gone make me wrong. I was like, that shit had failed me so I'm not even worrying about that no more. I'm trying to learn everything on my own, doing what I need to do to survive. And I didn't figure it out till like maybe twenty years later. I said, 'Boy, you just as stupid as they come. Them people did that to you and you let that affect your life for all those years.'"

School was over for him, but the streets rewarded smarts.

The completion of Pecan Grove imposed a territorial fervor on the area where before there was none. You belonged to either the Grove, the

Goose, or the Gap, gangs that claimed three or four streets (at the most) as territory.

Those relocated to the Grove belonged now to a turf that, as they saw it, needed defending. The streets west of Wilson in the direction of St. Paul's became the Gap. Starting at the Sisters of the Holy Family and running all the way to the highway was the Goose. You identified yourself as being from one of those three. Or else you were from Flake or America, single streets but gangs unto themselves. America Street produced the most crime.

The short end of Wilson did not, according to this map, belong anyplace, but the boys on the street (who were mostly my brothers) sided with those in the Grove. Carl met his best friend, Manboo, who lived in the Grove, in a minor fight of sorts over a game of football where the Broom boys were in a match against Manboo and his nine brothers. "They hit us," Carl said. "But we broke out of there. They chased us across Chef Highway, but everybody on the street ran them back. They were throwing bottles at us, but we had been here before the Grove was built." This lent an air of superiority. "They could never run us. They could never scare us." By virtue of this, my brothers fought on behalf of the Grove even though they went to school in the Goose.

Now that Michael was out of school, he wielded his body on the streets like a weapon. He had scoliosis, it was discovered, which required that he wear a body brace, a metal-and-plastic contraption beginning at the base of his neck and ending around his waist, to straighten his spine. There was no hiding it and no removing it before fights unless he had time to plan, and fights rarely came with warning. Getting the brace on and off required the assistance of another person and this would cause a show, draw the wrong kind of attention.

Inside the brace, Michael was straight up and down. When it was off—Michael spent more time outside of it than in—his body slunk down into a floor of excruciating pain. The cast was not well suited to his lifestyle; he made enemies and had to watch his back, which he literally could not turn his neck to do. In fights, he tried to grab his opponent's head in order to bang it into the metal sheathing on his body: that move could end a fight quick. The brace became a part of his mythology on the streets, spoke of the lengths to which he would go, making him a legend among the Grove, the Goose, and the Gap. Someone on the block said Michael damaged his back during an aggressive play session, when he was younger, playing Wolfman, his favorite version of hide-and-go-seek where he hid high up in Ms. Octavia's oak tree and jumped down on top of the heads of kids passing on the ground below.

Or maybe he got hurt the time he and a friend were breaking into the Municipal Auditorium on Rampart Street and the friend let go of the rope, plunging Michael five feet through a window.

These were the stories perpetuated by Michael and his brothers and his friends. They were better than saying he was born with scoliosis, a defect not gained by virtue of street heroics.

If Michael had worn the brace as the doctors had suggested, he could have avoided having a metal rod put in his back when he was a teenager. The metal rod was supposed to have been removed eventually, but it never was.

He punched hard, too, the hardest, so that people ran from his knuckles. He approached each row as his last—his punches let you know that—which is how he came to be called Boom, short for Tick Tick Boom. His always trying to release his body from its constant hurt gained him a reputation as wiry, snappy, liable to go off at the slightest. Family members said he was like his father, Webb, in that. When he laughed it was a fusillade, a gurgling back in the throat that sounded like a DJ scratching a record. Sometimes when he spoke to a person they felt cursed out even when he had not uttered a single profanity.

While Michael fought, Eddie moved back and forth between the house on Wilson and Lolo's house in St. Rose where he could act like the man of the house. He was tall and lean with a massive afro, had made it to eighteen without dying, and was spoiled rotten by Grandmother just as his uncle Joe had been. He was more comfortable in her house. For one thing, fewer people lived there, which made it neater. Eddie liked order and was easily embarrassed. The "millions of children" in the house on Wilson bothered him. "All my friends lived on the other side of Chef. All my friends had nicer homes," Eddie says. "That house and the East was a place where you grew up and you grew out. There was no staying for me. I think I got a sense of entitlement from my real dad's people. Because I know they had . . . I knew they had . . . you know what I'm saying?"

He knew they had money.

Eddie belonged in a distinct way to his father's mother, Mrs. Mildred, and her three daughters. They claimed him. He grew up, it could be said, a different class from the rest of his siblings and from his mother even. But it was Lolo who gave him the attention he needed that Mom did not have time for. He worked instead of going to school, supported at first by a small inheritance left by his father to all of the Webb children when they hit a certain age. Grandmother was the kind of woman Eddie admired, hardworking and concerned with having nice things. She had two cars parked in the garage of her house on Mockingbird Lane even though she could not drive (cars for people to drive her around in). She was contained but occasionally mercurial. She could go off on you in a split second. When the presentation of the body stands in for all the qualities the world claims you cannot possess, some people call you elegant. Grandmother was that, yes, but sometimes elegance is just willpower and grace, a way to keep the flailing parts of the self together.

Lynette Broom was born in 1974 just when everyone thought Ivory Mae and Simon were done having children. There were ten children already; the youngest, Byron, was school-age. Lynette was the sole baby in the house—for five years. The first girl since Karen ten years earlier, Lynette was pampered by Simon. He dared not approach the door to home without having something in his hand for her. If he was empty-handed, he'd turn back. A small thing—a single candy, a flower, a pretty rock, he knew—was always better than nothing at all.

Mom saw in Lynette a vision of her earlier self—except for the hair, a short afro that Mom called *lil bush*. *Lil bush* factors in most stories Mom tells of Lynette's childhood. Lynette had ringworm in her scalp, forcing Mom to cut her hair just when it was growing beyond *lil bush status*; how *lil bush* made its world premiere in the backyard of our cousin Geneva's house at a fashion show; how Lynette was so pretty even with her *lil bush*.

Deborah was wed not a year after Lynette was born, her reception held in the backyard of the not-yet-yellow house that she had left in haste a few years before. The morning of Deborah's wedding, Dad woke before the house to cut the lawn between our house and Ms. Octavia's. How many times had he had said jokingly to Deborah: "When you get married I'm gone *run* you down the aisle?" But now the day had come, and he was not happy to give his first daughter away. He fixed his sadness outside, while his sons, who were mostly young men now, set up tables and chairs for a hundred guests.

Ivory Mae and Deborah had spent hours together preparing for this day. The walls gleaming white after Simon had painted. Lynette's crib moved from the living room perch, replaced with a short bookshelf that held the *Encyclopaedia Britannica*.

Auntie Elaine brought the flowers. Ivory made the food—stuffed eggs and fried chicken. She made the look of the place, too—sewing cloths to dress the tables and the entire wedding party's attire, adding special touches (some with lace, some with collars, some without) to some of the bridesmaid's cloud-blue dresses made of fabric that looked like it itched. She sat at her seat beneath the kitchen windowsill working up these dresses until the moment the bridesmaids stepped into them. That was her way. Once her fire was lit she refused sleep and food to see her creations through, the entire kitchen transformed into a sewing room, her cutting board spread out over the table, pieces of cut-out patterns everywhere you looked.

A cousin had lent Deborah a white wedding dress and veil. In this way she and Ivory Mae were alike, wearing borrowed outfits at their weddings, but they did not speak of this. Nor did they speak of all that had come between them before that day—how Ivory didn't defend Deborah against Simon, for instance.

The smaller boys—Troy who was nine and Byron who was seven—shuffled through the rooms of the house meeting everyone else's demands, while the older boys stayed upstairs lifting weights, polishing shoes, touching up haircuts, whatever else.

Ivory Mae readied Deborah as she has not readied a daughter since, as she had not been readied on either of her wedding days. In photographs, there are only glimpses of her, half into her light-pink dress, foam curlers still in, hidden behind Deborah's veil.

Eventually Simon would dress, and someone would snap a photo of him posed with Deborah where he seems in a playful mood. Deborah in pale white next to her father in his slate tuxedo with a black bow tie larger than his pale-blue corsage. Like Deborah, he, too, had a narrow face. He had the hands that Carl has now, meaty, dirty, oil stained, balled up in a fist.

Dad's white best friend, Mr. Taylor, sat in the wooden pew of Rosemount Missionary Baptist Church crying like a man at a funeral, as if Deborah were his own child walking down the aisle. He carried on like

this through the entire service: before Deborah could make it down the aisle, her father's, my father's hand gripping her arm, both her hands strangling the bouquet. In the photos, Simon wears a look of confused surprise, his mouth slightly ajar. I have worn this same face.

While Mr. Taylor cried as if he knew something others did not, Deborah stood taking the hand of Henry Cooley in matrimony. She was tall and thin with an oval face that held seeking eyes and controlled lips that seemed to be clamping down on something soft.

The photos tell the story: My father in front of the window posing with Deborah. Walking Deborah down the aisle. At the wedding reception in the backyard of 4121 Wilson posing next to Ivory in her cropped jacket worn over her dress, her hair long and fluffy, coal black. They pose before a wooden fence that separates the houses from cottages behind, beyond which is a cargo shipment creeping along the Louisville and Nashville Railroad tracks on the Old Road.

There was dancing and music and Deborah was feted. It was a wedding reception like many others, except more so. Deborah had come back home to be married in the very spot that was sinking and needed to be constantly built up but that her father had made precisely for moments like this.

The reception mostly held to the outdoors, but people still wandered inside, to the bathroom, and then others went in *just to see what we had,* Mom was convinced. She had grown to believe that the objects contained within a house spoke loudest about the person to whom the things belonged. More than that, she believed that the individual belonged to the things inside the house, to the house itself. Maybe what bothered her was the large crowd, many of whom she had never seen before or had seen but did not know. Now they were traveling through her house. People coming inside had never bothered her before. It all felt to Ivory Mae like the start of something new, sticking underfoot, her first time feeling embarrassment about the condition of the place where she lived, the place she owned and thus belonged to. Here came the shifty settling in of shame.

# MOVEMENT II

## *The Grieving House*

*Strange house we must keep and fill.*
*House that eats and pleads and kills.*
*House on legs. House on fire. House infested*
*With desire. Haunted house. Lonely house.*

Tracy K. Smith

*Whatever nature do, this house do.*

LeAlan Jones, age thirteen

*This house is made of bone.*

Yance Ford

# I

## *Hiding Places*

*I* am five.

This small bathroom where my father sat on the toilet after work and died and where, before then, Mom took baths with green rubbing alcohol and Epsom salts to eat the weariness, is for me a playroom full of things no adult ever touches. The sheetrock leaning against the wall, smelling of mold, is my chalkboard, and the neon-green lizards crawling in and out through holes in the screen are my students. Standing on two bricks lifts me high enough to see out onto the alleyway running behind our house and over the fence that separates where I live from where my friend Kendra lives in the trailer park next door. Careful when coming down that my lavender jelly-sandaled foot does not step into the medium-size hole in the floorboard that will eventually become a large hole letting in more sound and outside creatures.

After this was the room where Daddy went quiet, it was a room with a washboard in the tub and then an actual washing machine, but Mom says *the plumbing was never right.*

Those plastic white tubes, contorted limbs twisting through exposed walls, are still here for me to look at, but the machines are not. The tub is gone, too.

There is still a heavy door that closes, with a hole for a knob where I have stuffed tissue paper for privacy. I like best to hear the voices in the house calling for me and not being able to find me where I am, here, where I can wait anything out until the night.

The other bathroom is in the second half of the house, in the add-on that Daddy started but never finished, next to the den with the wood-framed TV of my height, where the Flintstones and Jetsons live. Everyone uses this new bathroom just beyond the girls' room that is pink and mine since I am a girl, too. This bathroom is the only room in the house with a lock. I take full advantage of this, especially when I want to get away from my big brother Troy whose nerves are always bad. His right ear points and I fixate on it. The more his leg shakes when he sits watching football, the madder I can make him. I'll get up close to his arrow-shaped ear and yell, "Ear, ear, ear!" to rile him up and sure enough he (a seventeen-year-old boy) will chase me through the house from front to back—from the living room through Mom's room, through the kitchen and the girls' room where I sleep and into the second bathroom.

"That's why you Ear," I'll yell from behind its locked door. And since Troy will wait a long time outside it saying, "Wait till you come out lil gawl, you gon see, you gon see," I memorize the room's insides, learning right then and there the geography of hiding.

The second bathroom is also where I take my baths. The whole time I am in the tub, Mom is asking me whether anyone ever touched me down there, in my privates. *I don't care who it is, it could be your brother, your sister, your uncle, your cousin, your daddy, whoever, if anyone ever touches you down there you make sure to let me know right away. That is your and only your privates, that belongs to you, that is off-limits. I don't care who it is. The preacher or the teacher. You hear me. No one is ever to touch you in your privates.* She tells me this nearly every time my body touches the water. When my big sister Lynette is sharing bathwater with me, she hears it, too.

Mom's voice, when she is worried, has the same girlish sound as it does when she's entertained by whatever small thing I am finding hilarious.

*Your daddy, whoever.*

But I don't have a daddy, I think but never say.

It takes a long time for me to know why I don't have a daddy, but I am the *babiest*, I am told, last and smallest. Babies don't need to understand.

# II

---

# *Origins*

*I*n the story told to me and in the story I tell of myself, my father dying and my being born are the same line. I am born; my father dies.

One day, in my adult years, I tell my mother I want to know the story of me: "When you told Dad you were pregnant again, did he say something?"

*No.*

"What did he say?"

*Nothing.*

"Not a single word?"

*Here we go again!*

*You were born in seventy-niyen. They say you were in distress. All them children I had, ain't none of them ever been in no distress. And you been in it ever since.*

On the day I was born at Methodist Hospital, my father's brother, Junius, was buried in Raceland. It was New Year's Eve. Auntie Elaine stood witness in my father's stead, my mother silent in labor as she had been with all of her eight deliveries before. She didn't believe in making a show.

"You gotta holler, you gotta make some noise or them people won't ever come do nothing for you," Auntie kept saying. *You make enough noise for the both of us,* my mother said back.

Of all the children to appear from my mother's womb, I was her only cesarean section. My having been born this way relegated her to bed rest for two weeks, the longest she ever sat still after a birth, the longest she sat still in her thirty-eight years. Normally she'd deliver a baby, rest for several hours, leave the hospital, head to Schwegmann's Super Market to collect baby formula, then go home. This time, someone drove her to Grandmother's house in St. Rose where I could be handed over to Mom in the bed where she lay. Doctors had instructed her not to lift me or anything my size; at seven pounds, I was too heavy a lift. My mother prided herself on her high tolerance for pain, but no part of her had ever been torn or cut, not even for pierced ears. Over two weeks of immobility, her body seemed slow to heal. *The bed takes all your strength,* she started saying. From then on, she'd avoid it, except for sleep.

Simon Broom stayed back in the house with the older children, preparing the next youngest for school. Lynette, who was then five, remembers wearing torn underwear underneath her dress, which never would have happened had Ivory Mae been there.

I have the notion that a new baby come into the world ought to be cause for celebration. I imagine, then, that my father saw me and said what fathers say at the sight of their twelfth child. But I cannot know for sure because no one who came before me, the people on whose memory I must rely, has a thing to say about my father's reaction to me for the six months he and I lived in the same house, which is technically the six months I knew him, which happens to be the time when babies begin to see and hear the world, which is the time when they sit up alone, roll, rise up on hands and knees, eat solids, are smiling, laughing, and babbling. I have heard it said that a person is emotionally stunted at the age when major trauma hits. But what can the mind or body know at six months?

It was the summer of 1980. Simon Broom came home late that one night with ten pieces of Popeyes chicken (spicy) and apple pie for Lynette. On his way inside, a bottle of Old Grand-Dad slipped from his grasp and burst itself on the pavement. He sat down on the bed and told Ivory Mae he had a terrible headache. Unusual, him speaking about his body. He stood up from the bed. Went to use the blue-walled bathroom just off the kitchen. Stayed much too long. Mom went to check. She found him slumped over, head in lap, fedora upside down on the floor, and hoisted him, my father, Simon Broom Sr., onto her back. She, five feet, eight inches of woman, carried six feet, two inches of comatose man, saying not one word at all.

*To hear that much man be so silent scared me half to death.*

Hear the sound of her pulling him through the narrow shotgun house. Out of the bathroom, five gliding steps on polished linoleum, then left past the refrigerator with the lock on it, eight winded steps through their carpeted bedroom where Daddy's American flag sat folded in the bottom drawer, and into the living room where six-month-old me lay in the bassinet on the perch.

She eased Simon down onto the gold brocade slipper chair where he rested in his coma.

*You were a tiny baby, but you were the only one to witness me dragging him like that.*

*I called Deborah. I guess he was breathing. He had to be breathing. His eyes were crossed.*

*Simon, Simon.*

*Octavia came over.*

*I said, Let's call an ambulance. Deborah said, No, we're not waiting for no ambulance.*

Deborah and her husband, Henry, arrived at the house and drove him to the hospital.

At Methodist on Read Road in New Orleans East where I had been born six months before, it was determined that Simon Sr. had suffered a massive aneurysm. Now he was connected to a breathing machine, his room a swarm of family members summoned by his younger sister Corrine, whom Mom found overwhelming, having always been slightly distrustful of people she perceives as *biggity* or *trying to be too much*. It was not the *too much* part that bothered her, just the obvious trying. She liked to use the word "humble," silencing the *h*. Corrine, she felt, was the opposite of *umble*.

Mom shrank. Looking and knowing but not saying. The doctors sought her out and pulled her aside. She was Simon's wife. If he recovered, they needed her to know, he would be a vegetable.

She spent all of the first night there by his side. On the second day, Simon Jr., his eldest, arrived from North Carolina. It was his thirtieth birthday. Dad died shortly after 1 a.m., the next day, Saturday June 14, almost Father's Day.

There were too many people for privacy, but Ivory Mae was there standing next to him when he took his final breath, which she would not have noticed at all except for the trickle of blood running out from his left ear.

*Whatever it was, it had burst.*

His death certificate lists intracranial hemorrhage as cause of death, a brain aneurysm.

*Blood built up. He had too much blood.*
*I just kissed him and walked out the room.*
*And I said, That's it.*

He was fifty-six years old to Ivory Mae's thirty-nine. They had been married for sixteen years. The obituary in the *Times-Picayune* puts his death on June 14, 1980, at 1:35 a.m. Daddy is one of twenty-six deaths listed in the newspaper on this day, but because his last name begins with *B* he has the good fortune of appearing second on the page, his life summarized in one short column of newsprint, enough to fit between your pointing finger and thumb if you were to open them wide in the shape of an L.

After Simon Broom's death, Auntie Elaine went back to the house on Wilson, climbed the steps to the crown where the boys were, and told them that their daddy had "left for heaven." Carl, who was sixteen then, says he ran down those stairs "like oil spreads fire." Ran to Daddy's former room, but he was not there.

Simon Broom died on a Saturday (the day after Simon Jr.'s birthday) and was buried on a Monday (Valeria's birthday). Beecher Memorial Church on North Miro Street, where he was a sometimes member, was packed with friends from NASA, jazz musicians, and people Simon knew from around town. Strangers who only knew of him lined the perimeter of the church, leaning against the walls; others congregated outside its doors.

Mom dressed like a widow. Simon Sr. was dressed as if headed to a jazz gig. Mom had chosen for him a tie with red spots on it, but the Masons intercepted her desire, something about Masons and the color red at funerals, one of the men taking the tie from around his own neck and tying it onto Dad's corpse lying in the casket. This made a small commotion, getting a tie onto a dead body.

*Simon didn't look anything like himself. He looked ashen. They weren't fixing people up back then.*

Simon's and Ivory Mae's children took up the entire front pew. Simon Jr. was thirty. Deborah was twenty-six. Valeria, twenty-four. Eddie was twenty-one. Michael, twenty. Darryl was eighteen. They sat alongside Carl who was sixteen and Karen, fifteen. Troy was twelve. Byron, eleven. Lynette was five.

"Daddy bought all us boys a black suit before he died," says Carl. "Daddy said every man s'posed to always have a suit. Wore those same suits to his funeral . . . I wonder if Daddy knew he was gone die?"

Cousin Edward, Auntie Elaine's middle son, sat among the siblings wearing a brown suit—as if to break up the monotony.

I am told that of the twelve children, I was the one not taken to Daddy's funeral. *Nobody wanted to be holding no baby.* I stayed home with Joyce Davis, our neighbor on Wilson.

Except for a reading from Mom's favorite psalm: "I will lift up mine eyes to the hills from whence cometh my help," the service was overrun by the Masons whose Sir Knight, Ezekial Frank, "32 Degree Most Wise," took out a separate advertisement in the newspaper that called for members of "Amitie Axiom Chapter of Rose Crox" to attend funeral services of "our late Sir Knight SIMON BROOM." The attending men wore aprons and cloaks and wielded swords. "They were wearing little skirts," Darryl says. A cross of two swords lay on top of the coffin. As part of the ritual, they turned off the lights. One of their members rang a bell and intoned my father's name:

"Simon. Simon. Simon?" they called. "Arise.

"Simon?"

Just then, the swords fell, startling Karen, who, horrified at the thought that Daddy might awaken, rise up, and walk again, screamed at the top of her voice, betraying everyone's fright. The whole church jumped. Then quiet blew through the sanctuary. The walls froze.

"Why you walking on the backs of your shoes?" Simon Jr. asked Lynette. Her feet were hurting. He lifted her up over the casket to peer down on her father, who, for the first time in her life, offered nothing back.

Even though Daddy played in Doc Paulin's brass band, there was no jazz funeral. Doc Paulin wanted one, but Mom, overcome by the thought of yet another detail, said no. She regrets this now. I, too, wish she had said yes to this request and have sometimes felt that the absence of that detail somehow disturbed my own personal narrative. It would have been nice, for instance, to tell the following story: I am rhythmic because I have come from musical lineage. My father was so great an artist that he was honored with a jazz funeral. Horse-drawn carriages moved through the streets of New Orleans; people danced behind. To be able to say: "I have come from that."

For the repast after the funeral, most of Dad's family met at Corrine's house, less than a mile away from the house on Wilson where our immediate family gathered. *All the big, important people went to Corrine and them house.* Already, Mom harbored self-consciousness about her own home, and this only grew with my father's death, his absence illuminating the house's frailties.

After my father died in the small bathroom, the room folded in on itself: its dark-blue-painted walls peeling, the tub transformed into a storage bin, the socket hanging from the wall with pieces of electrical tape showing, the sink collapsing.

*No one tried to fix it back up.* The house becoming, around this time, Ivory Mae's thirteenth and most unruly child.

# III

## The Grieving House

$\mathcal{D}$addy did not, of course, wake to those funeral pleas ("Simon, Simon, Simon") or any of the ones that came afterward in the quiet of grief. The house at night was full of half-hidden sobs. Byron, the youngest boy, took it hardest, clinging to Mom wherever she went and then, after a time, going mute. When he started to speak again, weeks later, his body held his father's stalwart positioning, as if during the silence he had decided on a permanent way to be. As a boy, Byron wore the same fortified face he would wear seven years later as a marine.

Mom moved me from my bassinet in the living room to the space in the bed that Simon had occupied. I was a small dot lying where the great mass of my father used to be. During these cruel nights, Lynette woke from nightmares about the small bathroom where he died. The house, on some nights, would become a byway full of sleepwalking children on a voyage to Mom's king-size four-poster bed, which at times held all of us, sweating, splayed, entangled.

Dad's NASA coworkers had gathered more than a thousand dollars, the most money collected on behalf of any employee, but the relief would not last long. Mother was now keeper of the house. She had six adult children, two teenagers, and the youngest four who required constant attention.

*Simon's death was one of the most horrific things for me, but I had you. You were just six months old. So that was work to do. If I had gone to pieces . . .*

*The time when I would have really been mourning, really been sad, I was turned toward you. What more therapy can you get, running behind this one and that one?*

Simon was her second husband dead. *I figured I had two husbands and both of them died so it was time to do the single thing or people would be calling me the men killer. I had God on my side, that was my friend. I didn't have human friends. I was relying on Him.*

Her prayers became even more intimate: *Father God,* she began, *you know my heart,* like talking to her best friend.

*My main goal after Simon died was to raise all my kids and I didn't want anybody to help me. Another man wouldn't want to raise them like I wanted to. I said to myself, "It's up to you" and tried to do the best I could.*

And so she—a woman so striking that men routinely ran after her when we were out in public together—remained alone and forever untouched by another man. Deep down I think she, too, had come to believe that she, in her power, killed men.

In Simon and Ivory Mae's nineteen years together, Mom had never learned to drive, never managed money or bills. That suddenly changed. She worked small jobs, catering parties or helping at Corrine's home nursery. The Lafon nursing home, of the Sisters of the Holy Family, on Chef Menteur, where her sister, Elaine, already worked, hired her as a nurse's aide, but she would study to become a practical nurse like her mother.

When the reality of her new world was still fresh, she'd say aloud, *Simon will come round, he will be here any minute, Simon will be here after while.*

But he never came around the bend.

It was the survivor's season of firsts:

The Friday after the funeral, she shopped alone at Schwegmann's, seeking Simon in the aisles as she would a misplaced child, longing to hear his chatter, wishing for the ice cream to be melting in the basket while he spoke too long to every single body. *I wish, I wish, I wish. Everything we did together we held hands. He was my friend.*

At the end of Simon's death month, Darryl turned nineteen. Weeks later, he was arrested for stealing computers from Livingston Middle School. Darryl went to jail; Mom could not afford to bail him out. When Simon was alive she'd tell him to get on the boys, tell them to do right. "No, you need to learn how to tell them," he would always say. By dying, he forced her to do so.

Her form of discipline emerged from a keen sense of morality and a spiritual compass. You didn't blame others. Her voice never rose much, but her language and tone bent. When she was upset she cleared her throat. *Enough,* or *All right now you've run out,* she would say and that let you know. *I am your mother. My job is to instruct you on right from wrong. What you do with that is up to you. But I'm always going to tell you the truth.*

The August after Simon died, Carl turned seventeen. "Mr. Broom number two right here," he had started calling himself. He took a job at Morrison's cafeteria where Valeria also worked, washing dishes in the evenings after high school classes let out. He was a junior. Morrison's was the first of three jobs Carl would have in life. "Daddy had trained us. I wasn't worryin'," says Carl now. "You don't depend on nobody for nothing, you make your own money. Daddy had then built his clan."

A week after Carl's birthday, Lynette turned six. At the start of summer, just before her father died, she'd graduated kindergarten. Mom made her a white dress with ruffles at the bottom. She posed with her teacher, Ms. Serraparoo, in front of a bulletin board where "1980" glittered in teal, as if it were a year to be proud of. But the photograph Lynette actually carried around was the last one taken of her with Dad in which she appears as his musical sidekick, dressed in a colorful jean jumpsuit, her *lil bush* perfectly round, wearing oversize sunglasses and a heavy red necklace. On her feet, white Buster Browns, polished.

Earrings gleaming, hands in pockets. Dad next to her in a black Kangol hat, playing the banjo, his body arched toward Lynette. Both of them singing. Her lips like *ooooooooh.* They pose on the front porch, the door to the house wide open.

Who captured them, I wonder, in this special light?

After Dad died, that banjo stood alone in Mom's closet, behind all of the clothes she had made. Sometimes, when crouched in there, I'd lean against the cold banjo case.

In September, Karen turned sixteen. No birthday passed without a celebration; grief and celebration sometimes look alike. There was always a homemade cake and a gallon of Neapolitan ice cream sitting on a pretty tablecloth, always a small party around the kitchen table.

At first, Mom caught the bus everywhere she needed to go: to work; to church on Sundays; to Charity Hospital downtown for doctors' visits with the children; to Krauss, a department store on Canal Street for the home sales; or to the well-baby clinic on Almonaster Street. Or else, she waited for the older boys to give her a ride, but that felt too much like the past. *I was a little pathetic at first. I needed to make myself know things.*

Eddie, by then twenty-two, tried teaching her to drive, using the lid of her red beans pot as a steering wheel, but she tired of that ploy. *Put me in the actual car, boy.* He lost patience once they were behind the wheel: *He was the worst teacher in the world.* She enrolled at Victor Manning Driving School and made her way around town in a small red student car with a neon warning sign. She was a careful student, both hands on the wheel, thrilled that she would no longer have to wait for anyone or anything. *It was my Independence Day.*

My mother had always made a pilgrimage to Webb's grave on All Saints' Day, and after Simon Broom's death she continued that tradition, visiting her two dead husbands, leaving flowers on their headstones, mere feet apart. But a few years beyond Simon's death she decided to stop, feeling that some aspect of the dead men's spirits might accompany her in the car on the drive home.

The first Thanksgiving arrived, four days after Troy's thirteenth birthday.

Then came Christmas. The children retrieved the fake tree from the attic, carrying boxes of branches down the stairs, dropping them in a heap on the living room floor, before getting to work matching the color-coded stems to the base. Mom's job was to fluff the branches so that the tree looked full, so that the tree looked real. Afterward, she draped gold garland around it and hung balls made of golden threads that were always unspooling. She spread a white satin cloth underneath to hold the presents.

The ceramic statue that grandmother had made of our cat, Persia, was parked under the tree. This cat was a replica, a stand-in, for the beloved dead cat who had been white and fluffy with green eyes. I never met the real Persia, but the replica was white and hard with green eyes. Mom moved it around the living room whenever she felt like it, but it never traveled beyond. At Christmastime, Persia's likeness was always near to the tree, a recurring present.

In photographs taken on Christmas Day 1980, Mom and Lynette pose by the tree, leaning against the gold slipper chair that holds a blanket where eleven-month-old me is supposed to be.

But I am a wandering child.

*I used to always have to be finding you from somewhere. You never were a kid like Karen or Lynette, satisfied. They were more like kids who would want to be around you. You would play with something I gave you one minute, then throw it away. You couldn't just color, you couldn't do nothing in the lines, you would have to do the whole page.*

On the last day of December 1980, six months after my father dies, I make one year old. In the six Polaroids of me from babyhood, I am often on a brother's lap, my hair in three mounds, in the middle and on either side of my head, pout mouthed and trying to get down, eyes looking over at something outside the frame, as if saying, "I'll be over there, I'm coming." I am constantly being held against my desire, clinging to the side of the chair, knuckles reddening from holding on so tight, as if I do not trust my adult brothers to handle my baby weight. But when I am in my mother's lap, I am breaking my jaw laughing so hard, hands clapping instead of holding on. She is in a silk gown, both hands around my bare stomach, still wearing her wedding ring, braless, afro headed, delicate boned, golden colored, her chest and collarbones showing, her legs wide open as if in the act of bouncing me, smiling so that you can see to the back of her tongue.

*I had a lil baby. What can a lil baby know?*

In a picture taken outside the house, I am returning from elsewhere, barefoot and diapered, holding a decrepit baseball mitt. I am captured midstride, examining my found object, oblivious to the camera. My journeys away from home take shape, I am convinced now, in these early days.

# IV

---

## *Map of My World*

*M*y growing-up world contains five points on a map, like five fingers on a spread hand.

This world of mine, it must be said outright, is a blur. I can see, but only up close. This is how my big brothers, hiding in plain sight, can jump out from the open, yell boo and still make fright in me.

I hide my eyes' weakness from my mother for a long time. It is not hard, she is busy making her new world. My poor sight and the hiding of it shapes my behavior and thus my personality, becomes me in a way only time made me know. I needed, I always felt, to get out in front of things (people and circumstances) before they could yell boo. In photographs from these blurry years I wear a vacuous look, turned in the direction of, but not seeing the eye of the camera. My mother discovers all of this, the poor eyesight and my cover-up, when I am ten. But that is five years away from now.

The farthest dot away from me in this universe (the thumb) is Grandmother's house in St. Rose. We call her house the country even though there is little open land except on former plantations. In St. Rose, I see certain things for the first time. Like giant horses ridden on sidewalks or on top of the levees.

To get to the country, we drive on the interstate for thirty minutes, then down a narrow three-mile road that we call "long road," with swamp on both sides and no shoulder. We cross two sets of train tracks where every time I pray Mom's banana-yellow Aries won't give out the way Uncle Joe's car did when he was a young man and had to push his car off the tracks seconds before a train arrived. This is likely one of Uncle Joe's tall tales: *One of his stories*, Mom says. Grandmother always says, "Don't tell stories" when she means don't tell lies. I keep trying to know the difference.

After escaping the train, I latch onto other fears in the moving yellow car. We speed through night, Lynette and I in the back, Mom alone up front. In the dark, peering out the back window, my eyes make horror out of all they cannot see. This is the time of *Swamp Thing* and Jason from *Friday the 13th*. "ChChChHaHaHaHa, ChChChHaHaHaHa," Lynette is always taunting me, at home after we watch the horror movies where I sit right in front of the screen where everything is scariest. These are the days of burnt Freddie Kruger and his red-and-green stripy sweater, *The Thing* and *Gremlins*, who I am convinced live underneath my bed and in the kitchen at night.

When I think of Grandmother's house, I recall her in the bathtub, heat rising from underneath the door crack and moving into the hallway. I remember her sky-blue Daniel Green slippers, how her toes hang off the front. How in the bathroom mirror she dabs her face with a red puff that smells like canned cream. And her kitchen: Grandmother bakes a Bundt cake; Lynette and I fight over who gets which utensil from the leftover batter. I like the metal whisker where I can slide my tongue through the maze. Or else we—all of the grandchildren—are outside in the fenced-in backyard, pecans falling on our heads.

A skinny, burnt-looking man named Diggs lives in Grandmother's spare room with the twin beds. Grandmother calls him her friend instead of boyfriend, which is what he is. Whenever he sees me, Diggs riffles through a painted white drawer and gives me quarters, mumbling something I don't stay around long enough to hear. What happened to Diggs? I don't know. He disappeared from the house either by dying or by walking out the door. The same thing, he was gone.

The banana-yellow Aries that we take to the country is the same car we take to Schwegmann's Super Market on Gentilly Boulevard (pointer finger of spreading hand), which is one of my favorite places to act a fool. Getting there from our house requires that we drive down Chef Menteur and over the Danziger Bridge, which raises up like a backhanded slap when boats pass by underneath. One of Mom's friends kept driving even when the blinking lights warned cars to stop and plunged into the Industrial Canal below. That is the real-life scary story that grips me for the entirety of 1985. The woman survives; the woman becomes rich; but I still do not want to plunge into deep waters.

Each year I gain a new fear related to blindness or to water or to falling or to the soft ground that we live on, until I am older and shame mixed with wildness beats out fear.

The other three points on my map (middle, ring, and pinkie finger) are clusters: our house and the short end of Wilson Avenue where we live, Pastor Simmons's house-church where we go now that Mom is feeling more Pentecostal than Catholic, and Jefferson Davis Elementary. School is just across Chef Highway and church is just down Chef Highway, at the corner where the SkyView drive-in movie theater used to be but where the great big brown post office is now with our zip code painted across its facade in enormous numbers so that we can never forget: 7 0 1 2 6.

These are the places that make my growing-up world.

I become Sarah on the first day of kindergarten. My mother and I stand in the circular parking lot, just short of the entrance to kindergarten class. This Jefferson Davis school is shaped funny, like a split horseshoe. Each classroom has its own elevated ramp, like porches. Everywhere is painted royal blue and bright yellow. I am wearing the school uniform, a pressed white button-down shirt and a blue A-line skirt with ruffled socks.

My mother says to me: *When those people ask your name, tell them Sarah.* *Those people* is the phrase she uses for strangers (mostly white, mostly men) who decide how the world works.

I hear the big children pouring into the main entrance—which is where Black Santa Claus will sit for pictures in December—four doors flanked by a pattern of yellow and blue metal triangles pointed like arrows.

Up until this moment in my life, I was Monique. But now I wear a navy JanSport backpack with a blue mat for naptime sticking out from it with s. BROOM written in my mother's oversize print.

Near the ramp leading to my first classroom, a blur calls at me. "Auntie Monique, Auntie Mo." When we get close to the sound, I see that it is my nephew James, same age as me, a month older actually, standing next to his mother, my sister Valeria.

The teacher is at the door now. She is the same teacher who taught and loved Byron and Troy and Carl. The same teacher who taught and loved Lynette and Karen. Every one of my siblings except Simon Jr. had passed through these doors and now it was my turn. What's your name little girl the teacher is wanting to know.

*Tell those people . . .*

"Sarah," I say.

I have been named Sarah, I come to know, after Sarah McCutcheon (for her love of beauty) and Ms. Sarah from the Divine Mission (for her love of God) and for another Sarah, a nice lady who worked at the laundromat near the corner of Wilson and Chef. I have been told that I was named Monique because Michael, who was in Charity Hospital's psych ward tripping on LSD when I was born, insisted that the new baby's name start with an *M* so that we would be forever aligned, alphabetically at least. No one at home calls me Sarah until I am older and they want to make fun or put me back in my place. Later, when friends call home asking for Sarah and Carl answers the phone he will say, "Sarah who? You got the wrong number. Ain't no Sarah here."

There are only two people in this school who know who I really am. They are James (my nephew) and Alvin (my neighbor). But Alvin is in the third grade already, on the other end of the building, down a long hallway, past the cafeteria and the library, in one of the classes held in trailers, outside.

At playtime the boys, who are mostly Vietnamese—everyone in this school is black or Vietnamese—call me Syrup or Surrah or Searah. Because I know that Sarah is not my actual name, I don't correct them. I let myself go by all possible names. When I get home, I change out of the uniform and the name and meet Alvin in the giant oak tree in front of Ms. Octavia's house where he lives.

In the beginning, Alvin is my rough-playing next-door neighbor. By the time his mother dies when he is eleven—and suddenly so—he will be my soul brother and closest friend. Our relationship is so long that I cannot remember ever first meeting. He is hide-and-go-seek in wet summer air and five-cent Laffy Taffys with knock-knock jokes on the wrapper.

Alvin is the one who dares me to throw my elbow through the glass window of our den as a happy birthday present to him when he turns ten. I happily oblige, appearing afterward in the den where my brothers are watching a Saints game, Lynette's bedsheet wrapped around my arm, dripping with blood. One of my brothers (now I can't remember who, but the only one to stop and mind me) says, "Go head on now, you all right" and turns back to the game. Mom rushes me to Charity Hospital in the yellow Aries; the elbow is stitched. Alvin loves me in the way of a male buddy from then on, I think.

Alvin is brown skinned with red coloring and has soft, curly hair. His lips seem made for kisses; they are big and smothering. I call him Liver Lip in play; he calls me Olive Oyl after Popeye's rail-thin, awkward-walking woman. We go tit for tat like this. Hours go by.

Alvin is first to kiss my slivers of lip. I lean out the front window of our living room, over the cactus bush that Mom planted in the world before me. Alvin swallows my mouth whole. "Lean your head sideways, move your nose out the way," he keeps on saying. It is the grossest thing in the world.

On our long walks to school together we cross the sinister Chef Menteur Highway, just as Karen and Carl once did. The goal, Alvin says, is to survive Chef Menteur. Alvin, who is three years older than me, grips my hand and seemingly spirits me across. Once safe, off we go, running for no reason, past Ratville apartment complex on the long side of Wilson where Carl's first girlfriend, Monica, lives, past indistinct nubs of houses to where Gant and the long side of Wilson intersect, where we wait for the crossing guard to flag us across.

Alvin has a mother who we call Big Karen to distinguish her from my sister and a disappeared father whose name we never call. Big Karen is rarely seen, except for when she moves the curtain on the front window of Ms. Octavia's house, spots Alvin and me playing in the tree, then pokes the side of her face out of the door. "Get to school" or "Come on in here, boy" is all I ever hear her say. I see Big Karen's entire body exactly once: Buying candy in Ms. Octavia's house and using her bathroom, I run into Karen in the kitchen. She's wearing brown pants, the itchy-looking kind, with elastic at the waist. Black hair hangs down her back. She seems, in an illogical way, the most memorable adult in my growing up. I always dwell on absences, I think, more than the presences.

On weekends, adults seem to vanish anyway, and the short end of Wilson where Alvin and I live is overrun with children. Neighbor JoJo's daughter Renaya comes. So does Kendra from the trailer park next door. Valeria drops off James and Tahneetra. Toka, Darryl's firstborn, comes over, and so does Lil Michael, Michael's firstborn who is two months older than me. I am these people's Auntie even though I am still peeing in the bed. But I have the title and the title is what matters. Lynette teaches me that. "Lil girl, lil girl," she is always saying. "I'm your big sister. You need to remember that if you don't remember nothing else." Karen was the oldest daughter still living at home, but Lynette acted it. Her job, as she saw it, was to control me.

Mostly we kids play hide-and-go-seek, which we mostly call "It," in the grassy spaces between the narrow houses. There are few places to avoid being found. You can crouch behind a car until the driver backs out, as my brothers always do, leaving me in the wide open and exposed. Or sometimes one of my loudmouthed brothers sees me crouching and pulling up grasses in the time between hiding and getting caught and gives me away, something Troy does religiously. Or else I'll try to hide behind a tree that I've deluded myself into believing is wide enough to cover me. All of this to avoid the best hiding places that require getting close to the spongy earth, underneath Ms. Octavia's house, for instance, which looks precariously lifted, sitting on evenly spaced stacks of brick. Big Karen's dog is vicious too. If you run in the yard between Ms. Octavia's and Joyce's houses, he'll chase you to the limits of his metal chain, barking and drooling and nipping at the backs of your feet. Only the brave hide under Ms. Octavia's house where the ground seems to be melting. Everyone understands that no one will search underneath there; you'd be left in your self-inflicted misery for however long you could stand it. Who knew what you would come out looking like. No one cared if that's what you wanted to do to yourself. That spot is reserved for those more terrified of being "It" than being eaten by the squishy earth.

We tell stories of how the ground eats things whole. That ball you left outside, we say, where do you think it went? A certain section of ground is quicksand, we decide, over there, back by Ms. Octavia's shed. It will take you in if you aren't careful. When it rains hard, water collects and stays for days. In our child-wise minds, the seal between deep ground and our present reality above that ground is string thin.

I hate being "It." Searching for people who do not want to be found, who when discovered yell like maniacal banshees and then run from you, afraid of the invisible scourge you are trying to pass on. With my poor eyesight, I often find a hiding person by mistake, just bumping into them by accident.

For these reasons, I do everything "It" is not supposed to do. I count with one eye open to see in which general direction the others run. And, too, many times in the middle of the game when others are hiding out-of-doors, waiting to be found, I'll stop being "It" without saying a word to anyone except myself, go inside, and call it a night.

By the time I'm seven, our house has become a studious house. In the evenings, Mom studies for nursing exams. But she keeps failing the required tests after six-week courses, where she is always the oldest student, and restudying for them, still working, in the meantime, with Auntie Elaine at Sisters of the Holy Family, a facility she praises for not smelling like piss. She studies for her GED, too, and reads everything she sees. *I was always a person who desired to be . . . I recognize I'm a good mom, but I wanted to be more than that.*

On Sundays, at Pastor Simmons's church, she is often called up to the podium to read Bible verses she has nearly memorized, articulating every single syllable into the mic. I love it best when she says the number "nine," pronouncing it NI-YEN. And at home, how she calls lasagna LA-ZAND-YAY.

Lynette is the first to break family tradition when she tests out of Jefferson Davis and into Schaumburg Elementary, the school in New Orleans East for "gifted" kids, which is too far for walking.

I am already being given standardized tests in school, which I don't mind. Playing school has become my entire life. I unearth boxes of slightly mildewed paper from underneath the stairs at home. I love the smell and feel of paper. It stands for abundance. You can collect reams of it, even when you have little. People waste it, throw it out, take it for granted.

In the boys' room, I make up multiple-choice tests for my students, the inanimate stuffed creatures I've collected, including a black Cabbage Patch doll named Cynthia and Peter the Pink Rabbit, then take twenty-five pieces of paper, one for each student, and go through them writing the answers to each of the questions I have made up. With my bad vision, it is easy to manufacture random answers. After this harried exercise (timed just as the standardized tests in school are) where I fill out my imaginary students' tests, I pass the pages back to the waiting pupils who

eye me the way they always eye me—trancelike—then I collect them back
and pretend to grade them, sitting behind an ironing board that folds out
from the wall in the boys' mostly empty room upstairs in the crown. After
I grade the tests, I record the scores, then scold the students for their
carelessness, for their failing grades. Had they not read the questions?

From time to time, I talk James and Alvin into being my real-live
students, but when they are playing with me school lasts only half an
hour. James and Alvin do not like class—the real or imagined kind. And
I am too harsh a teacher.

Some days, I decide to make the kitchen a stop on a field trip with
my stuffed students.

My mother is always on the telephone, the cord twisting around her
waist. She spends almost all day on the line with Grandmother. Or else
speaking pig Latin on the phone with Auntie Elaine. *Isthay ildchay isway
ettinggay onway ymay amnday ervesnay. This child is listening to every
word I say.*

I am sitting in my chair, my back to the side door where the familiars
enter, watching her at the kitchen sink, steam rising off the dishrag. *Scalding water kills the germs*, she is always saying. She wipes the counters
down with bleach. *Sure Clean*, she calls it. In the window, where she is
facing, there is an ivy plant and, in a Styrofoam cup, an avocado seed that
she thinks will grow, but never does.

Mom throws away a chipped dish. *If a plate or cup chips, I don't
care how beautiful it is, throw it away immediately*, she is always saying.
When she talks to us like out of thin air, we are supposed to remember.
Underneath the sink where the cleaning supplies stay there are holes in
the wood that are wet and ugly and slippery like swamp mold, from the
pipe underneath the sink that leaks dishwater.

I fuss at the teddy bears who are seated around the table. At real
school, at Jefferson Davis, Yogi Bear shows up in the cafeteria with a
police officer to tell us "Just say no" to drugs. I hammer this message
over and over into my fake students. "Just say no," I say. I had learned
the word "rebuke" at Sunday school and liked it. "Just rebuke those

drugs!" *Get from round here with all that,* Mom says without looking at me. We will not stay long then, I tell the students. The kitchen table is oval with a white lace tablecloth draping down to touch my leg. On top of it sits a cake, high on a glass pedestal, with white icing made from lemon juice and powdered sugar the way Grandmother taught, drawn on in flourishes with a butter knife. Random cakes when it is not a birthday are for company.

"Can I have some?" I still want to know.

My mother stirs a pot on the stove.

I change tack.

"The teddy bear needs a pickle," I say to Mom who moves around seven-year-old me like I am invisible.

If the house is a kingdom, my mother is the rightful ruler and Lynette the despot. For this reason, play school does not extend to the girls' room where I sleep in a twin bed across from Lynette. In photographs, I am always holding up rabbit ear fingers behind her head. "Mah!" she is always calling out. When I taunt her about her Jheri curl, the abundance of spray she uses to keep it moist under the plastic bag she wears, "Mah!"

My mother rarely answers. Lynette yells out my transgressions anyway.

I am, on the surface, the opposite of Lynette, wild in how I do things, in a perpetual hurry, and unconcerned with physical appearance. When I am eight, I fall in love with a black sweater that has pink and purple psychedelic elephants marching across it and wear it every single day, never desiring another outfit. But Lynette is always on the verge of acquiring something new, if not in real life, then in her imaginary world. She spends all of her time drawing, lying across her twin bed, shaking her foot, one hand on her head, moving colored pencils around. The women all look like her, small faced and lanky, but dressed in ball gowns and gray suits, with top hats and high-heeled pumps. They all have moles on their faces, just above the lip, which Lynette wishes she had and sometimes draws on her own face.

Lynette is a member of various after-school and church clubs, admired for her looks. She loves mirrors. We have four of them posted up in our bedroom where she sits before them and makes a thousand selves. Lynette has taken all of Mom's quiet lessons about poise and cleanliness to heart. Through the years, the women on paper multiply, wearing their fancy box hats and pointy-toed shoes, living in piles beneath Lynette's mattress or as cutouts dancing across our pink walls.

She imagines herself a fashionista in a universe of styleless people, which lends her wardrobe the air of costume. Working with Mom, she sews a pair of red corduroy bell-bottoms, which hang in the doorway between our room and the kitchen for the longest time, swaying for all to see.

When she is fourteen and I am nine she starts wearing too much lip gloss. The stickiness collects and drips off slowly. "Catch it," I'll say. "It's running!"

"Mah!" Lynette calls.

On weekends, Lynette puts on talent shows in the backyard so that we become new people she likes and wants to play with. She gives each of us nicknames. James becomes Blacky Boo J. Blacky for his coloration. James took the name to heart, using it to describe himself even after he was grown. His sister, Tahneetra, and I have forgettable names. She is Prissy Pritina or some such thing and I am always a Princess Something. Lynette dresses us and following her stage directions, we parade around the backyard on the raised concrete platform where Mom hangs clothes to dry.

She has become the art director of family memory, organizing photographs and presenting the story of us in books with labels handwritten in her curlicue. Our differences have irked her enough that she begins labeling my pictures "Rosemary's Baby," which I find funny because I have not seen the movie. Several things lead to this unfortunate name:

On trips to Schwegmann's Super Market, usually Mom's away time, I make a job of finding things I need in order to teach my fake

classes—staplers and paper and chalk that we can't afford. When Mom
tells me no, I pitch a fit, get on the floor, and yell, ignoring the one time
Mom demands I get up. She says things only once. I know this. I also
know that there are two traits she won't tolerate in children: sneakiness
and embarrassment by them. I qualify for the latter.

These public behaviors make me a candidate for regularly scheduled
spankings, delivered by a switch in Mom's soft hands. I am responsible
for retrieving my own stick from the bay leaf tree in the backyard, near
Ms. Octavia's shed where the quicksand is, which also happens to be
where the dead dogs I heard about, but never met, are buried. My brothers always talk about how, in the world before me, there was a dog for
each child. If it rained hard, I reason, the animal carcasses would come
floating up and back to our side of living. This poses a problem for me
when it comes to playing outside in the wet, after it has rained, whenever
the ground is soft.

Mother spanks me in silence. Afterward I run into the living room
where we are not supposed to be and threaten to call "child protection
services" on the rotary phone. My mother says, *Go right ahead, please
call them,* and that deflates the whole thing.

For these antics, I am left at home a lot and find myself looking out
from the front French windows, crying, the two cedar trees in front seeming to heckle as Lynette and Mom back out of the driveway. I try to make
sure they see my face contorting even though I can't see far enough to
verify that they are looking at me. I claw and preen in the window, but
after they are gone and I am without an audience, I am happy to be alone
in the house with one of my brothers barely watching me.

If it is Christmastime, I get down under the tree and open the gifts—not
mine, but everyone else's. Afterward, I retape the packages as best I can, but
I am in a hurry, my heart racing, to move on to the next thing; I am sloppy.

One time, I am left at home with Michael who is supposed to be
keeping an eye on me. Michael is a grown man in his twenties, working
twelve-hour days as a cook in the French Quarter, but he is passing through
the house with a girlfriend. They are upstairs. I am in the den watching

Fred Flintstone make his car go with his feet. I like what is playing on the TV but become more interested in what is sitting on top of it. Underneath Michael's fist-handled hair pick sits a ten-dollar bill, which I go and take without a thought.

Ms. Octavia sells candy, pickles, and frozen Kool-Aid that we call huckabucks. My favorite things are Now and Laters, which I always eat now; and banana Laffy Taffys. For me, eating candy is an activity. If my body isn't moving, my mouth needs to be and whenever my mouth isn't moving, I fixate on the shape of certain things on my tongue. Just the thought of Laffy Taffys and my tongue would lust so much I could taste the sweetness in my saliva. Laffy Taffys have three knock-knock jokes inside the wrapper so while I am chewing through the candy—which I like to put inside my mouth whole to give it a filled-up feeling—I crack myself up on at least one.

Minutes after I take Michael's money, I appear at Ms. Octavia's side door. As usual, she's wearing her flowered housedress. The candies I want cost ten cents apiece. I present Ms. Octavia with the money, say I want as many as a ten-dollar bill can buy: that's one hundred banana Laffy Taffys.

"Where you den got all this money, girl?"

"Michael."

"Now I don't know . . ." Ms. Octavia is kind, but not a fool.

"He did, Ms. Octavia. Ask him."

I know she won't leave the house to ask. The house is her scene; she departs from it exactly once in the time I know her.

Ms. Octavia fills a white paper bag with yellow candies and this makes me happy to be alive. I go and sit on her front stoop, facing Wilson. I am busy unwrapping and swallowing and laughing. I am looking down, getting ready to open yet another, when Michael and his afro suddenly appear. He is outside in his white boxer shorts. His mouth is open like a striped bass and so close to my eyes that I can see everything precisely. I'm staring straight at his chipped front tooth. He has my shoulders in his hands and is screaming, "Where my money, lil girl? Where is my mutherfucking money?"

I grab the white candy bag and fly around Ms. Octavia's house. We go around in this way a few times until tortoise me tires out. I am wearing my favorite swamp-green long-sleeved jogging suit. I overheat; Michael catches me. The message has not changed: I'd better go get his damn money. I manage to make an exchange with Ms. Octavia and return seven dollars to Michael. Ate two dollars' worth. Hid one dollar's worth of Taffys in the backyard, for later on.

But the moment that solidifies the Rosemary's Baby title in Lynette's head is much more serious, as she sees it. One time, playing in the living room around Mom, who sits in the slipper chair, I pull the miniature grandfather clock by its cord from a shelf above and down onto Mom's head. Blood runs down the side of her face, but she does not raise up. She sits there, stunned, but says, *Go get a paper towel.* Lynette is hysterical, screaming and turning in circles. Mom needs stitches it's so bad, and this is the childhood story Lynette tells of me to other people for a long time. "That girl almost killed Mama," she starts. But Mom always seems forgetful of it when it comes up. As if it never happened. That is her way. Sometimes, because she always carries a lot of things at once—grocery bags, her pocketbook, a grandchild, the mail, someone's backpack—she slams her finger in the car door and immediately, to squash our fear, says, *It's OK, it's OK, my babies. Call Troy, go get one of your brothers. Lynette, calm down. It's OK.*

# V

## Four Eyes

*E*ver since Alvin's big brother Herman knocked half of Lynette's front tooth out, she has stopped smiling so much. Herman had done it in play, with a rock from a slingshot in the yard between the two houses, but the very sight of Herman revives for Lynette the traumatic moment and here he is now knocking at our side door.

It is Lynette's thirteenth birthday. I know this because she is leading me in an art project where I am to design several versions of her birthday card out of construction paper. We are in the living room that is meant for pose not play with glitter and glue and scissors, which is how I know with certainty that no adult was around. When Herman stood outside the side door and announced that his and Alvin's mother, Big Karen, had died of pneumonia we just stood there frozen, not inviting him in or knowing what to say. Lynette was the boss of me then.

By this point, fourth grade, I have acquired the nickname Tape Recorder for how I listen in on adult conversations and play them back almost verbatim.

For fifteen years, everyone was saying, no one had stepped foot inside those first two rooms of Ms. Octavia's shotgun house except for Big Karen, whose rusted car still sat in the drive.

I seem to remember (though I cannot imagine why I was chosen) walking alongside my sister Karen through Big Karen's darkened rooms, their walls painted black. It felt like wading; the memory is a strong, wrapping presence, feeling not fact.

It sounds like myth now, but someone said Carl's picture was found in a box, pins everywhere on his body. Carl had fought with Herman; this was true. One of them grabbed a crowbar and chased the other. They were back to talking, back to being friends soon after the row, but Big Karen still initiated a court case, leading a judge to decide that Carl could no longer pass in front of Ms. Octavia's house, where he had passed all of his life, to get to Chef Menteur. He either took the Old Road or crossed over to the other side of the street, where the trailers were, to walk past. Big Karen was into that voodoo, people were saying, and I took this to explain her meanness and every single thing about her.

After Big Karen's burial, her two oldest kids, Herman and Rachelle, Alvin's siblings, try mightily to paint over the walls, but the black paint is unrelenting. They paint three or four or five times and even then the wall stays dingy white, never pearl the way they wanted it. Back then, I took that as a sign. All of us kids did. Now, I think it had more to do with their painting skills.

One day after Big Karen dies, I find Alvin outside in the backyard, behind the houses. We halfheartedly kick sneakered feet together in a shallow pool of rainwater littered with tarot cards that I assume belonged to Big Karen. I want to use words, but none pass between us. Much of my childhood consisted of wanting to know things and this moment is no different but I don't know my question. Silence stands between us then and forever on the subject of Alvin's mom dying when he is eleven.

Even though it goes against what Pastor Simmons preaches about the body being just a container for what matters, I thought then and still think now: when a person dies in a place they become the place and nothing is ever the same again.

Big Karen's death makes her more real. That is how my world works. The ceramic cat named Persia, the dead dogs buried by the bay leaf tree, my father, and now Alvin's mother.

When I am ten, my mother discovers that I cannot see beyond a hand in front of my eyes. I have been acting a clown in school to distract from this nonsight. The children sitting all around me are annoying blurs, the chalkboard black waters with scratches of white.

Sometimes if I slant my head (the way Alvin had instructed for that kiss), close one eye, and peer out of the side of the open eye, I think I can see better. I love desk assignments because I can bend close in to the paper to work silently, but most of our lessons require looking at the teacher and the chalkboard in the front of the classroom, which forces me to act out to hide the truth. This is why I get an X instead of a check for "exercises self-control" on my report card that year. If the teacher asks a question based on something she's written on the board, I'll say something smart-alecky to hide the fact that I have no idea what she's written. It is hard to know what you cannot see. The teacher finally guesses something is wrong—maybe she sees my contorting face—and moves me to the front row where even while squinting my eyes into slits, I still cannot make anything out. I am not legally blind, but nearly. What's the difference when you can't see?

Mom and I drive together in the banana Aries across the High Rise and into "town," which is what Mom calls anything resembling the New Orleans that most people understand: uptown, downtown, the French Quarter, those places nearer to where she grew up. We park on gravel and walk the short distance to a storefront on Claiborne Avenue. The shop that contains the eyeglasses that would make me see is lit up with cold fluorescent bulbs. All of the buildings where we go for physical wellness have this dull quality. Plastic and metal frames glow from behind like crown jewels. Rows and rows of them. My eyes are examined, and I am directed to choose one of the ugly frames in the much smaller selection offered to children with broken eyes who can't afford decent-looking glasses.

"Trees have leaves."

According to Mom this is the first thing I say the moment I can see. My chosen glasses are large purple squares, plastic, the outer edges scalloped. The kind older teachers wear and let dangle from a chain around their necks.

That matters little now. On the way home, riding in the back seat of our yellow Aries I read aloud every single word we pass, from billboards along the interstate and from storefront signs. I read the numbers on the radio dial. The mile markers and exit signs have words, too. We arrive home and I read from the cereal box and from anything that is in front of my working eyes.

I annoy everyone around me by observing out loud what everyone already knows. Now everything is particular and distinct, the house a nosy child's dreamworld. I read the label on the bathroom sink and the covers of cassette tapes. There is the Abramson High School sticker in the window of Lynette's and my room that before was a smear of blue and white on glass pane. My siblings pass before me as if I am a space alien and stare, my eyes small dots behind the lenses. I can see detailed versions of everyone I thought I already knew.

Karen wears pinkish glasses that nearly match mine except her lenses stick out from the frame, Coke bottles we call them. I laugh out loud when I see the clear version of Karen—who was then twenty-five years old and had just had her first child, Melvin—for what seems like the first time. The protruding thickness of her lenses seemed to taunt: this is what you can aspire to, blind kiddo.

The walk home from Jefferson Davis changes. I see the scantily clad women walking Chef Menteur Highway as Alvin and I wait for the light to change. How Alvin walks now with the older boys and the switching girls, leaving me behind. Now, waiting at the light to cross over to the short end of Wilson after the school day, I can see Carl in the distance, milling about outside our house. Can see him looking in my direction and waving a hand.

Every night, I hide the purple glasses underneath my pillow while I sleep. During the night, they change position so that when I wake, I beat the mattress frantically in search of them.

Only when they are on my face can I know what kind of day I have awakened to.

By the end of my tenth year, my first year of twenty-twenty eyesight, one detail overwhelms them all. Our side of Wilson Avenue, the short end, seems a no-matter place where police cars routinely park, women's heads bobbing up and down in the driver's seat. I am struck with the wonder of this, how we live in a city where police take such peculiar coffee breaks. Walking home from school, I try not to see what is right in front of my face. Sometimes, when I want the world to go blurry again, I remove my glasses when passing by these scenes. In this way, I learn to see and to go blind at will.

# VI

## *Elsewheres*

$\mathcal{W}$e take photos because we do not want to remember wrong.

There are, in the handful of images of me from the start of my teenage years, glimpses of the child I once was. When I still smiled with abandon, goofy-like, forehead veins straining, and gave a laugh where my nose got involved. Standing on the perch, where we posed for picture-taking time, a white silk bow upright against the backdrop of my hair, I am holding a bright-red Edward Livingston Middle School Windbreaker with an eagle soaring across the right breast. In 1991, in sixth grade, I was an academic star, which had earned me the Windbreaker and the right to call myself a scholar.

In another photo I abandon the jacket to show off a royal-blue "honors" sash that showed how narrow I'd become. Mom stood beside me, matching: Her pale-pink suit against my pale-pink dress with its puffed shoulders and peplum hitting midthigh, far below my nonexistent waist. Mom's white stockings match my white stockings, a two-for-one sale at K&B drugstore. She is high cheekboned, smiling to show all her front and some of her side teeth, eyes closed, holding on to my Student of the Month certificate.

Lynette appears with me in one picture, holding her own plaque in one hand, a basketball trophy in the other. She is academic, athletic, and beautiful with a narrow toffee-colored face. She, too, wears a pink suit, but hers is bright coral. Mom stands between us, one hand on each of our backs, as if presenting us to the world. Her upper body leans toward Lynette, who is already six feet tall; her knees angle toward me. All of our clothing has been conceived of by Ivory Mae and sewn by her own hand. "Ivory's Creations" read the tags in back of all our outfits.

At twelve, I am the same height as my mother, but this will not last. Soon I will grow taller and she will never catch up with me. This will matter in some ways, when it comes to her disciplining me, but mostly it will not.

No photographs exist to document the rest of my time at Edward Livingston Middle School—grades seven through nine—because I won't accumulate any more academic achievements to brag about via snapshots on the living room perch. But Karen will take her place there, wearing a cap and gown with a pregnant belly pushing out from underneath. She will graduate from Southern University of New Orleans, then give birth to Brittany, her second and final child. All of us—Karen, her two children, Lynette, Mom, and me—stay living in the Yellow House together.

Nineteen ninety-one to 1996 is the half decade when my life is most defined by the comings and goings of my family around me. These are the years when I do not feel ownership of my body or do not yet know how to take ownership of it, when my limbs suddenly shoot out. During this awkward phase, I begin to cultivate an obsession with the house's windows and doors, the ins and outs of the place.

I am thirteen when Lynette is eighteen. I enter teenagehood when Lynette is leaving it. In her high school photographs, she poses in front of painted backgrounds wearing jerseys, holding a basketball or a volleyball. Or she is pictured at school dances in ruffled, strapless gowns—turquoise or glimmering white or royal blue—Ivory's creations labored over after her job at the nursing home, into the night, and through the morning and afternoon until the precise second Lynette steps into them.

Lynette worships Molly Ringwald, has done so since the late eighties, and feels that the film *Pretty in Pink* tells the story of her life. Her dresses, then, are part of her own movie's costume design.

In 1992, Lynette still lives at home in the Yellow House, but in a year she will be gone. Her departure builds as do the number of sketched women dancing across our now lavender bedroom. Lynette reads fashion magazines, mostly *Vogue*, voraciously, tears out those designed women, and hangs them on the wall alongside her own fashionable cutouts. She's fixing herself, too, bothering Mom about getting her chipped front tooth repaired. Mom finds a dentist on Chef Menteur who promises gleaming white, but in the end Lynette's implant, which costs in the thousands, grays. Instead of drawing so much, she fills out college applications for New York City schools, asking Mom for money to Express Mail packets she's procrastinated about.

While Lynette maps her escape from the Yellow House, I begin seventh grade at Livingston, which feels like another country. New behaviors are required. I enter a crew of girl-women who go by such names as Chocolate T and Red. Sometimes, they call me Slim.

Livingston faces Dwyer Road at the tail end of the long side of Wilson. A tan-bricked building, its cheerless facade reads more detention center, less school. Inside, we school ourselves and each other—that is the unofficial curriculum—calling each other names as a way of elevating ourselves among our peers. The goal of every school day is to avoid getting ribbed, which means you spend a lot of time scheming about how to rib another person best and first. You have to be prepared with a verbal comeback that will make the other kids laugh—not at, but away from you. You don't want to tease yourself into a physical fight, just verbal spar hard and loud enough so that the teacher breaks it up. Name-calling starts with phrases like "yo mama" and "yo breath" and "that's why . . ." The things that get you targeted have to do with the unavoidable conditions of our lives—how clean your navy-blue-and-white uniform looks, how you smell, who your parents are.

Occasionally, somebody would "iff" at you—make a fast motion pretending to hit you but stopping short—to test your fear and reflexes. We call it iffing because it is a game of what-if. The lesson: always be ready for whatever.

I don't remember what unenlightened things I said back then, but I perform these verbal jabs most consistently during Ms. Green's English class. She is a tall, unshapely woman we call Ironing Board. Her feet stretch out the square-toe penny loafers I fixate on as she patrols the class with her eyes from where she sits behind a large pecan-colored desk. Her hair is a frizzy red mass of fallen leaves. She speaks in a raspy male voice and carries with her a scent of cigarette smoke and peppermint mouth.

Often because of things I've said, name-calling, she raps my hand with several rulers bound with gray electrical tape. She grabs the tips of my fingers, pulls them back so that the flat of my palm stretches to trembling. The sting radiates out through my fingertips. If I jump too much the thumb moves involuntarily and that is a pain I would think about the entire day and the night, too. Ms. Green's ruler sometimes lands on the cartilage where my thumb bends, and this leads me to rage I feel cannot be helped. What was at first a simple chastening in front of my class would then become a fight, teacher against out-of-control child yelling profanities and whatever else would help me avoid shedding tears in front of my peers, which was the last thing on earth I want anyone to say about me: that I break, that I broke, that a teacher broke me. When she hits my thumb, and I've gone wild-child on her to suffocate the pain, Ms. Green sends me outside to wait in the hallway. Out there, she reasons, I can make all of the commotion I want.

But without my audience, I stand staring at lockers. From time to time, my nephew James and I meet in the hallways. Either he has already been put out of another classroom for bad behavior, or if we are in the same class, he misbehaves in solidarity with me. I am his Auntie Mo after all. In the hallway where no one is passing, we make each other laugh or we just sit sullen, the floor tiles cold beneath our bare legs, feeling like nothings and no ones while English class goes on inside the closed door at our backs.

Daily, the school hallways hold contests of a lurid sort. Mobs of school-children form concentric circles that pulse and grow, a boxing match under way in the inner ring. When the brawl is most dangerous, someone runs down the hall, yells "Fight, fight, fight," and all of us run toward, not away. We stand there believing that we want to see two people destroy each other. This is, for us, educational, entertainment, a break in the monotony of our day. "Fight, fight, fight," we call, revved up. A slight as simple as stepping on another's foot by mistake could put you in the ring just as fast. You have to be careful.

Some days we have substitute teachers who seem called in from off the street. Many times, the substitute puts a movie into the VCR that has nothing to do with the subject matter or with learning. Everything in the world feels stupid then. School feels to me like an unpredictable, malfunctioning parts factory. You can never tell when a piece will fly off, hitting you in the face, possibly blinding you for life. You fall in with the crowd or you stand out. Standing out, being recognized as I was in sixth grade as an Eagle Scholar, can get you destroyed. Everyone knows the verbal beatings are worse than the physical kind. It's hard to heal from scorn.

I begin disliking school, bored by its monotony, the way every class, even the one memorable math class taught by the bald Mr. Nero who had high expectations for us, devolved into a corralling of wayward students.

We had become a horde, to be gathered and made to "act right," indistinguishable from one another.

I develop mental crushes on hard, light-skinned boys, those seemingly impossible to get, to whom I was invisible, the boys who were now Alvin's friends. After school, I see Alvin with his crew but only for split seconds before he disappears into worlds I will never know. Alvin and I speak little now. He is never alone, and when we are back on the short end of Wilson, we act too old for games. I mostly stay inside, peering at Alvin from the kitchen window.

In the fall of 1993, Lynette leaves for New York City's Pratt Institute of Technology to study fashion design, and I inherit, for the first time, at fourteen, a room of my own.

My school attendance drops. Our crew of girl-women enters the school doors in the morning and walks straight out through the back, escaping Livingston through a hole in the schoolyard's wire fence. Sometimes, patrolling truancy guards see us and give chase. This evasion becomes the highlight and lesson of our day. While Alvin and James are in class, I lie watching soap operas at Red's townhouse, her mom away at work. My friends are with their boyfriends many of these days; they are becoming pregnant in the other room while I watch the television.

Sometimes when I am dawdling at the corner store close to Livingston, my sister Valeria, James's mother, drives by. "Get your black behind back across that highway," she says, taking off one of her flip-flops and wagging it in the direction of me and the short end of Wilson.

We don't cut school on assembly days when talent shows or subpar Shakespearean productions are performed in the auditorium with its flitting fluorescent lights shining on an awful art deco scheme of faded rectangular soundproofing panels around the walls. The wooden folding seats slam against the backs of our legs when we stand. "Ouch, dammit," everyone is always saying. The stage, dark even when lit, rises higher than normal, forcing us to tilt our heads back in order to see. When the entire school gathers in the auditorium it is guaranteed that a fight will break out. I never fight though. I like words but not the way my body feels when it is moving through space.

One day, midway through eighth grade, after I've missed an alarming number of school days, I walk the long side of Wilson toward home, past my former elementary school, Jefferson Davis. It is likely that I'm eating junk food, a kosher dill pickle and a bag of Elmer's Chee Wees. Whenever I am eating, I am happy; when I am happy, I haven't a care. I walk as slow as possible, trying to disappear my snack before arriving home where I would have to share. I saunter past houses with people sitting on porches and wave; pass the mobile home dealership hidden behind a high corrugated wall; speed up my pace to go by Ratville, boarded up and abandoned now, before crossing Chef Menteur. When I make it to 4121 Wilson, my mother is there in her work uniform, sweeping the kitchen floor, which seems an ordinary task. She sees me and raises the broom, wielding it like a sword against my backside. Vagrant, truant me cries aloud, "No Mah, no Mah," running and carrying on, begging her for mercy. I cannot run far. The end of the house seems also its beginning. I have to crouch down where I am, long limbs and all, and take my punishment.

"You want to be so grown," my mother says afterward, pitying me.

The next day, certain things change. For one, when I wake, oil is dripping down from my forehead. Mom has anointed my head overnight with cooking oil as if to cast out whatever rebellious spirit was in me.

Mom always thought words had enormous power, was always saying, *You have what you say.* In our house, "I'm dying" and especially "My head is killing me" were forbidden figures of speech. She'd interrupt you midword. *You'll have what you say.* To demonstrate this, each morning, from then on, I was to sit down with her at the kitchen table to read aloud from the Book of Proverbs, which, Mom reasoned, would grant me wisdom I didn't yet have. Proverbs has thirty-one chapters; we read a chapter every morning of each day, beginning again every month, for a year.

"Happy is the man that findeth wisdom, and the man that getteth understanding," I mumble, always furious at first. My mother sits across from me, drinks her cup of coffee. I slur the words, drag them, cough my way along. My mother never reacts. "How long, ye simple ones, will ye love simplicity? And the scorners delight in their scorning, and fools hate knowledge?"

Mom summons her firstborn, Eddie, to fix me—she always calls him for the seemingly impossible tasks—and he appears in the church aisles from his house in suburban LaPlace to talk sense into me. He walks like his feet hurt. He seems here against his will. His face tenses. He spoke then as he speaks now, always threatening a depth that rarely arrives. "I know I'm getting deep now," he is always saying. "Now look at this, what do you think you're going to achieve running around here with these knuckleheads? Now I know I'm getting deep, I know this is hard to see, but . . . they're not going to ever be anything," he says. Eddie is not part of my normal world. I barely know him. There are twenty years between us. I stare hard at him, admiring his golden skin, which sweats and glistens under the sanctuary's lights. I nod, dead eyed, a look that to this day scares Eddie when he sees it on my adult face. "You've had that look since you were a little girl," he will say when he sees it. "It means you're lying."

Mom begins driving me to Livingston's doors and waiting to see that I do not escape. She returns long before the afternoon bell rings out our freedom at three thirty and waits, parked across the street, her car's headlights facing the dingy school.

This doesn't last long, because next I know, she has enrolled me in private school at Word of Faith Academy, part of a megachurch. In the weeks leading up to this, I sense change is coming. Mom is on the phone even more, whispering about me to Lynette in New York City.

Where before my universe had consisted of a few square blocks of New Orleans East, getting to the new school requires that I travel farther east through Bullard, one of the area's wealthier suburbs, which includes a black upper class living in Eastover, a gated community with two-story homes built around a man-made pond and golf course. Passing through Bullard on the way to school makes me think that we had not settled eastward enough.

New Orleans East was no longer majority white as it had been a decade before. Everything in the East slipped—into stasis, entropy, full-blown disrepair. The oil bust in the late 1980s led to a surplus of empty apartment buildings meant for employees who would work for booming industries that never materialized. Those became subsidized housing for poor black people pushed from the city's center, where real estate was more valuable, to its "eastern frontier."

My classmates at Word of Faith Academy are no one I know from before, girls named after Christian values—Faith and Charity and Hope.

I am one of five black students. Word of Faith kids are popular not for their name-calling skills, but for how highly ranked their fathers are in the church. The teachers are the spouses of church ministers, which means the learning is spotty. Our Spanish teacher, the principal's wife, knows Spanish from a study-abroad session taken four decades before, in her youth. You don't need to know Spanish to know that she teaches it badly, enunciating every syllable with a Southern twang, her sharply bobbed hair moving into the side of her mouth as she speaks.

Mr. Chris is part of Word of Faith's church choir. He also teaches gym and history. When he writes on the chalkboard his whole body quivers as if the board is emitting shock waves. These are the things Livingston has trained me to notice. Writing on the board takes him forever. Once a week, in the mushroom-shaped megachurch, Mr. Chris holds chapel, leading us in goofy a cappella songs and too-earnest prayer.

At Word of Faith, I wear a red-white-and-blue plaid skirt with either a red vest or a navy-blue sweater over a white button-down. For my first year, ninth grade, I roll my skirt up three inches higher than the rules and speak in clipped sentences to kids who appear afraid of me. And this detail cannot be avoided: I wear a plastic rat-tail comb lodged in my hair. I had been doing that at Livingston. It is one way I pretend that nothing has really changed, yet the lodged comb also makes clear that I have arrived in this new context from a distinct elsewhere and this perception of myself—that I am misplaced at Word of Faith—takes hold of me in a way so impossible to shake that I am writing about it now.

I cannot walk to school. Getting to Word of Faith requires my catching the city bus; I lose physical contact with the streets. When Mom drops me off at school some mornings in her new Chevy Nova, I insist she not drive too close to the archway of campus where fancier cars idle, letting students out to mill about before the bell rings.

"Just let me out here," I say the moment we enter the parking lot.

I am ashamed of our car even though it is brand-new. I am ashamed if Mom wears rollers in her hair. She is gentle and kind and gorgeous, and she loves me. Sacrifices basic necessities to put me in this private

school we cannot afford. I understand those things. I know. But my feelings . . . We seem, in our car and in our lot, not to match the school to
which I now belong.

I never again lay eyes on any of my friends from Livingston. My
time there has come to an abrupt end. I lose track of Alvin and James,
too, the two people who always know which name of mine to call, who
have come into the house where I live and seen me there, the two men
from whom I once could not hide. Alvin was, by then, in high school at
Abramson on Read Road, which was the normal trajectory for all of my
siblings and everyone on the street up until me.

# VII

## *Interiors*

$\mathcal{S}$hame is a slow creeping. The most powerful things are quietest, if you think about it. Like water.

I cannot pinpoint the precise moment when I came to understand that no one outside our family was ever to come inside the Yellow House. During the Livingston days my mother started saying, *You know this house not all that comfortable for other people.* And that line seemed after a time unending, a verbal tic so at home with us that she need not ever complete the sentence.

*You know this house . . .*

Because Lynette was five years older than I and far more outgoing, and because she had a social life beyond the short end of the street, this mattered much more to her, at first. One time, in her middle school days, Lynette dared ask anyway. She wanted Kristie Lee to come over. All of her friends had been hosting slumber parties and now it was Lynette's turn.

*You know this house not . . .*

"I knew what would happen if you made friends," Lynette says, thirty-five years after the fact. "So I stopped making them. It meant that people were going to want to come into your life, and they weren't going to come nowhere near that house. Not even if it took everything in me."

Kristie Lee never came over.

In this way, we stayed closed, clutched inside. Without knowing how it came to be, we left every person in our world who was not family outside, unable to cross the threshold to enter in and see the place where we lived, which was still my mother's pride and joy. *The house was my beginnings. It was the only house I ever knew.*

We love interiors. My mother was raised by my grandmother Lolo to make a beautiful home; I love to make beauty out of ordinary spaces. I had not known this back when I was living inside the Yellow House, but I knew it in my adult years when I created rooms that people gravitated to, the kind generally described as warm. Once, a friend came to one of these made places, an apartment in Harlem, and sat in the parlor looking around. The room had made him feel alive, even happy to be alive, he said. And then, "You have things to make a home with." People are always telling me this. I was the same person when I lived in the Yellow House. I had those qualities that drew me to want to be in a beautiful place surrounded by people I loved, and what this is building to, what I am trying to describe, is the gut-wrenching fact, the discovery even, that by not inviting people in, we were going against our natures.

That is shame. A warring within, a revolt against oneself. It can bury you standing if you let it. Those convoluted feelings manifesting as an adrenaline rush, when I narrowly avoided letting someone see the place where I lived. By the time I was fourteen, the possibility of anyone nonfamily seeing our house was imbued with fantastical power, the anxiety sending my heart to racing, even now, thumping these words out across the page.

My fear at the mere thought of someone seeing the Yellow House (my home, the place where I lived and belonged) drove me to do frantic things. If a classmate was dropping me home from Word of Faith Academy, I kept them away from the short end of Wilson Avenue. I'd lie, say I needed to pick up something from the store first. Even in sopping rain,

I'd rather walk home in the wet. From the inside of Natal's where I perused the shelves, having no money to buy, I'd watch until their car backed out of the drive, until their car was out of sight, then walk Chef Menteur, to where the people I loved, my mother and siblings, lived, the whole while wearing the scent of deceit and wishing I were invisible.

One time, when Lynette was eleven years old she spent a wonderful weekend among nice things in her godmother Bonnie's uptown house. That weekend, Bonnie, an ex-girlfriend of Uncle Joe, had other relatives over. "They had been so impressed with me," Lynette remembers. Those impressed people dropped Lynette off at home. Another kid, along for the ride, needed to use the bathroom. "What was I gonna say?" asks Lynette. "I'm imagining these people in Aunt Bonnie's lovely home. The nightmare! Of somebody seeing our house falling apart and people like us lived there! I kept insisting, panicking, crazy like a maniac, 'I'm gonna go to the store and walk home from there.' But they were adults, they knew." When you are frantic, your behavior is more obvious than you think.

Lynette's godmother called Mom to tell of Lynette's fiasco, which led my mother to ask Lynette whether she felt ashamed of the place where we lived. Lynette had a hard time finding the words. She just said the obvious: "They were gonna come in to use the bathroom." Mom had to understand. She let it go.

"The kind of people that we were made it worse," says Lynette. "Because of the way Mama made us look, people began to have expectations. It's better to look homely if you live in a house like that."

We were composed children; my mother was a composed child. We looked like people who had money. In how we dressed but more than that, in the way we carried ourselves. We walked upright, possibly with airs, expecting great things of ourselves and everyone around us. Like her mother, my mother buried her rage and despair deep within, underneath layers and layers of poise. America required these dualities anyway and we were good at presenting our double selves. The house, unlike the clothes our mother had tailored to us, was an ungainly fit.

My mother rarely ever sat. She was always go, go, go. Except for sometimes after school when I'd do my Spanish homework on her bed. Mom, who was hungry to know foreign things, wanted to learn a second language too. Sometimes when she was reclining on her bed, her legs crossed at the ankle, I would lay my head on her stomach and listen to the sounds it made. Her interior sounds could become so loud. She would rub my forehead—her hands are unusually soft—and that particular memory is to me an airlift, transporting me even now to a far less exposed feeling.

My mother was, I can see now, the house that was safe. But even still, we carried the weight of the actual house around in our bodies.

In high school, I did not make close friends. No one came over to the house. In high school, I was the same person I am now: sociable and interested in receiving people. I did not make friends. I was acting against my nature.

I lost my best friend from church, Tiffany Cage, who couldn't understand why she was never invited over when I was at her apartment at least two Sundays a month. Her family of three lived in a small apartment. It wasn't lavish, but it wasn't falling apart, either. When she started demanding visits, I'd lie: "You will come" or "We have company now" or, again, "You will come."

When Tiffany persisted, I wrote in a notebook (my writing everything down having become, by then, habit): "All she cares about is coming to my house. How petty." After mellowing, I wrote the truth: "Tiffany was exactly right. She has gotten too close. Now it's time for our relationship to end."

I wrote anguished letters to Tiffany that were never sent: "I have felt really weird ever since you said that crap about me not being open. I was appalled by what you said. I don't feel comfortable being in a relationship with you anymore since you spend most of the time 'observing.' I will hopefully find new friends in my new life when I go to college. See you later. Bye!"

Mom was never satisfied with the state of the house. Not even in the days when Simon Broom was alive and insisted they join the Pontchartrain Park Social Aid and Pleasure Club, which required they hold at least one meeting at the house on Wilson. *I had to work hard to fix it up. I didn't have the nice stuff. Furniture was nice, but compared to what other people had. . . . We still had heaters when everybody else had central. It all looked real nice though. Everybody always had a good time, but I felt like I deserved something better. I tried to raise y'all, I don't care what it is, if it's yours, be proud. Whatever you have, make sure it look nice.*

There was the house we lived in and the house we thought we should live in. There was the house we thought we should live in and the house other people thought we lived in. These houses were colliding. And the actual house?

My memories of the house's disintegration have collided, the strains impossible to separate, its disintegration a straight line always lengthening, ad infinitum.

Simon Broom never finished the upstairs that was the boys' room, so there was wall framing instead of wall to look into. The ceiling showed unfinished beams. "Those were my monkey bars," says Byron.

*Your daddy didn't want to spend the money to do things right. Instead of taking up the kitchen floor if it had a hole in it, like anybody with sense, he'd just take boards and put over the hole so one part be up all crazy-like and you'd be walking up and down across the floor.*

That's how things were fixed when Dad was alive. Once he died, things continued on in that way or not at all. Traces of my dead father were everywhere in the house—a door sanded but unpainted; holes cut for windows, the panes uninstalled—like songs cut off right at the groove.

Over time, the house's electrical problems worsened; the lights in the add-on would short out while the original house stayed lit, the house a malfunctioning Christmas tree.

"Daddy was always doing something to fix up the house. That was an ongoing thing," Michael says. "Daddy would always go get something from somewhere else, something already been used, maybe if a lot of the stuff he built the house with wasn't used it might have stayed up. That's one way to think about it."

"A house has to be maintained," says my brother Simon now, after the fact, but back then when he was in the army, the house felt like falling apart and the older children didn't fix it back up. Eddie had left for marriage. Carl was married, too. Darryl found crack and its accompanying trouble. Byron had enlisted in the Marines. Other brothers were running after women or seeking work in order to get women. And then there were just us three daughters in the house: myself, Karen, and Lynette.

Mom was always trying to repair things in the way she knew. The light switch in the kitchen broke, the wires exposed. Mom put masking tape on the wall, made a perfect square around the switch, which—for a time—held the wires in place.

Sometime in the nineties, though I cannot remember or find evidence of exactly when, Mom refinanced the house and installed yellow siding. What's strange is how I don't remember what color the house was before—I have only ever called it the Yellow House. The siding, pale yellow, was delicate in appearance, but striking enough that it still made a show, made the house appear new for a time. Subtle and classic, our yellow. Also highly susceptible to dirt.

The contractors, taking advantage of a woman alone, didn't install it properly, either. They left the decaying wood underneath, installed the pristine vinyl siding on top of rot, which we would not know until more than a decade later when Hurricane Katrina showed the underside of everything.

Shortly after the siding, Karen's amateur-carpenter boyfriend installed a geometric-patterned linoleum on the kitchen floor, but the corners started curling a few years too soon. One minute you'd be walking around barefoot and gliding on the linoleum Mom had polished, then two steps later you'd suddenly feel yourself walking on wood patches where the linoleum had come up. The floor became pocked with holes. Around this time, the rats came to live with us, making so much noise in the kitchen while I was trying to read James Baldwin or sleep that I didn't dare get up out of bed to see what they were doing. I'd know in the morning, anyway.

Karen's boyfriend also built a kitchen cabinet, but never got around to making its doors. Mom did the best she could: white linen on the bottoms; fruit-themed valances on top. The house wore curtains instead of doors.

The plumbing was never right. We had buckets underneath the kitchen sink catching dishwater. The kitchen cabinets had big holes that led to the outside. Mom plugged those holes with foil after hearing somewhere that rats couldn't chew through. And still they did.

The room that imposed the greatest discomfort was the newer bathroom with the only lock in the house. Drafts came through the window that looked out to the back alley. Overridden by vines where lizards and snakes lived, it was plain wild. I imagined this greenery, twisted and gnarled, overtaking the house from the backside, enveloping us in a green canopy that would grow up over the roof and down to the other side. We would wake one morning wrapped in its cocoon, unable to bust out. A nonview can be a most torturous thing when the mind wants to wander and skip along a landscape. That bathroom and its broken faucets: we needed pliers to turn on the water. The more you used the pliers the sooner the grip wore off and so then you could not turn the water on at all. Is this why we resorted to boiling water on the stove and carrying it through the lavender room where I slept, saying, "Watch it, watch it, watch it now"? Or was it that the hot water heater had given up, the pilot light gone out?

What is important is our carrying boiled water through the house and to the bath in our red beans and rice pot, the pouring of the scalding hot water into the bathtub or sink. All of us still loving baths, the boys and the girls, baths being an everyday event for us, trying to relax in a room whose surroundings you did not trust and therefore despised. When would the rats come out from underneath the sink where the plastic bowl caught leaking water?

You could not say.

This is how your disappointment in a space builds, becomes personal: You, kitchen, do not warm me. You, living room, do not comfort me. You, bedroom, do not keep me.

Michael had married and bought a three-bedroom house on Red Maple Street in a brand-new middle-class subdivision in Michoud. His house had plush wall-to-wall carpeting and a dramatic arched entryway. He and his wife drove a brand-new red Dodge Dynasty, which stood for something. Michael was a perfectionist, creative, obsessed with the presentation of food. Of all the boys, he was most like Mom. He took Mom's most basic dishes and turned them into menu-worthy appetizers—for instance, putting Mom's bell pepper stuffing inside an egg roll with a sweet potato sauce on the side. He was always coming around to see how his girls— which is what he called me and Mom and Lynette and Karen—were doing.

Michael initiated several Yellow House home-repair projects. He went out and bought two-by-fours and was tearing down the rotted den walls, but eventually the project fizzled—whoever was supposed to help never showed up—and stayed stuck as if incomplete were the happiest of locales. *Nobody really wanted to fix the house. They was thinking about they own dream house.* It was easier for Michael to buy things that did not require rebuilding: a hot water heater and a new stove.

Some nights we'd return home from church to find termites or flying cockroaches gathered in our rooms and I'd stay up nearly all the night watching them fly, crawl, and fly.

To describe the house fully in its coming apart feels maddening, like trying to pinpoint the one thing that ruins a person's personality.

It seems to me now that as the house became more and more unwieldy, my mother became more emphatic about cleaning. Mom's cleanings were exorcisms. At the core of her scrubbings was her belief in meritocratic tropes. That hard work paid off, for instance. How could I still believe this was true after witnessing her down underneath the kitchen table cleaning—her frame reduced to a small bundle? Oh, to scrub raw a floor that will not come clean! There was always a bucket of mop water sitting around. She was always spraying the tub, wiping the counters down, scrubbing the burners. This was especially true at Christmas.

*It's beginning to look a lot like Christmas,* she'd go through the house singing, pulling down boxes weighted with ornaments, some of them glass and wrapped in paper from Christmases ago, some of them gifts from our grandmother, bought from places long disappeared. Gold was Mom's color, not silver, which made us laugh at her story of the year Dad bought a fake silver Christmas tree, which he sat in front of the den's row of windows at the back of the house. *It was the scariest little tree.*

Mom labored over the living room at Christmas as an artist would. No detail was lost on her: gold garland around the door trim; shiny red paper on the front door, which served the dual purpose of keeping the draft out and hiding its ugly tan color; a gorgeous bow in the center made the door a gift.

The room drew us in—beckoning to us from wherever we were in the house—suddenly you'd find yourself inside it just staring at the things Ivory Mae had made. At night, we lit the Christmas tree and sat on the carpet watching its blinking lights, not wanting ever to leave the warm, full room. For once, nothing was missed or desired.

*How about the Christmas tunes,* Mom would say, and someone would go get Lynette's old pink stereo. Mom sang "Silent Night" along with the Temptations in a voice straining for the operatic, soaring, trembling, cracking sometimes. When she sang, she always started off strong and then quickly faded as if disapproving of her own sound. When "Rudolph the Red-Nosed Reindeer" came on, things picked up: she touched her nose and stood to shimmy her hips. She balled her hands up and shook them, made her mouth tight, jigged and rocked. From the floor, we tapped our hands together and shimmied from the waist up.

One year, for a final touch, she threw snow from a plastic bag onto the tree. Another year, she sprayed snow from a can. But this happened only once or twice. The snow was too much of a delusion, and she hated the way it spread everywhere on the carpet.

In 1994, my sophomore year, the billboards sprouted, rising up over the great oaks and above the highways, Gothic text on plain white: THOU SHALT NOT KILL.

No one heeded the boards.

We watched the crime stories on the nightly news: police tape wrapped around trees everywhere in the city, like strings of unsolved crimes. That year, when I was fourteen, fear came to live, twisted in our hearts, and hid underneath my bed.

This was the year when we disregarded stop signs after dark and treated red lights as stop signs, when we did not pull over if the blue lights of the law flashed behind us, when we could not trust anyone or anything. New Orleans cops were renegades, carjacking and brutally assaulting drivers pulled over on routine traffic stops. One cop raped a Tulane student in his police car. In 1994, policeman Len Davis, also known as Robocop and the Desire Terrorist, who in his off time guarded a cocaine warehouse, ordered the murder of a woman who confidentially (she thought) reported his pistol-whipping of a seventeen-year-old to the police department. The informant was thirty-two years old, a mother of three. Her name was Kim Groves and she was dead. One of 424 murders that year.

Those are just the highlights.

Tourism rose.

Lynette returned, dejected, to the Yellow House after a year in New York City. She reclaimed our room, but not her position in it, so busy was she with finding work. She couldn't afford tuition and life in Manhattan. No one had told her what a life there would cost, because no one in our family knew.

She sought work in the French Quarter. There was no work in New Orleans East now. The Plaza mall where she had worked during high school was on its way to dead, having once been a vast labyrinth (eighty acres, one hundred plus stores). When it opened in 1973, a mariachi band played in front of Fiesta Plaza Ice Rink. "Whoever heard of selling ice skates to New Orleanians," a Maison Blanche department store ad read. "Does sound a bit like selling water skis to Eskimos, doesn't it?" But the skating rink was all the rage. And the movie theater. But now there were Night Out Against Crime meetings in the mall's parking lot. Going there put you at risk of being held up (before you could step foot out of the car) by a person with a gun. The big department stores that once drew people to travel across the interstate bridge from all directions—Maison Blanche and Sears and Mervyn's and DH Holmes—had mostly pulled out, leaving only Dillard's. The customers, now mostly high school and middle school students, stole their wares.

A local business advocacy group called New Orleans East Economic Development Foundation was formed, and they waged campaigns to save the Plaza and the East as if for the soul of man, launching a public relations campaign, "New Orleans East—It's Great Living," with ads on the radio and on the sides of public buses that would take Lynette to the French Quarter. They were fighting the East's increasing disenfranchisement, its abandonment. "Pull out your map of the City of New Orleans and if you haven't noticed already, a good portion of New Orleans East is not there at all," they said in a meeting, presenting a revised map of New Orleans that included the East.

Jazzland, a theme park now famous for the haunted look of its abandoned, rusting rides, was in the planning stages then. It was, in 1994, six years before opening, New Orleans East's great hope. Prostitution on

Chef Menteur Highway seemed the only industry still booming, no downturn in sight.

Lynette found work in the French Quarter at clothing boutiques and restaurants. It was normal in New Orleans to work two or three jobs at once to reach a decent salary—even for police officers who earned a mere $18,000 a year and were responsible for buying their uniforms and their handguns.

In 1994, Grandmother's mind was deteriorating at the pace of the law. It began this way: Grandmother was hiding money from herself, in old pocketbooks. That did not seem unusual for a woman in her midseventies, but then she was washing dishes in cold water and then she was cooking the dirty dishrag in a pot of red beans. On weekends, rather than our traveling to St. Rose for family gatherings, as we had been doing all of my life, Auntie dropped Grandmother off to live in the Yellow House with us.

My job was to keep Grandmother inside and to keep our brother Darryl out. Grandmother couldn't be trusted to know where she belonged. Darryl would scheme and steal for crack.

Grandmother would get it in her mind that there was someplace she had to be, people were waiting for her, didn't we understand, we who—suddenly—were not her people at all, judging by the confusion on her face.

Trying to keep Grandmother indoors was hard. While she was trying to pry open the side door with me standing in front of it, she spoke of women who were waiting to meet her, women who, my mother said, were from the world before me. Aunt Shugah was waiting, Grandmother was always imploring, and she didn't like to wait. Or Sarah McCutcheon. Sometimes, it was her birth mother, Rosanna Perry. Grandmother was a skinny woman with the strength of a weight lifter. I'd sometimes have to peel her fingers from around the door, one at a time, her nail beds cherry from holding on so tight. When it became this serious, I'd yell for someone else in the house to come. "Help!"

And still, Grandmother escaped one Mardi Gras morning. Troy was supposed to be keeping an eye out. Grandmother was missing for hours. Police finally found her marching behind a horse, in a parade, uptown. Clutching a moneyless purse, she'd left the Yellow House, evaded the prying eyes of Ms. Octavia next door, somehow made it across Chef Menteur and on to the number 90 bus to celebrate Carnival time.

The short end of the street ate whole members of its own body. Structures could disappear overnight and without warning, razed or carried off during our sleep. The land that had been Oak Haven trailer park was now bare, its out-of-the way status perfect for illegal dumping executed by people who were bold enough to do it in daytime. Eventually, it became an official business, junk cars lifted between steel maws and crushed, stacked high like game chips. The junk was winning. The short end of Wilson had become more industrial than residential. The view from our windows changed: a solid fence of salvaged sheet metal rose up around the junk, blocking one terrible view with another. The houses, hapless bystanders, could not make the ugly beautiful.

Joyce Davis and her family simply moved out one day, relocating to Gentilly, a middle-class neighborhood on the city side of the Industrial Canal. As if to dramatize their departure, the Davises' home was demolished days after they left in what felt like a single swipe, leaving a square patch of concrete that looked too small to ever have held a house. Three houses were left on our side of the street.

Some Sundays, we drove around looking at properties listed for sale in the newspaper. Karen mostly took the lead, urging Mom on. I remember the yellow highlighter on folded newsprint. Karen's blue Toyota packed and dragging the ground with the weight of us, Karen and Mom in the front. Me and Karen's two children, Melvin and Brittany, in the back. We drove to the marked addresses, but we never left the car to go inside the open houses. It was as if the sight of another, more promising space might instantly destroy our ability to continue living in the Yellow House. What if we weren't able to achieve the new dream house after seeing it? Then we would be stuck not only in the falling-down house, but even worse, in the falling-down house cradling a vision of what it could and should be.

If only, if only, if only.

We knew what dreams cost; we had been doing it—dreaming and paying—all of our lives. My private school cost us lights and home repairs and food on the table sometimes. Unrealized dreams could pummel you, if you weren't careful.

But still, Mom made notes describing the house she aspired to. "Living room, spacious dining room, two bedrooms, spacious den, kitchen, garage, sewing room, nice front and back yard, good location, preferably in the city, air central and heating central," she wrote in a notebook. "Ground level, lots of space for flowers and shrubbery. Brick and wood. Nice windows."

During her time back in the Yellow House, Lynette wrote a resolution called S*A*V*E: Mom's House Plan. From July through November, Ivory Mae's children would contribute monthly to a new house fund. Lynette laminated this document and hung it up so that it looked at us every day. Checks trickled in, but these did not add up to enough for Yellow House repairs or a new house. The plan needed a project manager, and Lynette was not that. We all felt guilt when the plan didn't come together, the laminated paper yellowing on the wall. We eventually took the paper down, but it has survived the years. House hunting would stop—for a time—but then revive, this load-bearing dream spurring on highlighting and drive-by house touring, again.

The one sign of progress on the short end of Wilson was the construction of a brick house just across the street from Ms. Octavia's—next door to the junk business. The sight of the house being built was mesmerizing, all of the hammering and lifting and comings and goings of the work crew. Wider than all three of the houses on our side of the street, it had two separate entrances in front framed by redbrick arches cut out of a brick wall tall enough to hide the house's occupants who could sit behind it, on the porch, undetected. The attic had a small window from which someone could look onto us. These details lent the lone house on that side of the street an air of mystery. Because I never quite knew who stayed there, never saw them moving about on the street, I put the owners on a pedestal: They of the Misplaced Brick House. There would come a time when I would know very well the man who would stay in that house long after its charm had faded. Everything that I am writing here now leads to that.

During her year in New York City, Lynette had met and befriended Deirdre, an aspiring model from Florida, whom she now wanted to invite home.

Lynette had left the Yellow House and had perhaps forgotten that we did not bring people over, or she had seen the folly of that and felt it was time for a new way of doing things. My mother said what she always said.

*Now, girl, you know this house . . .*

But Lynette rallied and changed Mom's mind, which surprised me and sent Mom into overdrive, doing all she could to the house except remaking it from the foundation up, which was the only important thing to do, the only way to hold the thing up, but we did not have the means for that.

For Deirdre's arrival, Mom changed curtains, cleaned the chandelier with its faux crystal teardrops, spray-painted the frame of the front room mirror gold again, polished the tables, Sure Cleaned the house with bleach so that we could barely breathe. The house just stood there, a belligerent unyielding child.

Lynette's friend Deirdre came one summer day. From where I sat inside the kitchen, just by the side door, I heard her tires roll onto our shelled drive. She was in a red Jeep Wrangler with a tan soft top. The moment I saw her car, I instantly longed for one of my own.

"The first day she came, she was overwhelmingly hot," Lynette says. "I should have told her: 'Listen, we live in a shack. Our house is completely dilapidated.'"

Deirdre came inside. Our welcoming her required that we move against everything we had practiced up until that moment. She confirmed for us, without knowing it, what we saw with our own eyes. She was deeply uncomfortable, complaining bitterly about those things that we ourselves hated most: heat, rats, and the bathroom.

It was our life. We felt judged, but we did not say so.

Deirdre stayed a few weeks, I think. She left just as she had come, backing out of the drive in her Wrangler. At the stoplight, she turned right, heading eastward on Chef Menteur to her own mother's home in Florida. She left, I think, not knowing in the slightest, owing to youth or personality, the gift of ourselves we had been desperate to give.

Deirdre confirmed what Mom had already known. *You know this house not all that comfortable for other people.* The house was not all that comfortable for us, either. The evidence stared back at us. We became more private then. In a way, you could say we became the Yellow House. Here is a riddle: What was worse? The house or hiding the house?

Shame is a slow creeping at first, a violent implosion later.

By the near-to-end, Sure Clean could offer no assurances. It was sure of nothing whatsoever. It was outdone by the house's need and so was my mother, Ivory Mae, who as Lynette put it "could save a rock."

I cannot recall another friend visiting the house again.

Just at the moment when Lynette was hired at the Court of Two Sisters restaurant on Royal Street, she was accepted into Parsons School of Design and left for New York City for the second and final time, never returning to live in New Orleans or to visit for longer than two weeks at a time. Weeks after she left, Officer Antoinette Frank robbed a Vietnamese restaurant on Chef Menteur that she guarded as a side job, killing another police officer and a brother and sister who worked there. This happened in March 1995, in springtime. I was fifteen.

I had just learned to drive. Carl taught me, taking me once on Old Gentilly Road, too narrow for two cars to pass at the same time. My second and final lesson was on the High Rise where I had to merge into speeding cars. "Drive, girl. Just drive," an unfazed Carl told me. I had no choice.

I had inherited Karen's former car, a blue Toyota Tercel parked in the yard between our house and Ms. Octavia's. I could peer at it from my bedroom window. It was the first thing I owned that I could make dreams for. But it never did run. Or even turn on. Still, I'd hung an air freshener from the rearview mirror, was readying a car that would never go, the grass underneath it dying, decaying, blocked from sun. I loved the smell of the fabric in the heat, newly conditioned by me, and the shut-in quality of it. Sometimes, I would close its doors, roll the windows all the way up, and sit inside until I lost my breath.

My siblings were all grown, most of them married, returning to the Yellow House for visits and for the lows, the in-between times natural to every life. Troy had left for marriage and had three children, but he, too, had come back after divorce and was living again in the crown of the house where he had grown up.

Darryl's return always began with him in the space of yard between the Yellow House and Ms. Octavia's, just behind my blue Tercel.

Watching from the kitchen window, I'd see Darryl's clothes on the ground, but no, the clothes were actually him lying down there, a ball of bones in fabric, knees huddled to his face, T-shirt tented, his head disappeared inside. Carl and Michael and Eddie's anger would fill the yard, their long legs moving in and out, a springy motion, Carl gnawing at the knuckles of his balled fist.

This beating belonged inside, but bringing Darryl in was dangerous now. The fury of the brothers made the neighbors disappear; no one was outside except for the fighting men and their cowering brother. All curtains were pulled tight except for a peeking hole in Ms. Octavia's bedroom window. I never watched for long. It is a terrible thing to see love misfire in a million different directions: we are beating you because you did a wrong thing as a grown man, because you hurt our mother who we love more than anything, because we can beat sense into you and addiction out of you even though of course we cannot, because if we do not beat you someone else will beat you to death and this will destroy us, too.

Mom would run outside each and every time in slippered feet yelling at the boys to stop—*Michael, Carl, Eddie, y'all going too far now*—her voice high-pitched and girl-like. *Let him be now.* She was thin, but curvy, many inches shorter than her sons, but she'd push her hips and legs against their bulk. When they backed away, Darryl was left lying on the grass. I'd stand there at the window watching him not move for the longest time. I never saw him stand up and walk away, but suddenly I'd turn back to look and find him gone.

Days later, he'd call collect from a drug treatment program.

"Hey Mo, Mama there?"

"Hold on. Mamaaaaaaaa."

*What is it, girl, why are you yelling?*

"Darryl want you."

And then the exact same thing would happen time and time again. This pattern—scheme, make amends, relapse, scheme—was who Darryl was to me for all of my childhood and teenagehood and for most of my adult years.

He stole our things to pawn for drugs: Mom's wedding ring from Simon Broom that she stored in her bedroom drawer. Dad's set of golf clubs. The banjo? He became responsible for any and all disappearances, whether he was the culprit or not.

We woke some mornings to find Mom's car missing, which forced her to walk the half mile down Chef Menteur to her job at the nursing home. In the days following, we'd hear stories about how someone else was spotted riding in our car. We understood the danger of this. Whatever slight was committed by whoever "rented" Mom's car from Darryl in exchange for drug money was also being committed by us. When the car came back to us and if Mom happened to be driving me to school, some-one could mistake us for Darryl or for one of his drug friends and unload a round. I became terrified then of being shot, especially in the head. For many years, in many different places, including my dreams, I nursed this fear.

When Mom worked overnight, the entire length of the Yellow House was empty except for me in the middle, in my bedroom. Those nights, when she was away, I'd lie in bed straining my ears toward the three entrances. The stranger I feared was my brother Darryl and whoever else might accompany him into the house to steal for drugs.

The farthest door in the living room was three rooms away. It had a sturdy lock, or maybe the door was nailed shut. The two states have merged in my mind.

The kitchen door, next to my room, was industrial size and too heavy for the frame. Procured by Carl—who, like his father, had a way of finding things—it poked out, its raw edges causing splinters when you grabbed it wrong. Because of its size, and especially because we used it most, locks always seemed to break off.

I lived those early hours of the night supremely aware, examining every sound, like someone walking in a strange forest for the first time.

As if to compensate for this attentive work, when I finally allowed my body and mind to rest, after a certain point in the night, 2 a.m. say, when I had reasoned that whatever could have happened already would have, I descended into a sleep so deep that nothing could wake me. I consider this type of sleep another self-defense. If you are sleeping this deeply, then whatever befalls you will overtake you without your knowing it. Sleep became for me the ultimate resignation.

One night I lay in bed. All about me were the circumstances of my life. The only light came from the kitchen, the next room over. The oven was on for heat. A dining chair leaned up against the heavy side door, serving as its lock. It took a tremendous suspension of disbelief for me to believe I was safe from anything whatsoever. I was fighting sleep, which meant that it was early into the morning of the next day, when I half noticed a limb moving out from underneath my bed. Then part of a male torso appeared. Was I dreaming?

He swung his body into the next room.

I closed my eyes. It was wintertime; my skin felt cold against the sheets.

I heard a familiar groan. My brother Darryl groaned.

The chair at the door fell across the floor.

I lay in bed for a long while, feeling the chill from the dark night.

When I finally stood up from bed, my arms wrapped about me, I pulled back the black curtain that separated my bedroom from the kitchen. The side door was wide open. The chair lay on its side.

Mom came home around six in the morning and discovered the trespass before I could wake to tell the story: Darryl had sneaked into the house and hidden underneath my bed until Mom left for work in order to steal the microwave, which was our last household appliance.

Darryl awoke in me a new fear, not of strangers whose faces I did not know but of those things, people, scenarios that were most intimate, most known. But I didn't really know Darryl, did I? He was my older brother. That was the fact, but facts are not the story.

I was afraid to look at Darryl in his possession, which is how I thought of his addiction. I did not look at him, had never truly seen his eyes. When I did, many years later, his was a face I had never seen before.

For the longest time, I couldn't bear to hear his voice. This is such a difficult thing to write, to be that close to someone who you cannot bear to look at, who you are afraid of, who you are worried will hurt you, even inadvertently, especially because you are his family and you will allow him to get away with it.

Darryl became "Praise the Lord" man whenever he was in recovery, saying "Praise the Lord" like a tic after every single sentence no matter its relevance. After rehab, trust regained, he would reenter the Yellow House and find temporary work—at a candy factory, say. He'd work until his second paycheck, then start back on drugs. I always knew when he was using because he was moody and jumpy, sleeping for too long on the couch. Sometimes, when I tried to wake him, afraid that he was dead, he'd call me Fatso. I had wide shoulders and big thighs.

"Who even uses that word?" I'd say to him.

The Darryl we loved, but rarely saw now, was extremely funny, a wordsmith, teller of the best tales. It was less what he said, more how he said it. He had a comedian's timing. He told tongue twisters using a lot of curse words, which made me crack up laughing, especially in those years when I could hear better than I could see. Sometimes, when we were younger, all of us who were in the house at any given time would end up in Mom's pink-painted bedroom while Darryl regaled us with ordinary stories made to sound fantastical. How a bullet grazed his face during a fight over a girl at a middle school dance, leaving a scar under his eye that looks like a folded leaf. "I just kept dancing, you know, baby, those legs kept moving. Ain't no thing," Darryl claimed. Sometimes we'd feel so free in our togetherness that we'd have the nerve to jump on Mom's bed. It would be all laughs and smiles and sometimes jabs and light wrestling when Darryl would interrupt with what we thought was yet another wry story. "I'm the black sheep of the family," he would say to ruin everyone's mood.

# VIII

## *Tongues*

By the time I was a junior at Word of Faith, I had gained an interiority, a place without strictures where I could live, and that inside space was the room I loved best. High school, for me, boiled down to my desire to leave it for an elsewhere that I did not yet know. I had adjusted, somewhat. Was by junior year part of the yearbook staff and had come to admire its leader, Mrs. Grace, a shiny-faced English teacher who spoke softly, pursed lipped, enunciating every syllable. My mother reading words aloud was my first memory of the pleasure I felt whenever care was taken with words; Mrs. Grace was the second. Writing, I found, was interiority, and so was God.

Church had become our main outing, a second home where we could make new selves. Now we went to Victory Fellowship in Metairie, a megachurch thirty minutes from home, which required driving over the High Rise, a great change from Pastor Simmons's tiny house-church just off Chef. We were at church twice on Sundays, in the morning and again at night, and on Wednesdays and Saturdays for prayer group, concerts, and guest ministers.

Pastor Simmons had baptized us in the Mississippi; we wore all white. At Victory Fellowship, I was baptized again by Pastor Frank while wearing an oversize T-shirt and school gym shorts in a whirlpool tub off to the side of the stage.

Victory, a salmon-colored monstrosity, called itself nondenominational. My mother was, I think, first drawn to the church's story, the absence of stark ritual and boundaries. The congregation called itself Victory Assembly at first, reflecting its founding by Frank and Paris Bailey, two former hippies whose testimony included living in a trailer park, roaming the French Quarter high on drugs, and stumbling into a performance of *Jesus Christ Superstar*, happenstance that transformed them into the sanctified. Their calling, as they saw it, was to find those who were lost, just as they had once been.

Spirit-filled, Victory's congregants spoke in tongues, a private language accessible only to God. I spoke in tongues as did my mother and sister Karen. Although I have not tried, I can, theoretically, still speak in tongues, as can they.

Tongues was interiority writ large. You had to do it without shame, with no self-consciousness whatsoever. The only control was in letting go. When you gave yourself over to it, it came bubbling out from you, this foreign language you did not need to study for, that was specific to you and your tongue, and that you did not know you spoke—until you did.

Shortly after receiving tongues, I joined Teen Bible Quiz, mostly for the out-of-town trips along the Mississippi Gulf Coast. Back in the Yellow House, I wrote scriptures on note cards, learning all of the New Testament and some of the Old Testament by heart. I became so good at memorizing these scriptures, taking these words inside me, that I was called up in front of the church to recite several chapters, which I did, the lights shining brightly, my mouth spitting the words like they were on a speedway, racing each other. "God is not unjust," my mouth was saying. I was a machine, afraid that if I slowed I would forget. The crowd cheered me anyway and the bright lights shone.

By the winter of 1995, the Movement began. That is what we called it, or else the Revival. The roots of this "once-in-a-lifetime Pentecostal outpouring" were in the distant past, Pastor Frank preached. He and his wife, who bragged about their former life as hippies, seemed suddenly academic, their sermons lectures on historical religious moments. They spoke of the First Great Awakening's heroes—eighteenth-century Calvinist Jonathan Edwards and George Whitefield, who preached nineteen times in four days until blood came out of his mouth. During the Second Great Awakening in the early 1800s, Pastor Frank told us, congregants made noises like Niagara—people jerking, laughing, rolling like wheels, crying, barking. I made these notes in a black leather journal Michael had given me. By writing things down, I had discovered, I could remove myself from whatever physical plane I was on and go to the room I loved best.

Victory's language changed to include the following phrases: Holy Ghost Fire, Drunk in the Holy Spirit, and New Wine. My favorite visiting preacher was Rodney Howard Brown from South Africa, who was always yelling FIRE. "Fi-yuh," he would say. When he was in town, services could last far past midnight.

Inside the doors of Victory Fellowship people were laid out on the floor, laughing uproariously for hours, coming to church to get "drunk" in the spirit. One lady, a white-haired retired teacher, jumped up and began sprinting around the sanctuary in midsermon. Soon, there would be mobs of people running spontaneous marathons while Pastor Frank preached.

I describe this without irony and without sarcasm for I was one of the drunk. This was the first drink, the first spirit, I'd ever had. I'd stand in the prayer line like everyone else, for the laying on of hands, all of us drawing an S through the church beginning at the altar and ending at the back near the exit doors.

When Pastor Frank came to you in line, energized and speaking in tongues, laughing and praying, you would almost immediately fall down, just from the sounds he made—unless your mind and body were set on resisting. Sometimes you'd rock from side to side until exhausted by the struggle, or by Pastor Frank's tenaciousness. He rarely moved on without a fall-down. Ushers also figured in your consideration of where to stand in the line: you always wanted to go where the strongest men were. Some, including my brother Troy, were notorious for letting supplicants fall too hard onto the thinly carpeted floor. Women ushers came behind the pastor throwing maroon blankets over the women who wore skirts or dresses or shorts. Those who seemed chilled and trembly got blankets, too.

I could be laid out for hours and hours, my mother sitting alone in the back pew of the church waiting for me to arise, the building having emptied out. The sanctuary was empty; even the pastors had gone home. Troy paced outdoors. I know for certain that I felt something, down on the ground, but what? That was so long ago I cannot say now whether I was taking a sanctioned nap or undergoing quiet transformation. The peace did not last long. Troy could always break my trance, afterward, in the car riding home when he insisted we stop at 7-Eleven for a Coca-Cola Icee and chips, an activity so banal it settled me firmly back in my reality, sitting in the back seat next to Troy's crunching and slurping and Karen's two sleeping children.

Word got around that I had been "touched." My spiritual drunkenness made me well known around the church. When I arrived in the building, at the sight of me filing into the pew, Pastor Frank would light up, I felt. Therefore, what came after will not surprise.

I got drunk on the Holy Spirit one day at Word of Faith Academy, in Mr. Chris's history class, while he was shake-writing on the board. The fact of my having done this outside Victory's four walls made me insane to Word of Faith's church members, an example of the vastness of God to those from Victory. Word of Faith had vehemently resisted the Movement, but it had come to them wearing a uniform skirt and red vest. Whatever came over me that day led me to appear drunk, my eyes squinted. I may have been laughing. I was carried off to the principal's office by both arms, past classroom doors, looking ill. Mom was called to come retrieve me. The principal called Pastor Frank to find out what exactly I had been drinking. He likely told the principal no, it wasn't drugs or beer, it was that Holy Ghost "Fi-yuh." I made it into Pastor Frank's Sunday sermons for a long while after that, as a shining example of God's grace— "the high schooler who . . ."

But nothing of our circumstances had changed beyond Victory's walls. And even more, and this is really the point, no one in the church knew where we lived. No one had ever been to our home, as much as my mother showed up, in the years I was there, those years I am speaking about now and the many years afterward; no one had any interest in the condition of our life. It was not entirely their fault. By avoiding showing people the place where we lived, we unmoored ourselves. No one did this to us.

By the middle of 1996, the Revival bore on. One day in church, after the prayer line, I met a bass player named Roy in the pews. He was the first man I felt lust for; I became infatuated with him. We hung out. No one in my house used the word "dating," but that was the idea. Roy happened to live in New Orleans East, just down Chef Menteur, not five minutes from the Yellow House. My interest in this bass player grew to take precedence over Holy Ghost Fi-yuh.

I was sixteen, but I lied and told Roy I was nineteen, like him. I had evolved from hiding the house to hiding the house of myself, obscuring details; secrets were cherished, earned possessions. I thought of it then as keeping some of myself for myself. I wanted to be old enough—if only in mind—to leave home. I had been taking correspondence courses in anthropology at Louisiana State University and this fact emboldened me to tell Roy that I was at a local college, a lie that I then had to support. Now, whenever I got off the bus and stood on Chef Menteur's neutral ground in my Word of Faith uniform, waiting to cross the street to home, I'd train my eyes above the cars passing by me, just in case Roy's was one of them, as if looking above, and not directly at, made me invisible.

Michael moved back into the Yellow House during this time, after his marriage ended. He carried little with him to the Yellow House except for a king-size four-poster bed that he let me have. The bed outshone everything else in my bedroom, and this I loved, mostly for how high it elevated me, far above the floor.

Michael came in from his work as a chef late at night. He had to pass through my bedroom to the upstairs crown where he slept. "Hey, baby girl," he'd say, plopping into the green velvet chair that sat against the corner wall. From where I lay in bed, I could see one side of Michael's drooping shoulder.

He spoke on and on. About the planets and the universe, about good and evil, about human failings. "Some people mind don't go all the way up," he said once. He recounted visions of black angels he'd seen in the upstairs window of the Yellow House many years ago, back when he was young, wearing a body brace, and tripping on LSD.

"Throw my ashes in Lake Pontchartrain, somewhere, or in the Mississippi . . . I wonder if you have memory when you die . . . I don't think you ever forget nothing. You might go blank if you lived a bad ass life. The whole world is about energy." He'd say these kinds of things; the next morning I'd write them in my notebook.

He spun tales, stories of his own life, how he became a chef: "Wilbur Bartholemy, he was a sous chef, real, real good chef, if it wasn't for that dranking and shit . . . He could cook his ass off. I used to be following his ass around . . . When I cook, I'm gone cook like my mama cook, the food I grew up on . . . I was a dishwasher at Shoney's at first, me and Darryl, everywhere I go and get a job, he'd come work with me. I love cooking. The thing is you get a high, say like if you putting out food, everything is clicking, the people outside is loving it, you start to feel invincible, whooping they ass, you have a rush, whoo."

Sometimes I spoke, too. Of private school and Birmingham, England, where I wanted to go and study for the summer. I had discovered Birmingham in a study-abroad catalog that came in the mail. In those days, the mailman delivered my dreams—shiny pictures in magazines and catalogs, Fingerhut and Spiegel. I'd call 1-800 numbers announced on television—"for more information," I would tell the operator—just to receive an envelope addressed to me. At least the postman knew that we, in fact, existed, situated as we were on the short end of a long street, some miles away from where tourists slept the night.

Birmingham was a picture of a castle with a price tag underneath. Birmingham, England, not Birmingham, Alabama, I explained to my family, from whom I hoped to raise money for travel. When I told Michael about it one late night, he pulled a hundred-dollar bill from his pocket and handed it to me, but that was the first and last donation. Getting to Birmingham required more hustling and explaining than I was willing to do. Still, Mom paid the application fee for my first passport. It would never gain a single stamp.

Around this time, I was discovering James Baldwin. I spoke of him to Michael. Michael and James Baldwin taught me to follow a crooked line of thought. Our conversations, more like philosophical meanderings, were, for me, a release from a great loneliness Michael did not know I felt.

"The world change every day," Michael would say. "Nothing stays the same. We all have to change. If we don't change, we perish."

"Right," I would say from time to time, middoze, so that Michael would carry on telling. Sometimes, I'd change it up, ask: "Why you say that, Mike?"

For a long time, I fell asleep to Michael's voice.

Michael would wake me in the wee hours of the morning—as Simon Broom once woke him—to drop him off at work in the French Quarter.

There he would be, standing by my bed in his black-and-white-checkered chef pants. In the car, he kept clearing phlegm, in between doses of Goody headache powders. I drove; Michael directed and critiqued. "Over here . . . Slow down some . . . Get in this lane . . . Watch yourself now."

We always entered the French Quarter by way of Esplanade Avenue, which felt like another world, the great oaks framing the mansions on either side of the neutral ground. Most of the drivers in the French Quarter this early in the morning were, like me, dropping workers off. I'd pull up in front of K-Paul's Restaurant on Chartres Street where Michael worked with Chef Paul Prudhomme, with whom he sometimes appeared in a chef's white coat on the morning news. When Michael opened the door, he'd grab the top of the car to lift himself out. AGHHHHH, he always moaned.

He'd wave me off and alone I took Canal Street to Claiborne to the interstate to the Yellow House.

Having Michael in the house did not stop Darryl from robbing us. He kept at it, brazenly stealing "every fucking thing that wasn't tied down" he'd later admit. This included Michael's large-screen TV and VCR, which we discovered one late night after church when we pulled into the drive, the headlights shining on Michael's things stashed alongside my blue Tercel that would never run, as if Darryl couldn't lift them all at once.

# IX

## *Distances*

$\mathscr{B}$y the start of 1997, I had sworn off church. They called it backsliding. There was a special prayer and altar call for backsliders like me who had tasted of the divine but shunned it for the pleasures of the world, which for me were the enticements of living in my head, thinking about men and cities in countries I had never seen, things that lay not in the present but far ahead.

Not yet seventeen, I had been building toward my departure, graduating high school with a nearly 4.0 grade point average. As yearbook editor senior year, I wrote in terrible clichés about how we should remember our "special moments in time." Of those special moments I cannot now recall a single one, except to say that my senior year was a long yearning for elsewhere. I did go to the prom that year, alone; the photograph exists to prove it to me. There I am posing with the three other black girls in a red satin peplum dress with an outsize white boat collar that Mom had sewn for a church event a year before. It no longer fit; it rode up my thighs the entire night.

I had chosen the University of North Texas, following behind Roy the bass player, who was attending the music program there. When he mentioned the school to me, it was the only university outside Louisiana that I had heard of. Even though I had been taking college-level correspondence courses and excelling academically, no one at the Christian school had ever mentioned the kinds of universities where I likely could have been accepted. I never heard the names Stanford, Berkeley, Princeton, Harvard, or Yale—or even Tulane, Loyola, or Xavier, which were only a few miles, a public bus ride, away. I do not recall ever sitting with a guidance counselor to discuss life beyond high school. It was as if life stopped there—for me.

I was not the first in my family to go to college though I am sure I wrote that I was on the college essay application. Karen had graduated from Southern University of New Orleans, but I had not asked her a single question about going there. My brother Simon Jr. and sister Deborah, who were living in North Carolina and Atlanta, he running his own business and she teaching, had gone to college, but when I was applying I had not known that; they were decades older than me. I saw Simon Jr. periodically when he visited us in the Yellow House at Christmastime, but I took him as I took Eddie—a disciplinarian you escaped and survived. Simon Jr. and I barely spoke. It felt unnatural to call and ask him a question.

Roy was not a full-on boyfriend, though I imagined him to be, at the time. We were affecting togetherness. Writing letters and speaking on the phone sometimes. Wishy-washy. Kissing and making out sometimes after church. He was trying to be a jazzman. I did not love him, but I loved the texture of his fingertip calluses and the musical props surrounding him in his basement room, loved how his face contorted—ecstatic!—while he was playing. I still went to Victory sometimes, but for the wrong reason, to watch Roy run his fingers along his bass while playing in the church band.

Roy could not love me either, not even if he'd wanted to. There were those lies of mine between us.

Carl and Michael drove me to Texas in Eddie's small pickup truck. I sat squeezed between my brothers even though my legs were longer than Michael's.

"Just hold down, Mo," Carl said, accelerating into fifth gear for the long stretch of highway. I contorted my body out of the gearshift's way.

My possessions rode behind us in the truck bed, covered by heavy black industrial-size bags from NASA, what Carl called body bags, that made a snapping turtle sound against the wind for the entire eight-hour drive. But Carl's cassette tapes, Johnnie Taylor, Bobby "Blue" Bland, Tyrene Davis, and Rod Stewart playing inside on rotation, buried the noise. Carl sang along in a bored voice, without lift. "Tonight's the night . . ."

He was against stopping for any reason whatsoever.

"Let's roll, we can hit this highway straight," he was constantly saying. He ate sunflower seeds the whole time, flicking their empty carcasses out the window.

From time to time, Carl made a noise that was not him singing and was not him talking: "Uhn, uhn, hn," he would go. It was the sound of making mental calculations. The three of us settled into what felt like separate universes on that one seat. Carl's conquering of the road seemed, for him, more than just operating a pickup. I felt he needed buttons to push, that with his abilities of concentration he could lift us off to someplace even beyond Louisiana road. He appeared in perfect control; in his company, I felt safe.

But Carl's agitation grew the farther away from New Orleans East we went. We crossed into Texas. Shortly after we passed the welcome sign, cops pulled us over, asking for all three of our licenses even though only Carl drove. Because I was in the middle and holding things in my lap, Michael and I were required to get out of the car so that I could move my arms enough to dig for identification. My brothers were stone silent, compliant, obedient men. Not themselves.

"Don't say shit," Michael whispered to my annoyed face.

Carl was ticketed for speeding.

Once we took off again, the bags flapping their noise, we complained bitterly the entire rest of the trip to relieve Carl of any bad feeling. He was just going with the flow of traffic, we said. Look at all those people speeding. It was my few things in the back, the black bag covering them, that alerted the police to us, I insisted. My things consisted of a word processor (an expensive good-bye gift from Mom), Dean Koontz novels, James Baldwin books, clothes with Ivory's Creations tags, a plastic see-through telephone, and not much else.

In Denton, Carl pulled up to West Hall, which lay at the edge of campus near the football stadium. We were either too early or too late; the place was deserted. We entered the dorm room I was to share with two women who had not yet arrived. It was a cement block. There was a single bed close by the door, which I immediately took, and bunk beds pushed against the far wall.

"We got to hit that highway," Carl announced just minutes after we'd arrived, my things deposited on the bed.

"Man, you don't want to stay a lil while longer?" Michael said. "Help Mo get settled?"

"For what? Let's hit that highway, bruh."

"Chill out for a second, man."

Michael thought they could drive me to Walmart where he would buy me a set of sheets and the small fridge I needed, but Carl fidgeted and flapped so much that I was glad to see him go. We patted each other on the back, our bodies side by side. I kept saying, "Thank you so much, Carl. Thanks, bro."

"Not a thing, bey," he said.

Michael was affectionate in the best way, calling me baby girl, telling me how he loved me and how he was proud of me, but I felt melancholy all the many times I thought about Mom, who I had left behind at the Yellow House, how we had not said good-bye. Seeing a person off had become, post-Webb, post-Simon, her least favorite thing in the world. She said, "I love you" before I left the house as if I were going to the corner store and coming right back.

The cost of my ignorance about college was high. I took out student loans to pay the astronomical out-of-state tuition my first year there, which I had not known existed until the bill came due. Because my high school was not ranked, not an "official" high school (I had not known this, either), I was forced to take a remedial study skills class, which I did not particularly need. From day one of class, I was ravenous about learning, nearly living in Willis Library, where I spent seven or eight hours at a time hunched in a cubicle reading books about subjects fellow students seemed already to know. I took up anthropology, drawn to ethnography and archaeology—cultural histories and artifacts—with a minor in journalism. When I finished the first semester with a 3.923 grade point average, I noted in a journal that I was disappointed with myself. "Good," I wrote, "but not good enough." I typed trite motivations—"Hard work pays off, remember that, Sarah!"—and hung them on the dorm room walls.

I had two roommates, but I only remember one: Bonnie was a short woman with hair nearly her length and feet that turned outward as if in a perpetual plié. She danced and, as proof, always wore a faded pink bodysuit underneath tights. She was a born-again Christian and was constantly praying for me, hoping I would "come back to the Lord." When it came to me, she seemed always to be shaking her head in disbelief. I was difficult to talk with, she said. I had moved on from Roy, found a Russian boyfriend, Sasha. I was obsessed with the library, with bills, with achievement, with coffee, those "things of the world," Bonnie called them. When I was not at my work-study job as a secretary in the School of Community Service or donating blood and plasma for money, I was collecting friends at Kharma Café, mostly men who reminded me of my brothers, friends from Los Angeles and Morocco and Congo and Indiana and Chicago. They were called Eric and Marcus and Muyumba and Khalil and D-Y. Samia Soodi was the one girl.

Partway through the second semester, my grinding ways drove Bonnie to flee. The other roommate had left early on, under forgettable circumstance, which meant I inherited the entire three-bed room. I opened the space to friends who came there to study while Billie Holiday CDs played on the stereo, affecting a sorrow not all the way felt, but I was perfecting an aura about myself. I was, for the first time in my life thus far, inviting people into my space without bad feelings or trepidation of any kind. I spread my things out, wallpapered the closet doors with magazine images (just as Lynette had done in our lavender room), laid a crocheted spread Mom made—burgundy, green, and red in an African motif—on one of the bunks. I hung a window-size Bob Marley poster on the wall near to where Bonnie had slept. I was glad she was gone. I set up my coffeepot on her former desk. A love interest wooed me by leaving coffee beans outside the dorm room door. Wilson Avenue was the furthest thing from my mind.

Until the summer of 1998, when I returned home to the Yellow House after that first year of college, determined, even at the outset, to spend future summers elsewhere.

"When I'm in New Orleans," I wrote in a notebook, "I feel like Monique. At UNT, I was Sarah."

Sarah and Monique, such different titles, in sound, in length, and in feel. I have felt for so long that those two names did not like each other, that each had conspired, somehow, against the other. That the contained, proper one, Sarah, told the raw, lots-of-space-to-move-around-in Monique that it was better than she. The names allowed me to split myself in two, in a way, as a decisive gesture. In its formality, the name Sarah gave nothing away, whereas Monique raised questions and could show up as a presence in someone's mind long before I did. My mother, understanding the politics of naming in a racially divided city, knew this back in the parking lot of Jefferson Davis Elementary.

I reclaimed Lynette's and my lavender room and hung heavy black curtains at the doors for privacy. Someone had installed an air conditioner in the bedroom window that did nothing to lessen the humidity and the heat. There is nothing worse than a trying-but-not-succeeding household appliance.

My college friends wrote letters to me at the Yellow House from their elsewheres, letters that I saved and stacked like paper chips. "Great that you got a camera," D-Y wrote from Los Angeles. "I hope you get snap-happy and take a lot of pictures. I would love to see your view of

New Orleans! It might allow me to get to know you better. N-E-Way . . ."
In letters back, I drew anecdotes not from my familial life on the short
end of Wilson, but from my life at work.

At first, I waitressed at a truck stop restaurant in the East, near to
Schwegmann's Super Market, landmark of my childhood antics, which
by then had shut its doors. The restaurant's $19.95 all-you-can-eat seafood
special seemed to draw every trucker in the South. I ran around refilling
platters overflowing with crawfish and shrimp, the juices running down
my arm and the side of my leg. That special—but mostly the appetites of
the customers—eventually drove the place out of business and drove me
out of its doors long before.

That is how I came to be working in the French Quarter. When I
began my barista job at CC's Coffee House, Michael, a veteran employee
of the French Quarter, explained which streets I was to avoid on the way
to the bus stop at night and demonstrated the forward posture in which
I was to hold myself in order to appear most threatening. Every day,
Michael broke away from his own work at K-Paul's Restaurant on Chartres
to walk the few blocks to where I worked on Royal Street. I fed him dark
chocolate–covered espresso beans and a frozen drink called the
Mochassippi.

From time to time, he'd look at me and say: "What, you don't like
to do nothing to your hair?"

My brothers were always asking me this about my hair, an unregu-
lated mass standing up and pointing whichever way. I was not interested
in hair, especially not in taming it. I wanted my hair to project a freedom
I did not feel. My brothers were vain men, all of them, starched like my
grandmother and her offspring: Joseph, Elaine, and Ivory. "Have you
seen Einstein's hair?" I had the nerve to say back.

Coffee orders at CC's generally came with a question, most reliably:
"Where is Bourbon Street?" On fifteen-minute breaks, I sat staring through
the window at passersby. During lunch breaks, I wandered the streets
with my camera, a good excuse to look. I froze the following scenes: a

man playing a horn along the Mississippi; a man wearing tight burgundy pants, twirling and dancing and Bible toting on Canal Street, an umbrella affixed to his hat; random street signs; and a crooked lamp in front of St. Mary's Catholic Church, the symbolism of which eludes me. I took photographs of Café du Monde and of a juggler on stilts leaning against the street sign at the corner of Royal and St. Peter streets. These signs and symbols were taken back to Texas with me as representations of the place from where I had come. Also photographed, but not shown: me in my barista uniform sweaty and gross, posing at the back of Carl's pickup truck, his arm around my shoulder; my cousin Edward, Auntie Elaine's son, there, too, cheesing to show all of his teeth.

I took no photos of New Orleans East, whose landscape I told myself was not what D-Y had imagined when he asked to see "New Orleans." Nothing in the landscape of New Orleans East signaled the New Orleans of most people's imaginations. No iconic streetlamps lighting blocks of brightly painted shotgun houses. No street musicians playing in the flat industrial landscape that contains very little arresting detail, being littered with motels, RV camps, and auto shops. No streetcars running, no joggers alongside them. Walkers here did not stroll. They walked out of necessity. There were few restaurants, no cafés to pass by or stop in. But none of those details made New Orleans East any less of a place. For the me of then, the City of New Orleans consisted of the French Quarter as its nucleus and then all else. It was clear that the French Quarter and its surrounds was the epicenter. In a city that care supposedly forgot, it was one of the spots where care had been taken, where the money was spent. Those tourists passing through were the people and the stories deemed to matter. Those of us who worked in the service industry all converged on this one place, parts of the machinery that maintained the city's facade, which did not seem like a ruse to me then. I found the French Quarter beautiful, its performed liveliness an escape from the East and where I lived on the short end of Wilson.

My summer at CC's was the first time in my life that I spent consecutive days in the French Quarter. The experience took on the boundlessness of all discoveries. On that one summer I based entire narratives about my growing-up years in New Orleans that played to the non-natives' imagination. I wrote scholarship essays and told stories about boys tap-dancing with Coca-Cola bottle tops on bottoms of sneakers and about how my mother shopped at the French market, which was a tourist market filled with baubles and very little food. Still, I came to lay much of what was wayward and backward about myself on New Orleans: I can cook and hold my liquor because . . . I love jazz because . . . I am therefore interesting, because . . . Defining myself almost exclusively by a mythology, allowing the city to do what it does best and for so many: act as a cipher, transfiguring into whatever I needed it to be. I did not yet understand the psychic cost of defining oneself by the place where you are from.

By evening, all of us who had traveled to the French Quarter for work from elsewhere wore the day's labor on our bodies. We could place each other instantly by our uniforms: Napoleon House workers wore all black with white lettering on the breast pocket; women in black dresses with white aprons and scalloped hats were cleaning women at one of the hotels. If you wore a grass-green outfit, the ugliest of them all, you worked at the Monteleone Hotel. Black-and-white-checkered pants like those Michael wore with clog shoes meant you belonged to the kitchen of any one of the restaurants. My uniform was khaki pants, a burgundy cap, and a matching polo shirt with a CC's emblem.

The malicious New Orleans heat could seem to crawl inside, affecting your brain so that walking felt like fighting air. New Orleans humidity is a mood. To say to someone "It's humid today" is to comment on the mind-set. The air worsened the closer you came to the Mississippi River and wet you entirely so that by day's end my hair was zapped of all its sheen and my clothes stuck to the body in all the wrong places. I needed a bathtub by the time I made it to work, so imagine how I looked at the end of the day, for travel home.

We workers collected together on the bus ride home, our facial expressions daring anyone to disturb our tranquillity, returning to where we lived and belonged. I was deposited at the corner of Downman and Chef Menteur where I waited to transfer to another bus. The stop, an uncovered bench the size of a love seat, was just in front of Banner Chevrolet car dealership's lot full of cars buffed to shining, prices on yellow bubble numbers plastered to windshields, deals none of us could afford. We who were waiting for the always-late bus stood still in our places while others flew by—off the Danziger Bridge, off the interstate onto Chef Menteur, heightening the reality of our immobility.

Sometimes I traveled to the French Quarter, not for work but because the lights in our house had been turned off for nonpayment and I needed to escape that scene for another, well-lit one. On one of these occasions, I wrote in my notebook: "I am home, this is my home, there is nowhere else for me to go if I want to see Mom. My times in New Orleans are loneliest and saddest maybe because I actually have to face reality, it's more difficult to hide without the fifteen-pound textbooks."

At the end of the summer, my mother, Ivory Mae, still a nurse's aide, graduated with a commercial sewing degree from Louisiana Technical College. She was one of six people to do so. "Success Is Earned" was the theme of the ceremony, held at Dillard University. Seeing Mom accept her certificate on a college campus, I thought about how she was such a natural at achievement. Afterward, Mom posed for photographs, smiling on the living room perch where the carpet was more threadbare than ever before.

High on pride, I spent that evening on the front step of the Yellow House waiting a long time to see Alvin, but he never came around. He had a girlfriend, his sister Rachelle had said as explanation. I didn't see him at all that summer. But I also didn't travel beyond the street to seek him out.

I still could not fall asleep many nights in the Yellow House. It was as if the collective heat of the house had converged in the very room where I lay. The window unit groaned its futile laboring, the temperature static.

# X

---

## *1999*

$Z$ora Neale Hurston said, "There are years that ask questions and years that answer." Nineteen ninety-nine did both.

I returned home to the Yellow House again, briefly, in the summer of 1999, between the ending of a summer school session and the beginning of my third year of college. I had spent all of my sophomore year in a student exchange program, attending school for a semester at the University of Massachusetts–Amherst, where I had gone because I heard James Baldwin taught there in his later years. I was still, in a way, following behind elusive men. I spent the spring semester as a visiting student at William Paterson University in New Jersey where I became a staff photographer at the school newspaper, taking bad photographs that paid little mind to composition or mood. I went from not having gone anywhere outside Louisiana to visiting eight different cities in the fall and spring of 1998 and 1999.

In this way, I came to know New York City, spending weekends with Lynette who lived with Deirdre on the Upper East Side. I thought of returning home then as returning back "to face poverty for the last time in my life," I wrote in a notebook. Home was a regression. New Orleans East without a car was stuck.

I had, by then, acquired a computer to replace the two-piece word processor. That laptop came under scrutiny one afternoon when two officers arrived at the front door of the Yellow House where I was working on a college assignment.

"Ma'am, where did you get the computer?" they wanted to know.

I explained that I was a college student; I'd bought it with student loans.

"Have you received any gifts of any kind, ma'am?"

I had not.

They asked questions about my nephew James, my sister Valeria's son.

I told them I hadn't seen James. I had not seen him for a long time. I could not recall the last time I saw James.

They left.

James arrived not a half hour later.

He drove a Burgundy Ford LT. I had heard talk about James's gift to Alvin, a matching Ford LT in silver.

That summer when James pulled into the drive, I did not tell him right away that he was wanted. He asked that I talk with him inside his car. He pulled into the long space of grass between the houses, almost near to the back door of the Yellow House, where we used to play hide-and-go-seek. With the doors closed, we sat inside. James smoked a joint. I had no worries, the car full of smoke. I had, by then, smoked weed in college. Knowing me, I am sure I mentioned having done this in order to equal things out. I would have cared what James thought of me. I would not have wanted to seem forgetful of who I really was.

"The cops are looking for you," I said. I was out of the car when I said it.

His eyes widened. He jolted alive.

He said something about tell Grandma (which he pronounced *Grum-mow*) bye.

He went from lurking to screeching toward Chef Menteur.

He had to go. I cannot recall whether we hugged. This was not a film. Nothing was going according to anyone's plan. No music was playing.

I remember exactly the Sunday my mother called to tell me the news about Alvin. I know that I was back at school, in a Denton apartment reading James Baldwin's *The Fire Next Time*. So captivated was I by the elegance and truth of Baldwin's writing that often I would live inside it for hours, highlighting phrases repeatedly, looking up words such as "conundrum," and writing their definitions in the margins; underlining a sentence about life in Harlem that read: "For the wages of sin were visible everywhere."

Sometimes when Baldwin wrote something that I felt in my core, I shut the book, stood up, and walked a circle. Sometimes while doing this, I would repeat the thing he wrote out loud or say "God damn" or "My God" to no one at all. At one of those moments, alone in my oblivion, the way I liked it, the phone rang.

"Alvin dead, Mo," my mother said.

I hung up without a good-bye. I became mad at the book, at Baldwin himself for grinning in his picture on the back cover, and ran up the stairs two at a time to go to bed, because there was really nothing more for me to do.

Alvin's funeral came close to two weeks after his car crash so that family and friends could raise money for a decent send-away. Some of the people at the funeral wore white T-shirts with a picture of Alvin taken at a high school dance and R.I.P. just above his beginning and end dates: September 14, 1976–October 24, 1999.

We sat around in metal folding chairs, just staring at my friend's corpse. I stole furtive glances at Alvin from the back of the funeral home.

It was an open casket that should have been closed. Not enough money for the best so the stitching on Alvin's face was clearly worked on, then worked on some more. There was so much powder foundation, especially under his eyes, making him five shades darker than in life. His hair was neatly braided in six parallel rows. No more of his smiling, though. This was a dark quiet.

I hesitated but then went to see Alvin up close—him and his eye makeup and somber gray suit with the one pink rose pinned to it—and became greatly afraid to see him like this, lying so silent.

James made it there that day, too, shackled legs and hands, head bowed. A pair of uniformed policemen escorted him down the aisle to see Alvin sleeping. James bent over, kissed Alvin's dead cheek. Before he could get a good long look at his friend, he was hurried back to prison to serve his second year of a twenty-year sentence for armed robbery.

Months before this death, on that summer break, I had seen Alvin and his mob of friends and waved from afar. I noted that they seemed up to no good, wore gold teeth, and smoked. I was sitting inside the Yellow House holding the kitchen door halfway open with my foot as my mother cooked. Alvin broke away and I met him in the yard between our houses for a hug. My grasp was loose, as if I longed to escape. I beat his back a few times like it was a drum instead of holding on to him tight, the way he held me.

I was slightly taller than him with broader shoulders. He wore blue jeans and brown leather sneakers with a rounded toe on smallish feet.

"You must like it there, in Texas," he said, that toothy grin widening into form.

"Been busy," I said, addressing a question I thought he might ask, but did not, since it was mine to begin with.

"You too much for us now," he said, searching my eyes. I laughed it off, looked into the ground, but it hurt the way true things do.

Alvin tapped my forehead once, playfully. To snap me out of myself, to make *me* comfortable, I am sure.

"I'll see you" is probably what I said then instead of good-bye. That was my rhetoric, my mind-set then.

Now—if I had known that Alvin would be leaving me—I would have porch-sat with him in the still of that night, told him how I'd been growing, how I was moving into myself. We would have shared our stories, in the way kids do. "Alvin," I might have said, "do you know they have white sand dunes in New Mexico?" I would have asked him about his own days (What was his life, his world? Who do you love?), about New Orleans East, would have wondered aloud about the hurricane I saw taking shape in his eyes, would have called home on those Texas Sundays instead of underlining passages that no longer make good sense to me. And then I imagine that there would have been more between us, more between the boy and girl who sat in tree branches for hours watching the world go by beneath us, maybe we would have even talked hours before Alvin's drive to the grocery store, a journey undertaken when he was high, on heroin, where his car had spun out of control, slammed into a pole just a street or two away from Wilson, instantly breaking him into two. All of this on Chef Menteur, the exact same highway he vowed to protect me from—and did.

After Alvin's death in the fall of 1999, I never again laid my head down to sleep the night inside the Yellow House; from then on, I laid my head down to sleep in other people's houses. Where you sleep the night speaks a great deal about your position in the world. I observed the life of the house from a distance, from Texas apartments at first, then from California apartments, and finally from New York apartments.

My mother, Ivory Mae; my sister Karen; and Karen's two children stayed on in the Yellow House long after I'd gone.

Troy and Carl returned there, too, between loves. They, Carl and Troy, were the final inhabitants of the house, posting up on either end of it after Mom and Karen had moved closer to St. Rose. Troy lived upstairs and Carl in the living room, always our best room. I commented on and observed this from a distance during regular phone calls with my mother.

I began to say things Mom used to say: You know that house not comfortable . . . What were Carl and Troy waiting for? I'd ask to Mom's silence. For the house to fall down on their goddamn heads, I'd answer. Later, my words would come to feel like a summoning.

But of the house's near-to-final days, it is for Ivory Mae, its sovereign, alone to tell:

*The roof of the house in the bedroom where I was sleeping, it was raining in there. It had caved in. We had to put a piece of plastic up, and they had a tub catching water. I had to push the bed over to the closet some when it rained. That went on for quite a while.*

*In the wintertime, by them having that big hole in the roof, at the top of the house, we had a space heater in my bedroom, and if it got real cold I would have to put up a blanket or something by the door.*

*The front room, I used to try to keep that as clean as I could. The rugs was all discolored.*

*Even though it was a rag, it was beautiful. I always tried to put a bright curtain, I tried to put a rug.*

*If a book comes out, people are gonna say, Well this can't be the people I knew.*

*You know what I'm saying?*

*I was living a lie, you know?*

*I was portraying this image, which it wasn't no image, it was me.*

*That was the whole story that nobody knew, where you were living. Everybody just assume by you always looking nice and driving your car and all, everybody just assume that whatever place you was in was, you know, the way you look. Because when people would come the outside of the house was always clean.*

*I always thought I was gonna be able to get the house done. At that time even with my brother, Joseph, being a carpenter, there wasn't really any money to buy materials.*

∞

*I feel like everybody grown up should have a legacy, like a house or something, to leave for the next generation. Just like my mama left a house, I feel like God had blessed me with a house, that's the way I should go out.*

*Everybody was saying, Why don't you go out there to California by Byron, Byron wants you to come. I went and I felt some relief about being in a house that was nice. But after a while I felt like what am I really doing here?*

*Is there really a place anywhere for me?*

*Then Elaine asked me to come to St. Rose, to our mom's house. I never liked the country. I wasn't no country person, but it was a nicer house and I could be close to Mom.*

*I'd still go to the old house to pick Troy up. Sometimes I would go in there and no one would be there. If I saw the bathroom needed to be cleaned or something, I'd do it. By that time, Carl had painted the tub black.*

*The den part . . . they had so much storage stuff, they'd made it just like a junk . . . And even the yard. My flowers . . . the plantings . . .*

*I would go in the closet to get stuff I had left. I wanted to get your daddy's flag, but when I went to get it, it was all raggedy and the rats had . . . It had holes like something had been tearing away at it.*

*The kitchen, they had that big brown table and all the chairs. I wish I had gotten some of those because those were good pieces of furniture.*

*The last time I went in there, Carl had that bed in the front and it look like nobody was . . .*

*I figured they wanted to live there.*

*I don't think this is something that I really want to remember. It just look like Simon was a part of my life that just disappeared, was gone, and look*

*like that's what this was, too. The house was there, and then it wasn't.*
*That's strange, how something could be and then it's not.*
      *If you could fathom that.*

*I could have done more. That's the way I feel. It feels like I was the cause*
*of some of these things. And you don't want to be the cause.*

*If I had . . . If I would have been more particular . . .*
      *I missed a lot of opportunities that were so open to me.*

*And then you see the lives of the children and they become the living people*
*of the house, the house lives in them. They become the house instead of*
*the house becoming them. When I look at you all, I don't really see the*
*house, but I see what happened from the house. And so in that way, the*
*house can't die.*

# MOVEMENT III

*Water*

*Far off from these a slow and silent stream,*
*Lethe the river of oblivion rolls*
*Her wat'ry labyrinth, whereof who drinks,*
*Forthwith his former state and being forgets,*
*Forgets both joy and grief, pleasure and pain.*

John Milton, *Paradise Lost*


*The City of New Orleans exists in a very watery world*
*. . . surrounded by lakes to the north and east*
*and bisected by the Mississippi River . . . surrounded*
*by water above (humid atmosphere and sixty inches*
*average annual rainfall) and below (a high water table).*

Unified New Orleans Plan
(UNOP, 2007)


*You guys are not from New Orleans and keep throwing it*
*in our face, like, "Well, how do you feel about Hurricane*
*Katrina?" I f-king feel f-ked up. I have no f-king city or home*
*to go to. My mother has no home, her people have no home*
*and their people have no home. Every f-king body has no home.*

Lil Wayne

# I

---

# *Run*

*August 27, 2005*
*Harlem–New Orleans–Missouri–Ozark, Alabama*

*F*ind Lynette and me at the Charlie Parker Jazz Festival, swinging out at Marcus Garvey Park. Spot us in the crowded amphitheater. It's frenetic. I am wearing a bright-orange halter dress with a wide-brimmed hat, its long black ribbon a vine running along its circumference, then snaking down the middle of my back.

Lynette and I are neighbors on 119th Street in Harlem; we live three houses apart. I am one inch shorter than Lynette's six feet, but she is still five years older. Men on the streets catcall us, say, "Y'all must be twins." Neighbors say they can tell us apart from behind by how and where we walk. Lynette, a makeup artist now, takes Lenox Avenue to the subway, a route that requires you meet eyes and talk. To get to my job at *O, the Oprah Magazine*, I mostly take quieter Fifth Avenue, switching along in high heels (Lynette says I am still playing school, like in the Yellow House). But today, we sisters are seated next to each other and Harlem is the only place in the world where we want to be.

While I am tapping my foot to catch the rhythm my mother is gathering up her things. While I am egging the music on, my mother is evacuating Grandmother's house in St. Charles Parish where she moved to be closer to her mother's nursing home and to my sister Karen and her two children, Melvin and Brittany.

Troy has left work early and is supposed to be making his way to them from the city. Karen has gone to retrieve him at the midway point, on Airline Highway, but he is nowhere to be found; someone has dropped him off in the wrong place, and everyone is trying to be elsewhere.

Like Eddie, who calls from the highway en route to Missouri, saying what everyone already knows: "Get out."

Getting Troy takes a long while; he has always been a pain, but the confusion lends time. Everyone packs a bag apiece. My mother makes sandwiches and fills a cooler with drinks. In the slow hurry, seventeen-year-old Melvin forgets the eyeglasses he needs to see.

The five of them—Melvin, Brittany, Karen, Mom, and Troy—head to Hattiesburg, Mississippi, the home of a cousin, together in the one small car. Mostly sitting in traffic. What is normally three hours becomes seven. Night descends in an instant and Karen does not like to drive in the dark nor does she like to drive on the highway, never having lost the horror of Chef Menteur.

My sister Valeria heads eastward in an untrustworthy car with her two daughters, one of whom is pregnant, and their children. When she finally stops driving, after the gas runs out, she finds herself in Ozark, Alabama.

Lynette and I call Michael on the walk home from the Harlem concert. He claims he's crossing the Texas border: "I'm out of there, baby," he is saying. This, it turns out, is the lie you tell your baby sisters.

Carl gathers up his family—his wife Monica and three teenage daughters—and heads for Monica's office at the Regional Transit Authority building, now an employee shelter. He ties his green motorized boat to the back of his pickup. At the shelter, Carl tells them to go on in, "Go head now, I'll be all right," then turns around and goes back home to wait.

Grandmother's whereabouts are not known. What we think we know: she, along with the other patients in the care of Chateau Estates nursing home, is being evacuated. In the flurry, Mom has called them, and this was the promise made over the line. Grandmother is gone, but we could not tell you to where.

All told, we scatter in three cardinal directions, nine runny spots on the map.

# II

---

# *Survive*

*August 28, 2005–September 4, 2005*
*Harlem–Hattiesburg–New Orleans–Dallas–San Antonio*

**CARL**

*You gotta realize . . . the Yellow House was up and running.*

A few years after the Water, Carl reconstructed for me what happened.

Carl and Michael sat outside the house, near to the curb. They were grilling, a half gallon of gin between them. The Mississippi River on one side, Lake Pontchartrain on the other. They were in between water. People who were evacuating drove past the intersection where Chef Menteur met Wilson, heading west toward the city; from Chef Menteur Highway they could see the smoke rising off Carl and Michael's grill.

*You gotta realize, Mo. It's August. It's beautiful. A Sunday. I then cut all the grass, weed-eated and everything. Had it looking pretty.*

*Mike, I don't b'lee I'm going nowhere,* Carl had said.

"I know I ain't going," Michael said back.

The city had imposed a 6 p.m. curfew.

*It got dark, got to be eight, eight thirty, still no rain or nothing. Shit, see bout eleven, eleven thirty at night that's when it started to rain.* When Carl tells a story he always gives two close options for the truth.

He packed his ice chest and told Michael good-bye, nothing memorable, and drove off in his pickup truck. Michael left to find his girlfriend, Angela, at their house on Charbonnet Street in the Lower Ninth Ward to see where they might head. It was already too late; he knew he was not going far.

The Yellow House, where Carl lived off and on when he had fallen out with Monica, stayed behind. Cords stayed plugged into the walls. His boil pots sat underneath the kitchen sink. That's what "the Yellow House was up and running" was meant to say.

Carl took Chef Menteur to Paris Road to Press Drive to the brick house where Monica lived with their three girls. The street was empty and quiet, not unlike its normal self. Carl did not know if anyone else was around. Why should he have needed to know? He was feeling good.

Mindy and Tiger, his Pekingese dogs, did not appear at the door when he entered, but soon they were running by his slippered feet. The house phone was already ringing. Even though it was 2005, Carl still did not have a cell phone, having no desire whatsoever to be reached.

*Mama and them kept calling, Boy, get your ass out the house.*

He sat in the recliner and watched the television.

*Well fuck, by my drinking I had then fell asleep, full of that gin.*

He woke and moved from the chair to the bed, but before he slept again he made small preparations, just based on feeling.

*Monica had a big ole deep attic, so I put the steps down. I had already mapped it out in case I had to get out of there. I had a hatchet up there already with the bottled water. Had my gun, the same gun right there, had my water and everything, the meat cleaver.*

*See bout three, four in the morning, the dogs in the bed scratching me, licking on me.*

*Damn, it's dark.*

*You could hear it storming outside. I put my feet down.*
*Water.*

*Sound like a damn freight train derailing. Shit crashing. Shit flying, hitting shit.*

   *I can't see nothing, but I know the house. I throw Mindy and them up the attic steps.*

   *I go in the icebox take the water out there. Shit, bout five minutes later the icebox come off the ground. The icebox floating. I got to go up now myself, the water . . . I got pajamas on.*

   *I took a pair of jeans, I still got them jeans, my Katrina jeans. I go up there. Just waiting. Just riding it out.*

   *Sitting there looking at the water coming. I got my gun, I got a light on my head, I say damn the hurricane rolling out there.*

   *That water coming up higher and higher.*

## IVORY MAE

My mother calls Harlem from Hattiesburg, says, "Water is now coming into the house. We're calling for help." The phone line cuts out right as she is speaking so that is all I have to go on for three days. Those two lines keep replaying in my head—during half sleep, at dinners where they seem to issue forth from mouths of people concerned with entirely different matters, at my magazine job where I appear to have it together, and at every single moment of quiet.

   *Water is. We are.*
   *Calling. Help.*

## CARL

*It's been bout four, five hours. All a sudden, the water don't look like it's coming no higher. It just stopped right there, bout six or seven feet. You could hear all kind of birds then came through all the windows.*

   *See when daybreak come, that water it start coming again, it start coming all the way now.*

*I got to start cutting now.*
*The water coming.*
*It's daytime now. I can cut now.*
*The water steady rising.*
*I said, Shit I gotta get through this attic now.*

*Never panic, Mo. You can never panic.*

*I'm cutting through that sucker. I got an ax, I'm cutting through that son of a bitch.*

*I was gonna shoot my way through it if it wasn't gone cut. I was gonna blow some holes through that son of a bitch. I'm getting out that roof.*

*Once I got my head out, I looked round.*

"Hey man, I thought y'all was gone," someone on a roof several houses down called.

Water edged the roof. Carl's green boat was nowhere in sight.

*It's hot outside now, you gotta realize. They had a bucket floating. That's how I kept the roof at the pitch cool.*

*It's beaming on that roof. That attic don't cool down until nine or ten o'clock at night. We'd stay up and talk all the way till about midnight. Survival shit. If them people don't come, we have to swim out of here or this or that. I said whenever y'all ready but let's give it a couple days.*

*Back then, the old folks across the way was telling stories bout they had a big alligator in the water. I mean if I had to swim I would have but you ain't gone get in no water and people saying they got an alligator. We'd sit out there talking until we get so tired. Sometimes we'd straddle the roof, sideways like this so you don't roll off.*

*Some nights we were in the attic when it had done cooled down good. I'd pull the stairs up—you didn't want anything from the house to climb in there. Mindy and Tiger knew something wasn't right. They running all through the attic, barking at anything, never slept, lil wild mutherfuckers.*

*After three days, me and another dude got in the water.*

There were still rules in the new Old World.

> *You swam up the middle of the street. You knew the neighborhood. We never dove because you never knew if they had a post or something down there. We swam to where them old people was. We made sure they were all right. We stood there a couple of hours, one dude had food and was grilling and smoking cigarettes.*

"You must have been hungry," I say.

> *But if you eat you got to use the bathroom.*

On the way back, swimming, saltwater rushed into Carl's mouth.

Two, three more days passed in the same way with nothing changing.

## HARLEM

Five days since the levees broke. There is nothing to do here except to feel helpless. All the windows of my duplex are wide open tonight, to let the outside sounds come in. I am being particular about this because my loudmouthed neighbors remind me of home. I sit cross-legged before the television set in my swamp-green painted room, watching CNN on mute, searching only for Carl's white cotton socks pulled up high, size 13 feet. In the day-to-day, I neglect serious consideration of any newspaper article except to scan for names and faces of my beloveds—Michael, Carl, Ivory, Karen, Melvin, Brittany.

Imagine this being all that you can do. It is as paltry as it sounds.

## CARL

*We knew they was coming but you go to getting mad anyway.*

From the roof where he sat, Carl could see the staging area on the interstate where the rescued were dropped off. The airboats came straight through the area where before you could see a fence, where before you could see a car dealership and the train depot where freights docked for loading.

This new Old World seemed boundless.

*They finally come get us, some white guys from Texas. They pulled up in an airboat to the pitch of the roof.*

Seven days had gone by.

Carl was deposited on the interstate right before the point where the bridge rose. This was not the quiet of the roof. Carl saw many people he knew, people from all over, out of the East, out of the Lower Ninth Ward, out of the Desire Projects.

Army trucks were taking people from the bridge to the Convention Center, which had become an impromptu shelter, but there were the old and infirm who needed to go first and Carl was in good health with legs he could use. *Mindy and them wasn't on no leash. I had some Adidas tennis on, but they was so tight. I took the shoestrings off and made leashes.* He took the dogs on a long walk to the Convention Center, joined by several men, bending his six-foot-three-inch frame down to better grasp the strings. From New Orleans East, they walked the five miles to Martin Luther King Boulevard, then back around to the Convention Center, a long route to avoid Orleans, St. Bernard, and Claiborne Avenues, all of which were underwater.

The walk took all day. But Carl never went inside the Convention Center itself. He stayed on the perimeter watching the clamor. For him, nighttime was not for sleep: a certain time of the night dogs would run loose from sleeping owners, sprinting through the dreaming masses.

Beyond the dogs' motion, things seemed dire and unmoving. But then Harry Connick Jr. appeared with TV cameras and buses showed up.

*I wasn't worried about getting on no bus,* Carl said, opening another beer. *Look like a movie, like the world coming to an end, people was just running. People just trying to get the fuck out of Dodge.*

"What about the drug addicts?" I want to know.

*All them was out there. Shaking like a fucking leaf.*

After days as part of a growing crowd that seemed to go nowhere, Carl set out from the Convention Center with two men he knew from the Grove. They headed toward the interstate where they found a boat with paddles sitting at the base of the ramp at Claiborne and Orleans Avenues, close to where Carl normally spends Mardi Gras day.

*Whoever left it must have kicked ass. I said, Let's take that mutherfucker and get the fuck.*

*Me and the two dudes pattlin.*

*People stranded on balconies in the projects,* his brother Michael among them, but he could not know that then. *I thought Michael was gone.*

The men paddled down Orleans away from the Convention Center, away from Canal to Broad Street.

*The water was so high you couldn't even much see Ruth Chris Steak House. This shit was amazing.*

"Hold on, bey," Carl says, answering his cell phone. He has come a long way since 2005. He says to a man's voice, "I was doing a lil interview with Monique about that Katrina shit." He does not know how to operate the phone fully, only ever answers it on speakerphone so that whoever calls talks to Carl and whoever else is around.

Back in the boat, Carl and the two men moved through the watery city, one boat among many, down Broad Street and back down Canal before night.

*You thinking that's mannequins floating by you, but when you get by it that body smell so bad, it then swoll up big. Man that ain't no mannequin, that's a dead body.*

*Now water leaking in the fucking boat. One dude got a bucket throwing it out, two of us pattlin.*

They headed down Canal Street toward the Regional Transit Authority building where Monica worked, but by then it had already been evacuated. That night the men stayed in the boat, tethered to the massive metal rollup gates in front of the building's parking lot, stranded cars and buses just inside.

*Just like we were fishing somewhere. We just sit up in the boat all night smoking cigarettes and talking. Nodding off, fighting sleep.*

That next morning they woke to the same watery city as the day before, but now there were boats with motors. That was the sound that woke them.

From the boat, Carl tried to *see the next stage of things. The Dome— wasn't nobody moving out. Convention Center, same. So now we all the way up Broad Street and Tulane. Now, what you think is there? What's there, Mo?*

I hesitate. It's a geography test. I don't know.

Orleans Parish Prison where inmates—some of whom were evacuated four days after the water rose to their chests—waited on top of the Broad Street Overpass in orange jumpsuits. Carl pulled his boat up to the bridge where other boats idled.

After the helicopter took all of the inmates, Carl headed to the top of the bridge instead of milling about at the foot with the others.

*Helicopter was a big ole sucker, bigger than this damn house here. They always land at work, but I never rode on none of them hard-riding bastards. I say hey to the dude who was flying, Man where you taking us.*

It was a rough ride. Mindy and Tiger bucked and pulled. Tiger was Mindy's son and they acted it.

*I'm home free now. I'm there now,* said Carl, placing himself in the landscape. He knew exactly where he was: *Int'national Airport.*

Louis Armstrong New Orleans International Airport.

## MICHAEL

It was the balcony that saved them. At night you could go out there and sleep. Or in the dark night you could sit watching explosions coming from the direction of Lee Circle, an oil refinery, maybe, but you didn't know, or watch houses burning down furiously across Broad Street. "Like fire from hell," Michael said. Everyone seemed to have guns. The balcony could feel like a box seat: Across the street, men with weapons shot grocery store doors open. Down below, two men argued over who would pull the boat while the other sat, one of them brandishing a gun to pull rank.

Michael and Rodney, Angela's brother, the two eldest men of the group, went out every morning in search of food, waking before daybreak, while the others slept. They were fifteen people in a two-bedroom apartment in the Lafitte Projects, which were demolished in 2008, rebuilt, and renamed Faubourg Lafitte, but that is now and I am still speaking of then, that September of 2005 when Michael was one of two self-designated lieutenants of the group that included his girlfriend's children and her mother.

The men walked or swam the streets, depending on the water levels.

More than four thousand people were stranded on the interstate where Carl spent a short time. Michael and Rodney avoided the masses, staying down on the streets figuring they were much better off in the housing project, protected from the elements at least and with toilets that they flushed by dipping a bucket down into the water and pulling it back up, an emergency well that served pure filth, but still.

The men foraged for food and other items from broken-in stores, eventually finding an air mattress and two boats. Whatever you needed and the last thing on earth you needed could be found, it seemed, in the dirty, fetid water. When they arrived back at the apartment before sunset, havoc-wreaking time, the men doused themselves with Listerine scavenged from shelves of abandoned stores. Closed their eyes and poured the entire bottle all over everywhere.

But the food in the house and on store shelves was "constantly getting less and less," said Michael. The men had less stamina for the daily journeys to forage. As time wore on, they had to travel farther and farther away from home base. The farther east, the deeper the water, the wilder the stories: "This crazy dude was whacked up off of some angel dust, lady police trying to help him," said Michael. "He grabbed her gun and shot her in the head and all kinda shit like that." For instance.

In the apartment, one woman among the fifteen people had taken to stealing food for herself and her daughter, hiding it from the rest who were rationing small bits. The clamor that broke out when this was discovered had no place to go but within the apartment walls. And this was the sound everywhere, a collective groan born from waiting shut inside.

Days later, after the Superdome had been evacuated, helicopters began circling the Lafitte. When they hovered low down to where the men on the balcony could see, the rescuers were pointing guns. Michael refused to separate his group; several times they turned down would-be rescuers who did not have sufficient room for the entire crew.

When they were finally rescued, it all seemed to begin and end in the same instant. The group, still intact, moved from the boat that pulled up to the apartment steps to an army truck and then to an idling bus.

"Where we going?" Angela asked the armed man standing at the head of the bus. Only silence.

## IVORY MAE

Hattiesburg, where Mom and her crew had arrived, was no escape. It rained so hard that water started coming into cousin Lisa's house. At first, it rose to ankle height. They raced to lift furniture onto tables, but the water kept coming, forcing them to flee to the neighbor's house on higher ground. They waited and waited—one then two days—until it was safe to drive to the airport where they would fly to another cousin in Texas.

Troy had never flown. Nor had thirteen-year-old Brittany. But grown Troy was the one to act a fool, proclaiming how he would die not from the Water but from this. "Dammit, dammit, dammit," he chanted the entire flight, his leg furious and shaking. He was getting on everyone's nerves.

The Dallas/Fort Worth airport was full of arriving New Orleanians who were asking, "Where we landed at?"

## GRANDMOTHER

A yellow school bus full of ailing nursing home patients made its way down the highway, which highway? Van Gogh said yellow is the color of divine clarity. Was Grandmother sitting on a seat, was it plush, was it fake leather like on school buses where when you sit the air releases, or was she lying on pillows on the floor? What of her arthritic knees? Were they hurting at all, did she say a single word, did she sing like normal, did she look around, did she have a flash of clarity? That is the thing I want to know: Did she have a moment of lucidity in her Alzheimer's-ridden mind? Can the body feel the crossing of a state line, even if the mind does not grasp? Was Grandmother's forgetfulness like drinking from the River Lethe? Did it cast her into oblivion, I wonder, erase the landscape of her former life, and is this the only condition, this unknowing, under which one should cross over state lines, leaving your familiarity behind? Is this the only way to properly leave home?

# III

## Settle

*September 6–September 29, 2005*
*Vacaville, California–St. Rose, Louisiana–Tyler, Texas*

*B*yron's two-story house on Dawnview Way in Vacaville, California, fifty-five miles north of San Francisco, was spacious under normal circumstances in that suburban way that grants illusions, with three bedrooms and an office. But there were nine people living in it now: six adults and three children. Like addresses everyplace in the days following the Water, it appeared as house on the outside but was shelter for the dispossessed within.

The minute Byron, Ivory Mae's youngest boy, learned that our mother and her crew had made their way through Mississippi's flooding to dry Dallas, he sent them five one-way tickets. He also sent a ticket to Herman, Alvin's big brother, our neighbor on Wilson who sling-shot Lynette's front tooth out. Herman, who was stranded in Baton Rouge, was like a brother to us.

Shortly after everyone arrived in Vacaville, so did I. I came not only because I couldn't figure out what else to do with my body but also because I had been assigned the difficult task of writing a "Katrina story" for the magazine. My assignment was to write about what my family had

come through, which required that I put myself in the impossible position
of reporter. I knew it was ridiculous, my writing down what everyone
said; after every conversation I hid myself away in the bathroom, writing
scenes into a notebook instead of feeling.

Mom shared the room downstairs with Karen. Brittany, Karen's
daughter, shared a bed with Byron's only daughter, Alexus. The men
shared a bunk bed upstairs in the former office, where if you closed the
door in the evenings it grew so musty you could barely breathe.

On the first night in Vacaville, Herman had a nightmare that woke
the house. He was a dehydrated, overweight thirty-four-year-old who
could barely walk on swollen feet. In California, Herman claimed to have
sat one whole day on the roof of the Yellow House until it split into two
underneath him, forcing him to swim to safety. But he is always making
shit up. Herman spent his days in Vacaville on the phone exaggerating
his exploits to gullible local radio stations. How he kept getting found by
these journalists, no one knew. Sometimes we joked about whether another
person was on the other end of the line at all.

Carl and Michael were still somewhere out there; ten days had passed.
The only time we cared about was the minute when we would hear from
them.

Herman swore he saw Carl in a boat helping people near the Superdome. This sounded like exactly the kind of thing Carl would be doing,
so almost everyone believed him, except for me. I kept saying, "I need to
hear from him." Whenever Herman repeated his Carl-the-rescuer story,
I looked at him, angrily.

Herman was loud in the day and loud in the night, his hauntings
persisting. "He had some real standout moments," niece Brittany says
now. Herman told tales, but everybody knew those were the best enter-
tainers. He seemed able to transport us back to a feeling of home, which
was Wilson Avenue. In Vacaville, he performed silly, momentous feats
like racing small Justin, Byron's ten-year-old neighbor who was a track
star. Herman, who was overweight by at least seventy-five pounds (and
with swollen feet), who was asthmatic and stroke prone, challenged

small Justin to a race down Dawnview Way. Somehow Herman's bluster grew into an event. At the designated time, around six in the evening, people on the block came out from their stucco homes, some of them with chairs, to watch. The whistle was blown and off they ran in the direction of Cedar Crest Drive. Herman was OK for the first thirty seconds, but then small Justin left him a wee bit behind, which led Herman, who did not like to lose or be shamed in front of a crowd, to pick up his pace. It seemed his legs might collapse. For a moment it could appear Herman was gaining, but small Justin left him far behind, so far that for a long time Herman was running against himself. Justin seemed to fly and disappear while Herman, bent over in the street, huffed and puffed for his life.

All the spectators were bent over, too, laughing uproariously. No one paid attention to Herman's recovery. We were all tickled by how serious he had been, to believe he might actually win! His performance brought levity to a grave, sinking reality. For the time it took Justin to beat Herman, no one thought about the Water. This was how Herman became a hero.

This story, "Herman's Race," was revived during every depressing moment in the long days ahead.

When neighbors brought over piles of used clothes, my family, who I had never seen ask for anything, slowly looked for things they liked, though it was mostly about need:

*Herm started out real, real strong,* someone would begin.

When Melvin, a teenager, sulked around all the day in a perpetual fog, dismayed and dispirited by the new arrangement, this foreign world:

*Justin flew, that was too much, seeing a grown-ass man up against a lil boy. Herman wouldn't give up though.*

When the news channels (which were always on) blared updates on the city and the storm that did not address the whereabouts of our two lost men:

*Next thing you know Justin wasn't nowhere to be found. Herm made his point though.*

∞

One week after they arrived in Vacaville, Melvin and Brittany enrolled at the local high school, the only two *Katrina transports* as my mother called them, their names and travails announced one morning over the loud-speaker. "I just want to fit in. This is high school," said Brittany. "It was a top story. Everyone was trying to figure us out," said Melvin who was called Louisiana by his football teammates.

Herman said he was moving to Austin, Texas, where "I'll never have to evacuate again," but then he took a job at the local auto parts store on Nut Tree Road.

Troy started unloading boxes from Walmart trucks for eight dollars an hour, far more than he earned in seventeen years of furniture making at Walter Thorn and Company, a job he had inherited when Byron left for the Marines. That job had been Troy's habit for a long time, since he was twenty years old: catching the Broad bus on Chef Menteur at 5 a.m., getting off by Louisa Street, then catching the Desire bus to Poland Avenue.

The men found jobs before Karen, who could not recall the last time she was without work. She had already decided the moment they arrived in California: we are never going back. After several months of searching, she—who had spent her professional life as a social worker—applied at UPS for holiday work scanning and retrieving packages. The job was surprisingly fun, a relief actually.

My mother cooked big pots of red beans and rice, meat sauce and spaghetti, cabbage and rice, things the household could eat off the whole day. Life tried to settle.

## MICHAEL

Eleven days after Carl and Michael went missing, I dialed Michael's number again. Instead of voice mail, Michael answered, said, "Wo nah, baby girl. Where y'all at?" as if we had been the ones missing.

At the New Orleans airport where they'd been carried on buses, "They had it written on a white piece of paper where you were going," said Michael sometime later. "They'd say this plane is going here, this one is going here, and that one is going there. They say you could go to Atlanta, Houston, Dallas, San Antonio. Which one y'all want to go. We got on the first flight out of that mutherfucker."

The fifteen of them boarded the plane to elsewhere, San Antonio. And that was where he was now.

## CARL

When Carl arrived at Louis Armstrong International Airport he saw that it had become a hospital, patients on stretchers everywhere on the floor, some rolled around on luggage carts. Some of the infirm had arrived from the Lafon nursing home on Chef Menteur Highway where Mom and her sister, Elaine, spent most of their lives working as nurse's aides. The evacuated patients were the survivors; twenty-two had already died.

Carl was miserable watching the old people lying everywhere, the sight of them reminding him to get on with his journey. At the airport, he ate his first solid meal since the barbecue and gin outside the Yellow House, fourteen days before. Full up, he embarked on the final leg of his journey, walking down Airline Highway with Mindy and Tiger still on shoelaces, across the overpass to cousin Earl's house on the snaking River Road.

*When we come round the bend, Earl and them was out there barbecuing. When they seen me coming they was so happy. I went to telling them the story.*

Carl called my cell phone two days later and related this story. My mother and I were in the parking lot of a grocery store in Vacaville where we had come looking for coffee and chicory. I yelled into the phone, "CUUUUUUUUURRRRLLLLLLLLLLLLLLLLLLL."

⚯

After arriving at cousin Earl's, Carl was dropped off at Grandmother's house on Mockingbird Lane in St. Rose, the only house in the family saved from the storm's devastation. It never lost power. Carl was alone in the house, mostly sleeping, until others heard of his good fortune and came to share in it. His longtime friend Black Reg, whose New Orleans East home was still underwater, came, the two of them splitting bills and responsibilities. Carl would return home to St. Rose after work at NASA to cooked food and, sometimes, waiting women. Reg kept the yard clean.

It rained more than usual those days. From his small room in Grandmother's house with the row of windows against one wall, Carl imagined the water topping the levees along the River Road. He stayed up all night watching to see what the rain would do. Now he knew: even after it quit, it could still do something.

He was a forty-year-old man living in his grandmother's house. He had a room now. And a short hallway to roam.

His stomach hurt constantly, and he suffered from headaches, but he blamed his physical calamities on the Water. It just needed, he figured, to run through him.

## GRANDMOTHER

A week after Carl reappeared, my cousin Michelle discovered Grandmother's name on the internet: Amelia. Briarcliffe Nursing Home, Tyler, Texas. "It is a nice place," Auntie Elaine said after having gone to see her there. In the scattering, Grandmother had suddenly fallen ill, but it was hard to know exactly how her illness came to be or how it progressed to the point of death rattles, but suddenly her organs were failing and Grandmother had trouble breathing.

Byron called me in Harlem where I was trying to make a story out of life as it was still unfolding. "Grandmother dead," he said straight up. He had already told Mom, he said.

Not an hour later, he called back. Grandmother's heartbeat was so faint that the doctors only *thought* she had died. She was, in fact, still alive. I squeezed my eyes closed and pushed my nose up trying to shut off tears.

A few days after this conversation, Byron called me again in New York City. I was sitting hunched over in my cubicle, at work. "Grandmother has one day left. For real this time."

By the time he told me this, Mom was already on a plane to Texas, arriving hours before her mother, my grandmother, Amelia Lolo, would *actually* die. It was a month to the day that the storm hit. September 29, 2005.

# IV

---

# *Bury*

*September 29–October 2, 2005*
*St. Rose, Louisiana*

*B*efore the Water, I had six siblings outside of Louisiana and five in or near New Orleans. In the After, there were two siblings in Louisiana; neither resided in New Orleans. Now ten people had to fly back home instead of six. Most all of us came for Grandmother's funeral, as if on pilgrimage. Grandmother's burial would be the last time for a long time that this many of us—ten of twelve children—were gathered together in the same room.

Michael arrived from San Antonio where he had already found work as a life insurance salesman, his days spent driving up and down roads where "it would stop being pavement, start being dirt, and then turn into water," for US Credit Union, which "wasn't government, but sounded like it."

Byron and Troy and Karen and Herman drove from Vacaville together, thirty-six hours straight. They retrieved Darryl from his home in Southern California along the way. Grandmother's funeral marked Darryl's second time back in Louisiana after leaving New Orleans eight years before when I was a senior in high school. It was my second time seeing him and talking to him since, the first time that I could remember meeting and holding his eyes.

Our eldest brother, Simon Jr., drove the thirteen hours from North Carolina.

Lynette and I flew in together from New York City.

All of us children, which is who we adults became in the presence of our mother, stayed together in Grandmother's house. This was the house that used to receive us regularly on weekends, for holidays and birthdays, for celebrations of all kinds. It was not lost on us that Grandmother's house, which she had bought and intended as a family home, was the very place that would keep us now.

Lynette and I were charged with designing a funeral program. Much of New Orleans was still underwater—the funeral homes were overbooked and stretched too thin—but we made a simple tribute to Grandmother using Microsoft Word. To print the programs, Lynette and I drove one hour each way to the nearest working Kinko's in Baton Rouge, Louisiana's capital.

Michael kept everyone fed. When visitors from the neighborhood stopped by to pay condolences he always asked, "How y'all flied through the storm?"

We wanted to memorialize Grandmother in the newspaper with an obituary, calling the *Times-Picayune* frantically, day after day, at every mundane moment, on our way to the grocery store or seconds after pulling into the driveway, just before getting out. But the line stayed busy; no one ever answered.

Far fewer people came to Grandmother's funeral than would have if an obituary had run. My mother mentioned this over and over. It felt wrong to me, too, not to have Grandmother's death in newsprint for someone other than those of us in the family to know or for someone to dig up years later, just as I have found evidence of my father's having lived—and died.

The evening before Grandmother's burial, my brothers gathered in the garage of her house on Mockingbird Lane. I could hear their sounds from the hallway and through the closed door. I opened it to feel less outside. The door, when I pushed it, made a loud grunting noise. My brothers sat around taking turns cutting each other's hair.

The boys huddled together in there reminded me of times before, in the Yellow House, when Byron would return home from the Marines—from Okinawa, Japan, where he had been stationed; or from a stint in Operation Desert Storm—how my brothers would meet him in the yard, pushing and fighting. *They act like animals,* my mother would say. *That's their way of saying hello and I love you.* The older boys were reminding Byron of his place in the family as the youngest no matter how big his muscles, no matter how far from home he'd gone.

Three months before the hurricane, in May, eight of us had gathered, my seven brothers and me, for a photo shoot to accompany an article I had written for *O* magazine about growing up with so many brothers. The editor had chosen the Riverfront, on the Mississippi, for the scene, just in front of a gazebo, in sight of steamboats passing by. My brothers were dressed alike in blue jeans and loafers and button-down shirts. There are several versions of the same image, but I love best the one with Darryl in front of the group, his mouth open, chanting, "Iko, Iko" like on Mardi Gras day. He had not been home in so long, had not been down to the Riverfront for much longer than that, and was happy to be back. I saw then how Darryl could dance, saw it for the first time. I danced, too, not enough to outdo Darryl, but enough to impress my big brothers. Somehow, I thought then, my ability to dance well would signify that I had turned out all right and was one of them.

This was the first time I could recall being physically surrounded by every single one of my brothers. In the photograph I leaned against Byron at the edge of the frame, my elbow crooked high to reach his shoulder. The men held small yellow umbrellas, a New York editor's idea of a second line parade, I guess. We smiled for the camera. Carl wore his trademark wire-framed Duckie sunshades, perfect round circles. The image appeared in *O* magazine, a full page. Carl took it to NASA to show off.

Now, four months later, I stood watching my brothers from the hallway of Grandmother's house. They paid me no mind, or they did not know I was there. Byron pushed against Darryl, his arms making an X across his chest, the movements less brusque, more tender. Michael was drunk and outside the house peering through the glass doors into the garage, my brothers pretending not to see. Carl, already a twig, was gaunt eyed, socks to his kneecaps, his face hiccupped in an ongoing laugh. I can still hear him laughing at everything, Simon Broom's shadow.

Suddenly a sound—deep, guttural—rang out through the house. *UgggggghhhhhAhhhhhh.*

The noise seemed to come from someone who had not spoken for a long while. The whole house ran to the back bedroom. Mom was on her knees pulling the sheets down off the side of the bed. None of us children had ever heard her cry.

Mother wore shock to the funeral. Her hair was black frizz, her normally wet curls, sapped. Her usually red lips, bare. Lynette had drawn black eyeliner on her eyes, which seemed not to connect to the eyes of anyone else. At the funeral at Mount Zion Baptist Church on First Street, Mom sat in the front row before Grandmother's casket. Auntie Elaine sat on one side of her, Byron on the other, where I knew he would. He was too young a boy, eleven, to do anything when his father died, but he would make up for it now. I stared at the side of Mom from where I was sitting across the aisle, a few rows behind. Her gone look made me cry harder than the gone look of Grandmother in the open casket.

The preacher spoke in vague terms, as they do, about Grandmother's goodness, congratulated her on graduating into the arms of her heavenly hosts. I thought about the white van in which her body was transported back to Louisiana from Tyler, Texas. I thought about the yellow school bus on which she was evacuated from Louisiana to Tyler, Texas. Yellow, I thought again, the color of divine clarity.

I heard my name called, then took the stage to read a letter to Grandmother, a collage of sentiment gathered from my siblings and

Joseph, Elaine, and Ivory. "Tennis," Eddie told me. "That was her thing." "Grandma was the first person to take me to Texas. Now I'm living there," Michael had said. "Grandma was," said Lynette, "beauty combined with elegance, inside and out, your home, the way you dress, your posture, every detail, the way you treat other people, the way you see the world, her jewelry box, tons of hatboxes, that armoire, huge bed with white headboard, red sponge for face powder. Someone you admired and wanted to be like."

Her son, Joseph, said his mother taught him to dress, to have impeccable style and taste. Her daughter Elaine said that she was generous, "housing so many people, relations, people married and misplaced." Ivory Mae wanted it to be known that Lolo was *a grand lady, my best friend*. These things combined made a woman of Lolo so that she was not only Mother, so that she was not only Grandmother, so that she exceeded her titles and her roles to become a person, and this was honor.

At the final viewing of the casket, Mom broke all the way: trying to climb into the casket, *Lolo, Lolo, Loli*. It was the most awful calling out of someone's name. Then no longer *Lolo* but *Mom, Mom* then *Mommy, Mommy. Don't go*, she was screaming. *Do. Not. Go, Moooooooooommeeeeeee*, she dragged the word out, became her younger girl self, stumping out the words. She might as well have pounded her feet on the sanctuary's plush red carpet. Mommy. Do. Not. Go.

All of us children stood there watching Byron, her baby boy, the young strapping version of his father, Simon, trying to hold his mother up. She was Jell-O sliding down his black suit. All of her body seemed loosed, each limb disconnected and moving away from the others.

I was wearing contacts, but if they were glasses, I would have taken them off in order not to see.

My mother sheltered bad feelings the rest of 2005, seeming immune to those things that generally lifted her—being surrounded by her sons, for instance. She has always loved men, feeling a certain ease and power around them. When one of her sons was especially well dressed and handsome she'd say, *You look like your father did when he was trying to woo me.* Certain of the boys, Michael and Carl and Byron and Eddie, live for this recognition, having inherited much of Ivory Mae's looks and vanity.

*Had I gone with her,* she had started to say in the days following. *I still don't feel like Lolo is gone. She had gotten to be such a part of my life. I centered everything around going to take care of her.*

*I should have taken that bus with her. Maybe Karen could have just went on, her and Troy and them, by themselves. By not seeing me every day or seeing some familiar face she just gave up. You know what I'm saying?*

After retiring from the Lafon nursing home on Chef Menteur Highway, Mom had moved to Grandmother's house in St. Rose and nearly lived in her mother's nursing home room, keeping Grandmother's bag in her car trunk at all times, full of nice-smelling lotions that she loved to run along Grandmother's arms and hands and legs. I can recall Mom's hands distinctly, slightly wrinkled, ringless, how she'd grab her mother's arm with one hand and rub all the way from the shoulder joint down to where their hands interlocked, Mom moving her fingers in and through Grandmother's.

She painted her mother's fingernails red. She braided her hair, two gray plaits hanging back along Grandmother's neck, the way she had done ours as children but with a new gentleness. Grandmother sucked sugar-free candies while Mom tended to her, moving the hard balls around in her mouth, patting the arm of the chair with one hand.

At a point in the course of her Alzheimer's disease, Grandmother forgot how to eat. Ivory Mae showed up to feed her. When she began developing bedsores Ivory Mae showed up to turn her. She could not abide Grandmother lying in bed all day in a gown. She did all the things the nursing staff would not. The nurse's aides at Chateau Estates were deplorable in Mom's eyes, unfazed, crowded around their stations, walking, some of them, like they were drugged worse than the patients, their reflexes slow. You yelled for them. They came whenever they pleased. Nothing was ever an emergency.

She'd get Grandmother into clothes if the staff was short, telling them don't worry about it, she had it, and she would have it. Grandmother would appear dressed and sitting in a leather armchair by her bed like she was someone with life to live.

Grandmother's clothes were labeled by Ivory Mae's strong hand: "Amelia Lolo" written on everything. And: Do Not Wash. In the nursing home, Mom moved around, packing dirty clothes to take home and wash lest the nursing home fade their colors, speaking with the staff who she reasoned would treat Grandmother better knowing someone was always coming around.

When Lynette and I came home for Christmas, we'd go along on these visits. Seeing Mom enter the room, you understood how she gained the reputation of being incredible with her patients at Lafon nursing home.

*Loli, Loli . . .*

And when Grandmother didn't respond, a sterner voice.

*Lolo!*

*This your baby, Ivory.*

*Ivory Mae.*

*How you feeling today, Lo?*

Grandma would make eye contact.

*You remember Joseph, Lo.*

Grandmother lit up, as if anticipating her son, Joseph, who she had not seen for a time. He said it was too hard to see his mother like this; he rarely visited.

On these visits, Lynette and I stood back, along the walls of Grandmother's small room, waiting for Mom to tell us what to do and how to behave. We'd bring ice cream, which Grandmother always loved. Mom asked me to feed it to her and I did. Lynette lotioned her hands and then her legs. Mom still told us, her adult children, exactly what to do and we did it.

There was a certain gentleness necessary when handling Grandmother that I had not yet practiced. On these visits, Mom was teaching us how to touch.

# V

## *Trace*

*October 3, 2005*
*New Orleans East*

$\mathcal{T}$hose of us who wanted to see the Yellow House crowded into Byron's car for the drive to New Orleans East. It felt like an out-of-state trip; there were roadblocks everywhere. But because Carl had returned to work at NASA not long after the storm, his work ID procured us entry. When we arrived at the checkpoint on Chef Menteur, Carl pressed his work badge up against the window. "I got a Michoud badge," he said to the officer through the closed window. "I'm legal." Even with windows rolled up, the post-Water smell (chitlins, piss, stale water, lemon juice) forced its way through the air-conditioning vents. We drove on, along Chef Menteur Highway, where instead of working traffic lights there were stop signs planted low to the ground. Like flowers. The actual flowers were now dead. We drove past Lafon nursing home where Mom used to work. The lot was full of abandoned cars, the building empty inside. I don't remember the rest of the sights on our way to getting there. Remembering is a chair that it is hard to sit still in.

We arrived at Wilson Avenue and made the right turn.

Herman jumped out of the car before it made a complete stop. We laughed at this. He disappeared into Ms. Octavia's house, where the great oak that Alvin and I had climbed as children lay in the front yard, its roots upright. Herman rummaged through soaking-wet dresser drawers for photographs of his dead brother and my childhood friend Alvin. Searched for intact images of his mother, Big Karen, and his grandmother, Ms. Octavia, who had died of old age two years before. Came up short.

Mom wore a white surgical mask. I glimpsed her through Byron's front windshield, her body parallel to the Yellow House, facing Old Gentilly Road, her shoulders slightly tilted, sunk in the buttery leather front seat, a hand cradling one side of her face. We, her children—Byron, Lynette, Carl, Troy, and me—jolted to the house.

Birds were now living in our childhood home. When we approached it with its broken-out windows, they flew away, en masse.

The house looked as though a force, furious and mighty, crouching underneath, had lifted it from its foundation and thrown it slightly left; as though once having done that it had gone inside, to Lynette's and my lavender-walled bedroom and extended both arms to press outward until the walls expanded, buckled, and then folded back on themselves. The front door sat wide open; a skinny tree angled its way inside.

And the cedar trees: once majestic, at least twenty-five feet tall, and full of leaves that I hid in as a small girl. An impossibility now, for the sole surviving one was puny and on the way to dead.

We poked our heads through the house's blown-out windows— peered into the living room through the wide-open frames. Walked along the side and stood in front of the new entrance, a fourth door designed by Water. The house had split in two, just as Herman said, the original structure separated from the later addition that Simon Broom, my father, built. On the original section of the house, the yellow siding hung off like icicles, revealing green wood underneath. That was the house of my siblings, a green wooden house, not the Yellow House that I knew.

We did not enter, even though the house we knew beckoned. We stayed outside, looking through the one big crack.

Somehow, standing as we were—spaced perfectly apart—made me think of the time, a few days before Grandmother's burial, when I wandered through Providence Memorial Cemetery with Lynette and Michael. It was an impromptu trip. Michael said he knew where our fathers were. "I got two daddies in one cemetery," he bragged as we turned into the graveyard on Airline Highway.

Michael gestured toward one of the only trees in sight. Webb, his birth father, was buried over there, he seemed to know. It was a month after the Water; everything was still ruined. There was no grave tender to ask.

We walked and walked. Over to the tree then past the tree to the rows of graves beyond it.

"My daddy not buried too far from your daddy," Michael kept saying. It was strange, his separating us out as siblings. It felt unnatural.

When we did find the men, they were nowhere near where Michael thought, but they were close together in the ground. I had never seen the burial spot of my father, Simon Broom. I learned his birthday—February 22—for the first time on that day and saw that he had died on June 14, 1980.

The three of us stood apart saying nothing whatsoever. I didn't know what I was supposed to do.

At the cemetery that day, there was little to look at, unlike this moment outside the Yellow House where there was too much detail for the eyes to make sense of: The white plastic art deco chandelier dangled from a white cord in the girls' room. A pair of Carl's pants in a dry cleaner's bag hung from the curtain rod. The white dresser that was painted over so many times that the drawers were permanently shut, the dresser Lynette and I used to pose in front of, where I would make rabbit ears behind her Jheri-curled head. I felt that old, childish shame again. I did want the Yellow House gone, but mostly from mind, wanted to be free from its lock and chain of memory, but did not, could not, foresee water bumrushing it. I still imagined, standing there, that it would one day be rebuilt.

∽

The House called.

*This is how you, Sarah, wanted it.*

You, House, are nothing but a crack—you are wide open and showing. You tell on yourself.

My mother stayed in the car, refusing to look. I recognized this behavior of hers as disappointment. To whom, I wonder, was it directed? My siblings and I who had let the house weaken, or the limping, fractured structure itself?

Before we left, I entered the front door and took baby steps forward, afraid the weight of me might collapse the house. The farthest I went was into the living room, where it was all dust, wood chips, waterlines but also the light switch by the front door: cream colored, gold scrollwork making an intricate design in the center. Pretty.

After a time—short or long I do not know—we joined Ivory Mae in the car that she had not left. She was still wearing the white mask over her nose and mouth.

Carl needed to go back to Monica's house, from where he escaped the flood, for his weed eater, he announced after we were settled back into the car. At Monica's, Carl entered through a wooden fence, crumpled like an accordion. I photographed his every movement as if to save him from disappearance. Mom kept yelling from the car: *Just leave the damn thing, Carl. I'll get you another one. Come on now, boy.* Her voice was resigned, muffled by the mask.

But Carl always does what his mind wants. Next we saw, he was up on the roof walking with a loping stride.

Picture a man set against a wide blue sky, wearing a bright-red Detroit Pistons hat, blue jean shorts that fall far below the knee, and clean blue sneakers. In the first frame, he is bent down, holding himself up by his hands, entering the escape hole, a rugged map carved through the roof, feet first. By the second frame he is shrunken to half a man. In the last frame, we see only his head. Then he disappears inside.

Carl reappeared holding a weed eater in one hand, a chain saw in the other.

Now he was pointing at the hole in the roof.

He was performing, his movements quick, wild but measured; he was earning his nickname. Rabbit. We formed a semicircle, looking up at him from the ground, as if poised to catch him.

*Come on, boy. Carl, come on now, get your ass down now. Leave that goddamn mess behind,* my mother was still yelling. It was rare to hear her curse, but still we stayed watching Carl. None of us obeyed her command.

We were here, it was apparent, as witnesses to what Carl had come through. To retrieve, in some way, not the weed eater but the memory.

# VI

---

# *Erase*

*July 2006*
*Wilson Avenue*

$\mathcal{M}$y mother, Ivory Mae, called me one day in Harlem and told me the story in three lines:

*Carl said those people then came and tore our house down.*

*That land clean as a whistle now.*

*Look like nothing was ever there.*

The letter from the city announcing the intended demolition, the planned removal of 4121 Wilson, had been sent to the mailbox in front of the exact same house set to be torn down, its pieces deconstructed and carted away.

The Yellow House was deemed in "imminent danger of collapse," one of 1,975 houses to appear on the Red Danger List, houses bearing bright-red stickers no larger than a small hand.

The notice in the mailbox in front of our doomed house read in part: Dear Ms. Bloom: The City of New Orleans intends to demolish and remove the home/property and/or remnants of the home/property located at 4121 Wilson . . . THIS IS THE ONLY NOTIFICATION YOU WILL RECEIVE. Sincerely, Law Department-Demolition Task Force.

Not one of us twelve children who belonged to the house—not Eddie, Michael, or Darryl; nor Simon, Valeria, or Deborah; nor Karen, Carl, Troy, Byron, Lynette, or myself—was there to see it go.

*Look like nothing was ever there.*

Before our house was knocked down, Carl had overseen its ruins, driving by almost daily, except for the day when he suddenly fell sick in the driveway of Grandmother's house where he was living. One minute he was revving his engine for the drive to NASA in New Orleans East, the next, his head lay down on the steering wheel. A neighbor saw this, a busy man's head down, and became alarmed. Carl was rushed to the hospital for surgery. "Crooked intestines," was how Carl interpreted the doctor's diagnosis of intestinal obstruction. "They had to chop a large section of me out. I was all twisted inside from all that bad water I was swimming in," Carl was convinced.

He stayed in the hospital an additional thirty days postsurgery after incurring an infection from the hospitalization itself. This was how it came to be that he missed the letter in the mailbox and the house was demolished without our knowing it.

Everyone else was still displaced. The only one to see our house go was Rachelle—Herman and Alvin's sister, Ms. Octavia's granddaughter—who we called Ray. She was the inheritor of the last remaining house standing on the street. Ray snapped Polaroid images of the Yellow House's demise, instant evidence that she misplaced and could not find when we came back around, months after the fact, asking, "Did you see it? Did you see the house go down, Ray? Did you see?"

Perhaps there is a trick of logic that fails me now, but to deliver such notification to the doomed structure itself seems too easy a metaphor for much of what New Orleans represents: blatant backwardness about the things that count. For what can an abandoned house receive, by way of notification? And when basic services like sanitation and clean water were still lacking, why was there still mail delivery? But we were not the only ones. Lawsuits were filed against the city on behalf of houses that unlike ours stood in perfect condition when they were knocked down. There were sanctuaries, actual churches that deacons prepared to move back into, only to discover them gone. A newspaper article headlined NEW ORLEANS' WRECKING BALL LEVELS HEALTHY HOMES asked the simplest and thus most profound questions, such as: "How do you not inquire before you knock a place down? How do you not knock on the door first?"

During a later trip to New Orleans, I retrieved the file from city hall that told the story of the demolition. I carried it around in my purse and wrote "Autopsy of the House" in large letters on the front page. The cover letter held the following disclaimer: "The subject property was not historical in nature." The report tells this story: The house was displaced from its foundation. Structural displacement was moderate as opposed to severe, which would have required that the house float down the block and settle in another locale entirely. City inspectors deemed the house "unsafe to enter." There was asbestos everywhere, in the living room walls, in the trowel-and-drag ceilings that Uncle Joe had painted, in the asphalt shingles, in the vinyl sheeting on the floor. City inspectors noted that the left wall framing was severely "racked."

I called on an engineer friend and described the house, told her I was trying to learn from reading the autopsy which of the structural problems were waterborne and which were just the dilapidated house. An engineer would not use the word "dilapidated" to describe the house in its post-Water state, she told me. Dilapidated is a judgment. From an engineering perspective, she explained, the house was stable after the hurricane. It just wasn't contained. All the cracks happened so that the house could resolve internally all its pressures and stresses.

Water entered New Orleans East before anyplace else. On August 29, 2005, around four in the morning, water rose in the Industrial Canal, seeped through structurally compromised gates, flowed into neighborhoods on both sides of the High Rise. But that was minor compared with what would come two hours later when a surge developed in the Intracoastal Waterway, creating a funnel, the pressure of which overtopped eastern levees, destroying them like molehills. Water rushed in from in the direction of Almonaster Avenue, over the train tracks, over the Old Road where I learned to drive, through the junkyard that used to be Oak Haven trailer park, and into the alleyway behind the Yellow House, which may have served as a speed bump. The water pushed out the walls that faced the yard between our house and Ms. Octavia's. The standing water that remained inside caused the sheetrock to swell. Water will find a way into anything, even into a stone if you give it enough time. In our case, the water found a way out through the split in the girls' room.

"Water has a perfect memory," Toni Morrison has said, "and is forever trying to get back to where it was."

The foundation of the Yellow House was sill on piers, beams supported by freestanding brick piles. Not an uncommon way of building in Louisiana, this foundation did not stand a chance against serious winds and serious flooding. The autopsy report testifies that our sill plate was severely damaged, that the connection was "pried or rotated." It could be said, too, my engineer friend told me, speaking more metaphorically than she was comfortable with, that the house was not tethered to its foundation, that what held the house to its foundation of sill on piers, wood on bricks, was the weight of us all in the house, the weight of the house itself, the weight of our things in the house. This is the only explanation I want to accept.

The only structure that was stable at the time of demolition was the incomplete add-on that my father had built. The house contained all of my frustrations and many of my aspirations, the hopes that it would one day shine again like it did in *the world before me*. The house's disappearance from the landscape was not different from my father's absence. His was a sudden erasure for my mother and siblings, a prolonged and present absence for me, an intriguing story with an ever-expanding middle that never drew to a close. The house held my father inside of it, preserved; it bore his traces. As long as the house stood, containing these remnants, my father was not yet gone. And then suddenly, he was.

I had no home. Mine had fallen all the way down. I understood, then, that the place I never wanted to claim had, in fact, been containing me. We own what belongs to us whether we claim it or not. When the house fell down, it can be said, something in me opened up. Cracks help a house resolve internally its pressures and stresses, my engineer friend had said. Houses provide a frame that bears us up. Without that physical structure, we are the house that bears itself up. I was now the house.

# VII

---

## *Forget*

*August 2006–January 2008*
*New Orleans–Istanbul–Berlin–New York City–Burundi, East Africa*

*T*he large, close family is like an amoeba. To disconnect from its slithering mass is to tear. A friend once told me that it is easier to cut than to
tear. I learn this, but slowly.

At first, I drew closer in—to the city and to my family—returning
from New York where I lived to New Orleans seven times in three months,
more times than in the past three years. It was not the ruinous structures
that drew me—or even the city's failing infrastructure. Those of us who
were born to New Orleans already knew its underbelly. Storms, of all
sorts, were facts of our lives. Those images shown on the news of fellow
citizens drowned, abandoned, and calling for help were not news to us,
but still further evidence of what we long ago knew. I knew, for example,
that we lived in an unequal, masquerading world when I was eight and
crossing the dangerous Chef Menteur Highway with Alvin. I knew it at
Livingston Middle School when I did not learn because no one was
teaching me. I knew it in 1994, when we were petrified, afraid the law
might kill us—knew it before, during, and after the Water. Katrina's

postscript—the physical wasteland—was only a manifestation of all that ailed me and my family in mind and spirit. When we spoke on the telephone (and all of us were always on the phone with one another) we said all of these things in so many words.

Tallying up the cold, bare numbers provides some measure of clarity. Before August 29, 2005, my mother, six siblings, and seventeen nieces and nephews lived in New Orleans. Now, I had two brothers in all of Louisiana. The rest were scattered among seven states. When I flew to New Orleans, there was no one to retrieve me from the airport. Every time I arrived on these seven visits, alone in my rental car, I made a ritual of touring city streets, getting lost without trying—crawl driving down Marigny, Marais, Roman, Burgundy, St. Claude, Governor Nicholls, Mirabeau, Paris, Elysian Fields, Louisa, and Florida Avenue—with John Coltrane chanting: "A love supreme, a love supreme . . ." The deserted houses I passed along the way spoke their messages from beyond, words transmitted by spray paint on brick and wood. Some of the houses asked rhetorical questions: "Michael, where are you?" or "Does this feel right to you?" Others said the obvious: "We have moved." Some spoke Spanish: "Con Todo Mi Corazón!" There were the stern houses: "Please remove your car from the boat without crushing it," and the defiant, name-calling ones: "Hey Katrina: That's all you got? You big sissy." The religious houses quoted Bible scriptures; the guilty ones cursed; the sorrowful, leaning and crushed, wailed and moaned.

On one of these drives, I spotted a man and woman in masks and blue bodysuits. They waved and I returned the gesture. The only other movement that day came from a pack of scraggly dogs fighting over a foam to-go plate. When my car approached, they didn't bother to look up. They were hungry. They had been left on the scene to duke it out. They had nothing in this particular world to lose.

I made these seven trips back home for shaky reasons, grasping at the slightest thing. Attending, for instance, Tales of the Cocktail, an annual event held by the spirits industry. For the conference, aptly themed "Sip for the City," I stayed at the Monteleone Hotel on Royal Street in the French Quarter. In the elevator, the bellhop, an older black man with a pockmarked face, said, "Is it hot like this where you come from?" Overly sensitive to any implication that I was not a New Orleanian, I became annoyed at his question.

"I come from here," I said.

I mostly stayed hidden inside my hotel room, which had been named Vieux Carré Suite. It was not special, the room, and I was no mixologist. I had no business hanging around there. My brothers taught me long ago that a mixed drink should be the color of alcohol, not of the mixer, and that was all I needed to know.

The French Quarter, chosen by the city's founders for its high ground, was one of the only areas spared the Water. I spent my days wandering its streets, as if for the first time. The city was still mostly devoid of its natives, but the tourists always come. Visits to Bourbon Street were justified as an act of economic good. "Do your part for the recovery of a great American City," an editorial suggested. "Fly. Order. Drink."

I flew. I ordered. I drank.

Then there was the grand opening of Harrah's Hotel on Poydras Street where I was part of the press junket. I knew that *O* magazine would never cover this hotel, but its publicists wined and dined me in my large luxury suite and I did not resist. Sometime during the visit, I drove the twenty minutes to see Carl at Grandmother's house in St. Rose.

A year had passed. Our mother was still in California, but I heard from her that Carl had developed a hernia. At the sight of him, I launched into question mode, asking about doctors and health insurance. "It just started, Mo, this nagging-ass pain, stabbing sometimes," he said. "It don't hurt unless you know it's there." I knew that this was only half the story but was careful not to irritate. I was still the baby girl and Carl, my big brother. I sat for a while and watched him clean while the TV played. "My ma might walk in . . . any moment," Carl said, wishing.

"Don't worry, baby sister," Carl said after a silence. "I'm gon get that bastard out of me."

For dinner, Carl fried us redfish that he'd caught in Lake Pontchartrain. Dinner was drowned in cooking oil, with no side dish. We watched the television.

"Well, make sure you handle that doctor thing," I eventually said. "Cause that freaks me out, the hernia thing."

"Sure be glad when Mama gets back," I said as if her reappearance might, like magic, fix Carl.

He stood up to wash the dishes. I stood up to go. "Oh, you bout to roll?" he said. "Trying to beat that traffic," I said, then headed back to lonely Harrah's Hotel.

During those trips back, I visited Wilson Avenue where our house used to be only once, during the Louis Armstrong Festival. My friend David and I stood facing a 160-foot-long burrow in the ground beginning near the curb and running the length of where the Yellow House used to be. David asked where certain rooms were, where Ivory and Simon had slept. I tried to pinpoint, but found myself confused.

"No, *that* was the kitchen," I said.

He asked where the side door might have been. Like me, he had the blaring feeling that it was wrong to stand outside a family house unable to enter into its commotion, sit down comfortably, and introduce yourself by name: David and Sarah, here together. Or have the option to stay and sleep the night in a place that you know.

This friend, overwhelmed by helplessness, dug into the ground and recovered two artifacts from the land that once held the house: half of a yellow-and-blue fleur-de-lis plastic wall decoration that hung in the bathroom and a silver spoon bent and used till paper thin. On our way to the rental car, he fell into an open sewerage hole that neither of us had noticed. I yanked on his arm trying and trying to lift him out. When he surfaced, the entire bottom half of him was covered in muck.

When he dropped me off at the Creole cottage in the Marigny where I was staying, I fled the car, leaving the artifacts on the passenger-side floor. David honked the horn, calling me back to them.

I took the artifacts back to Harlem. Once, the spoon went missing from its place in the windowsill of my duplex where it had sat for months. I found it washed in the utensil drawer and thought, *No, you have been misplaced, you do not belong in there with all of the others, you have not come from where they've come* before retrieving it and putting it back on the windowsill where silt and dust could re-collect. When I left that house, I put the fleur-de-lis and the spoon in a ziplock bag and placed them in a box with Misc–Fragile written on top. I wondered, *Where, if at all, might I store these two things?*

My returns to and departures from New Orleans were a vexed motion, like a thick rubber band pulled almost to the point of snapping before contracting back.

More and more I craved forgetting. I tried and failed. Trying better, failing to forget better, just like Beckett said. Remembering hurts, but forgetting is Herculean.

This bent toward amnesia, my search for a haven, finally led me away from New Orleans altogether. I stopped asking my mother questions about the state of things in the family, in New Orleans. The government-funded Road Home, intended as a path back into lost homes for the displaced, was frozen in bureaucracy amid heated debates and politicizing about which areas of the city were worth rebuilding.

For Katrina's one-year anniversary, President Bush urged New Orleanians to return home. As if it were that simple and not about ingrained historic and structural inequities, the giant matter of who could afford to. "I know you love New Orleans, and New Orleans needs you," the president said, referring to the city in the feminine, as often happens when the place is sentimentalized. "She needs people coming home. She needs people—she needs those Saints to come marching back, is what she needs!"

But his speech, delivered in the picturesque Garden District, failed to address levee failure or the lack of clean running water or bus service, trash pickup, mental health services, jobs. At the moment of Bush's speech, signs of trauma were everywhere. Crime and suicides soared. Parents were still separated from their children. "They are raising themselves," one teacher said of students. What Bush said was: "It's a heck of a place to bring your family. It's a great place to find some of the greatest food in the world and some wonderful fun." One thing was clear: to some, the city's delights mattered more than its people.

In Harlem, I no longer followed what news about New Orleans there still was and instead spent my time planning trips to faraway places. In October of the anniversary year, I flew to Istanbul, Turkey. Found myself wandering in a small Ottoman village called Jumalakizik. In the outdoors there, drinking fresh raspberry juice and eating masa, a stuffed pasta dish, unable to speak Turkish beyond the basics presented in the guide-book, I fumbled around with words, searching for a way to say how the meal's perfect presentation and taste reminded me of two women, one dead—Grandmother—and my mother, who was still alive.

I tried—in vain—to train my attention on anyone anywhere who was not my family because . . . that hurt less.

In November, I took time off from work and traveled to Berlin, still searching for that which I could not name. I visited a Turkish hammam there, to remember Istanbul. A Turkish woman bathed me, scrubbing every crevice, and this called up memories of being bathed by my mother in the Yellow House, the place I wanted only to forget. The water made a sudden, rushing sound as the woman poured it from a bucket high above where I lay; she was wetting everything, every single spot of me, and for a second I let go of what scared me about being submerged, in memory and feeling, but especially Water. For an instant, I surrendered. I must have looked at the Turkish woman with sadness or longing or fear because something prompted her to say, "Turkish Mama." Was she asking or telling? Either way, I felt something nearly like love for her.

I began to wish I had proper time and money for trips to Papua New Guinea, South Africa, Mali. I collected articles about these places instead of articles about the aftermath of Water, placed them in a file folder called Destinations, and dreamt about them in daytime. At night, I dreamt about the Yellow House. I was naked in it. Or cooking grits for a lover who never appeared at its door. Or else there was a commotion outside, in the yard between our house and Ms. Octavia's, but I couldn't find a door to exit or a window to look out from. My sister Lynette dreamt about the house, too, in nightmares where she was chased by a dragon along its back alley. For her, too, there was no escape. Troy and Michael dreamt of the house, I learned many years later, but, not wanting to know, I would not ask for details.

Inside my Harlem apartment, I painted the kitchen Mardi Gras yellow and hung paintings and photographs of Tuba Fats and Doc Paulin's Brass Band in the parlor. Every piece of furniture had the appearance of age. Friends remarked on how I had summoned up New Orleans in Harlem. Many of them had never been there, to New Orleans, but all of the cues existed, I suppose.

A narrative of me had by now developed in the family. When my siblings called, the first thing they asked was: "What adventure you on now?" They said this and laughed, but I felt it as judgment. Around this same time, in the year after the Water, Carl began to call me Sarah instead of Monique. "What's up, Saaaarah?" he would say. His calling me by the name reserved for nonfamily made me feel separate and apart from him, like I had somehow changed—in his eyes. "Why you calling me that?" I always wanted to know, but he never answered.

Even though I knew that nothing would ever be the same, displaced and fragmented as everything was, I tried not to let on. At the magazine office, when people asked how my family was—and they always did ask, sometimes multiple times a day—I said fine or so-so or making it. I did not completely know; they were still reacting to Water. As was I. One day, I took a stroll down Harlem's Fifth Avenue toward Central Park to hear Joan Didion when a heavy, mean rain started, sending everyone darting for cover, nearly knocking each other over, reminding me what a hard and treacherous thing it is when Water has got you running.

Whenever someone asked where I was from and I said New Orleans, they asked, "Were you there?" "I was not," I always said. "But my family was." That absence, my not being there physically, began to register in me on subtle emotional frequencies, I can see now, as failure.

I no longer used the word "home," did not feel I had one. How could I know what it meant? The house had burst open; I had burst open.

My frustrations with the magazine job grew just as I faced up to the limitations of a failed love life. Satisfied with nothing, I felt trapped. Harlem evenings, I spent hours devouring war correspondent Martha Gellhorn's letters for the datelines—Tanzania, London, Mexico City. Wanted only to go, make a life, even if temporary, in distant elsewheres. Did not yet understand how movement—rivers, oceans, new sky— could be a place-holder, just another distraction holding one apart from the self.

In the winter of 2006 I met Samantha Power, who would later become the US ambassador to the UN, when she gave a talk at the New York Public Library. I had loved Samantha's book *A Problem from Hell*, about the history of the United States' nonresponse to genocide throughout the world. A good friend, the same one who told me how it was easier to cut than to tear, knew this, and invited me to dinner with Samantha afterward. Eight of us were seated around a fancy carved library table. Samantha was at the head, to my left. Magnetic, red-haired, and freckled, she had a way of conjuring instant intimacy. I told her about my urge to travel in order to "understand more broadly the displacement of my New Orleans family." I had said this line so much that it had become like saying my name. I was genuinely interested in placing what happened in New Orleans in a more global context to understand how loss, danger, and forced migration play out in other parts of the world. I was also finding, I can admit now, anthropological, academic language for the urge to distance myself from the fate of my family, which of course was my fate, too.

Samantha and I were meeting for the first time and already I was asking her for a compass.

"Burundi," she suddenly said. "Where is Burundi," I wanted to know but was too embarrassed to ask.

"Burundi," Samantha kept saying, "You must go to Burundi." With each iteration, the place seemed bored into me. By dinner's end, Samantha and I had drummed up the distinct feeling that there was no time to lose. I had to go.

At home that night, I typed, "Where is Burundi" into the search engine and discovered that it was a mountainous, landlocked East African country the size of Maryland, most famous for where it is in relation to another, more widely known place—Rwanda. The country's citizens know this so that when Burundians are asked, "Where is Burundi," I would learn, they always answer: "Next door to Rwanda." In that way, it is a country always framed in another's light, a shadow of itself. Burundi is known for very little in the world beyond its borders, not for its locally grown coffee beans; not for the fact that within it resides the mouth of the Nile; nor that it suffered a twelve-year genocidal civil war, ignited in 1994, the same year as Rwanda's more famous one, when the plane carrying Burundi's and Rwanda's presidents was shot down, killing them both. Rwanda's hundred-day massacre received attention that Burundi's twelve-year war never would even though both were predicated on an arbitrary class system imposed by Belgian colonialists. In the nineteenth century, those European foreigners twisted the peacefully interdependent system of human relations between the Hutu, who mainly tilled the land, and the Tutsi, who mostly tended cows, into a murderous one by designating one group superior based on physical differences: the width of noses, span of foreheads, height, gradations of color.

There were no guidebooks to Burundi for me to consult, except for PDFs of outdated manuals designed by NGOs for employees who had long fled for cheerier assignments. *Lonely Planet* had a small section on Burundi in the back of its Rwanda book, which advised: In case of medical emergency it is best to leave the country. In *Lonely Planet*'s East Africa guide, Burundi was summarized in a few pages covering the dire political situation and the dire restaurant situation, the dire health situation and the dire economic situation. This was, it seemed, the place you passed through on the way to Elsewhere, East Africa—Tanzania or Rwanda or Uganda.

Burundi was and still is on the United States' "Do Not Travel" list, along with Afghanistan, El Salvador, and Iraq. Because it feared an al-Shabaab terrorist attack or another civil war, the US State Department designated Burundi a "danger zone" in which "Americans travel at their own risk." Even though Burundi's long civil war had ended in 2005 when 81 percent of Burundians elected Pierre Nkrunziza as president in their first-ever democratic election, the country was still an economic invalid hovering on the brink of war. The Forces Nationales de Libération (FNL) rebel group, I read, still hid somewhere in the countryside, ready to pounce, threatening a coup, perpetrating ambushes and banditry.

That night at dinner, Samantha Power had raved about Alexis Sinduhije, "the Nelson Mandela of East Africa" in her view, who had won a fellowship to study at Harvard's Kennedy School where Samantha taught. Alexis founded an independent radio station in Burundi called Radio Publique Africaine (RPA), she had told me. Most Burundians owned little, but everyone had a radio. Alexis had transformed fifty former tomato sellers, child soldiers, farmers, and teachers into well-trained journalists who reported the truth about corruption and human rights abuses; such reporting was a rarity and risk in a country of fragile peace. As a result, Alexis had been imprisoned by the Burundian government, kidnapped, and viciously beaten before escaping to Belgium where he was leading the radio station from exile. Now, Samantha had let me know, he and his team at the radio station needed help creating human rights programming, training journalists, and fund-raising—none of which I had any experience with. She thought I would be perfect for the job.

Three days after that dinner, I sat hunched in my cubicle on the thirty-sixth floor of the Hearst Tower having a whispered phone conversation with Alexis Sinduhije, who delivered a sermon to me from his exile in Belgium, the line breaking up the whole while. He spoke to me as if my fate had already been decided, my life in Burundi drawn up for me in the present tense. We are paying you six hundred dollars monthly, he was saying, and this was a high salary in Burundi. I would be "la directrice du développement," mostly fund-raising—writing proposals, searching for new foundation money, and meeting with ambassadors and other diplomats—to support new radio programming that would advance human rights in Burundi. Burundi is right now at the precipice, Alexis explained, you can see how it needs your vision and spirit. So decided, charismatic, and charming was he on the phone that after our call I walked, nearly dazed, the five steps into my boss's glass office, cradling a new ambition, and announced, "I am quitting and going to Burundi."

She gazed over the piles of books walling her in at her desk, said, "Where is Burundi?"

In spring, I packed my Harlem apartment. I was twenty-seven years old. I left behind Lynette and her newborn, a girl named Amelia after our grandmother Lolo. Before my flight to Burundi through Paris and Addis Ababa, Ethiopia, I flew to St. Rose to visit my mother who had returned from Vacaville and was staying in Grandmother's house with Carl. Mom looked at me a lot in her studying way. I pretended not to feel her eyes. Carl mostly stayed in the next room with his door closed. We could hear him whispering into the telephone. Whenever I picked it up to make a call, I'd hear a woman's voice. "Sorry, Carl," I'd say, then hang up. It was not easy for Carl and me to speak to each other. I was unwilling to perform the role of baby sister whose duty it was to assess and lighten everyone's mood whenever needed, and Carl as big brother was off duty, too. He seemed to carry a great silent load and was concerned with getting back into a place of his own.

The pouring-down-raining night before I left, both of us anxious and not sleeping, we'd met in the hallway.

"So, Mo, I hear you going to Africa, huh."

"Yep," I said.

"Don't let them lions getcha," he said.
"I won't, Carl," I said back.

The next day was Michael's forty-sixth birthday. I called him in Texas from the Louis Armstrong airport. Carl and Michael always saw me off for major life events—they drove me to college in Texas and then four years later, drove me cross-country to graduate school at the University of California–Berkeley. On the phone, I avoided talking to Michael about Burundi because it was hard to explain why I was leaving my job at a national magazine in New York for a mostly unknown place. I couldn't say with a straight face: I'm going far away from you and I don't quite know why. Or: I am so rattled and destroyed by what happened to our family that I don't know how to help or what to do with my body and mind. I sought oblivion: the opposite of knowing. These feelings of mine seemed impractical, ethereal responses to what was real. I had only watched everything that happened from a distance. What right did I have to react this strongly? I felt guilty about not being "there," not knowing exactly what my family had gone through, but also about moving to Burundi. This feeling was childish and old in me, tied to the original guilt I felt leaving Alvin and James for college when they had both dropped out of high school. Leaving home, I had learned, meant a loss of the illusion of control. You could never know all that happened when your back was turned, which, ironically, is the appeal of leaving, too. What the gone-away-from-home person learns are not the details that compose a life, but the headlines—like Alvin is dead, or the house is gone. *Look like nothing was ever there.*

I asked Michael questions about his life in Texas, where he had found work as a chef in a popular hotel near the Alamo. To end my interrogation, he said, "Safe trip, baby girl." When I complained about how none of our other siblings had called to say bon voyage, Michael said, "You worry too much about the little shit that don't matter."

∞

Of the things I carried that April of 2007, most notable were my clothes and shoes, for how wrong the pieces were—the shoes soft and thin soled, gold and animal skin—Miu Miu sling backs and green suede peep toes that the Burundian ground devoured, straps first, soles second; the tops and skirts and dresses were too dark, mostly black, or too revealing. The fabrics weren't light, nothing blew according to the wind. Everything stuck.

The smell of Bujumbura, Burundi's capital, greeted me first: burnt rubber and banana peels, I thought; later I would learn that it was unprocessed palm oil and coal, trash burning in backyards. I did not know my coworkers' names or where I would live, only that someone would meet me at the airport. A woman headed to Rwanda mistakenly exited the plane in Bujumbura, an error she was horrified to discover but quickly did, Burundi's airport lacking the facade and accoutrements of Rwanda's—Wi-Fi, free luggage carts, air-conditioning, red-painted cafés, and duty-free shops. When Burundi's airport closes, and it does close, the lights power off and the building, designed in the shape of a village hut, dies in one great exhale.

My lost look must have given me away. A uniformed man shuffled me through the visa line, delivering me to four men in a white Toyota pickup truck—all radio station employees. I would not see Alexis Sinduhije, who had convinced me we'd be making a radio revolution, for many months.

The road, red like rust, seemed like a video game. Phil Collins was playing on a cassette tape the whole while we flew by boys driving motos with baseball caps for helmets and a man on a bicycle with a door balanced on his head. We swerved wildly to avoid potholes, driving onto small bits of sidewalk where people knew not to walk. Some drivers sat behind steering wheels on the left sides of cars; others were on the right. Phil Collins sang on: "One more night. Give me just one more night . . ." At first I thought the driver played him to make me feel comfortable hearing a language I knew, but Phil blared from rolled-down car windows everywhere and would be sung on karaoke nights from stages where live bands performed covers. The men who worked for Alexis were singing

along now, too. People here loved Phil Collins. By the end, I would like
him, too.

The scant travel literature, none of it written by Burundians, called this
a francophone country despite the fact that 90 percent of the population,
those living outside Bujumbura, spoke Kirundi not French. In the city
people spoke French mixed with Kirundi, sometimes mixed with Swahili—
three languages I did not know. Those who spoke French spoke it badly.
But not as badly as I.

I had arrived in Burundi with a well-honed and much-practiced
description of myself that I spoke often in poorly constructed French: I
was from New Orleans. (Where? they asked.) It had been a declaration
in my life before this point, requiring no pause, conjuring its own fantasies.
I had gone to UC–Berkeley in California. (Where, what?) I had worked
for *Time* Asia in Hong Kong and Oprah's magazine in Manhattan. (Who,
what, where?) I had absolutely nothing to stand on except my name and
the fact of my having been born.

When I said my own name someone would always ask what the
name Broom meant; beyond the practical they wanted to know *why* it
was my name and what the name foretold. I did not have a philosophical
translation for the name, as did the Burundians I met whose last names
were decided at the moment of birth: Ntahombaye, "he who lives nowhere."
Or Mpozenzi, "I know but won't say." I'd try to explain American slavery
by saying, "I do not know what my last name means. It is the name of
my family's slaveholder," but my capacity for language was not sophisti-
cated enough. People asked about my siblings, and this was the one detail
that excited them, that I had come from a mother bearing so many children
who were all still alive. Did they know their meanings? people wanted to
know. No, we are all named the same, I'd say, behind our fathers, Broom
and Webb. A family of children in Burundi could not be identified as kin
by their last names; you would not know who was born into a clan unless
you knew the family personally. To them, I must have seemed as unmoored
as I felt—calling myself by a name whose meaning I did not know. One

late night in a bar, a few of the radio journalists decided I would go by the name Kabiri, twelfth child in Kirundi, but the name did not stick. I wrote it down in my notebook and forgot about it.

For the first time in my life, I was mostly silent. When I did speak, after much mental calculation, my voice trembled. When I listened, my ears strained and still did not interpret rightly. I was exhausted by translating, sometimes catching only the words around the perimeter of sentences, which were generally not the key words. I prayed that no one would ask me a complicated question because then I'd be forced to prove just how little I understood, which made me feel unintelligent, a fool for not knowing.

In Burundi, I was *l'étranger*, without language; I was without the sound of my voice. This was slightly romantic in the beginning. "I desire to dream in another language, which would place me in a different world altogether. Ultimate displacement," I wrote in a letter to a friend.

At first, I lived in Alexis Sinduhije's gated house, which contained hints of him, photographs posted on a wall in a room whose door mostly stayed shut. A wild, unkempt place on the outside, the gate falling apart, the garden untended, but inside I had a neat sky-blue room with a low bed and mosquito netting. In that house, my waiting life began. I could pass hours sitting by the window staring outside, through burgundy-painted security bars.

Everything was done for me. A man opened and closed the gate, which I never entered or exited without someone having come to take me someplace that they had decided upon. In the mornings, the chauffeur arrived to drive me to the radio station, but the time was never fixed. It was whenever he showed up. I could never say who would be in the car when he came or where we would stop along the way.

Even at the office I was a wanderer with no fixed place to sit.

Because we were just across the street from the executive offices of the president whose corruption charges, human rights abuses, and self-serving policies RPA's journalists investigated, it was not uncommon for our lights to be mysteriously shut off, or for Kirundi-speaking soldiers with guns on their shoulders to appear in the newsroom while we worked. When RPA's journalists reported criticisms leveled against the president, the following types of things happened: The spokesman of another political party had his house demolished while he was *in it,* a crane lifting off his roof as if it were a playhouse. Five other local politicians had grenades thrown into their homes.

There was a single bulb hanging in the wide-open newsroom and one cord that all sixty of us shared to connect to the internet, which was mostly how I did my work—searching for grant opportunities, writing emails, things that required the world beyond Burundi. My work at Radio Publique Africaine would never provide the feeling of achievement that I was used to, but I worked steadily, chasing down money and designing along with the journalists new radio programming—a show called *Connaître Vos Droits* where reporters would read the Burundian constitution in Kirundi over the air so people knew their basic rights. Another show would cover the parliament live, a first for Burundi and a major step in holding politicians accountable to voters. The station, whose tagline was "Voice of the People," was a kind of open-air market for those in need. Women routinely appeared when their children went missing. Radio hosts would stop midshow so the parent could describe the missing child on air. One time, a man robbed a local bank and then came to the radio station, dressed neatly in slacks and a button-down shirt, demanding airtime to rail against the country's discriminatory lending practices. He ranted *live* on the air until the police arrived.

Burundi's heat was work, too. Every day I was driven home for a meal and nap only a few hours after arriving at the office. After which I was driven back to the station until someone could give me a ride home, and thus my days had no measure.

At dinnertime, Alexis's houseman, Robert, five feet three, with an afro larger than his head, spoke to me in French. He was a former schoolteacher, alcoholic, I heard someone say. I understood him because he spoke slowly. But still, I had to burn a hole in his face with my eyes, could not look away and understand at the same time, which he didn't seem to mind.

As days went by, Robert advised me over the dinner table, saying, "The black are mischief, the lighter-skinned ones are gentleman. Don't get darker," he told me. "Then you'll just be like everyone else." It was too early in my stay to know the depth of his warnings. All I noted then was that he sounded like a New Orleanian, obsessed with gradations of skin color. Early on, everyone I encountered in Burundi was someone I already knew from New Orleans: the skinny boy at the restaurant was Carl; my boss, Emmanuel, reminded me of Manboo. This was psychic grounding.

At night, lying in bed underneath the mosquito netting, I seemed unable, at times, to remember why on earth I had decided to come to Burundi. In notebooks, I wrote: Je suis libre ou folle? Free or crazy?

One night, at bedtime, a month after I'd arrived, a drunk Robert banged at my bedroom door. He was wearing only boxer shorts.

"Je t'aime, Sarah," he said. "Je t'aime."

He spoke the one simple sentence that I understood. He was a man in love.

I could take him, I knew. Still, I locked the door. The next day, I moved into a house of my own, helped along by two new friends who I met at Cyrille's Bar, where I'd begun to spend my evenings after work, nursing Amstel Bock and Primus, the local beer whose factory never closed, even during the worst days of the war. I am not a beer person, but it was the only thing in unlimited supply, unlike drinking water, petrol, bullets, and sugar, the procuring of which required bribery and government connections. At Cyrille's one night, I met Gregoire, a native Burundian who had returned to his country after thirty years in Germany. He was an architect, father of three girls, quiet, and watchful, who had come to rebuild many of Burundi's schools and banks. Gregoire became like a brother to me. Through him, I met Laurent-Martin, who grew up with Gregoire in a small village, up country. Laurent fled Burundi after the war and spent years in Nairobi, first working as a taxi driver, then covering sports for the BBC. He rose through the ranks to become a political correspondent for the station. He was composed and extremely vain, his forehead always shining, clothes creased, cowboy boots polished. Together we formed a small family of three, inseparable, like Joseph-Elaine-Ivory. Gregoire and Laurent were my local historians, educating me, helping me to locate the nuance. I can see now that I was collecting brothers. Both men reminded me of Byron: mostly silent with strong protective urges.

My new house was part of a community called Kinanira III, in Bujumbura's flatter terrain, where the roads were unpaved and dust flew. Up above us, high in the hills, lived the president of Burundi and the ambassadors—of America, Norway, South Africa, France, and Belgium. Those houses, in stark contrast to ours, had terraces, stone walls, generators, guard towers, cable television, and landlines, which were not available elsewhere because, per the local news, "The country doesn't have enough wire."

Burundians called the place where I moved a compound. It had a tall white metal gate that stayed closed except for a few times during the day when the security guard I inherited opened it to let the car from the radio station enter. My house was a squat concrete block notable for its security bars and its many keyed doors. It cost three hundred dollars a month, which was half my salary. There were three bedrooms. I had one, and another belonged to Consuelette, the housekeeper who came with the house. The third was for my expected guests, friends who would never come, who would change their minds after they read travel warnings or learned the cost of a ticket.

The floors of my house were gray concrete—unpolished, like my mood. In photographs taken shortly after move-in day, I wore pink lipstick where it belonged and the same lipstick on my cheeks, as if to liven myself, but my large eyes looked shocked by something. Dull, like my new floor.

The bathroom in my bedroom was huge. Someone had painted the tub sea green, and now the paint was flaking; you could peel strips off, like dead skin. Sometimes, out of desperation, out of a deep need for comfort, I'd fill it until the hot water ran out and sit down in the peeling tub anyway, but never for too long.

The house's bareness was a spirit that muted all I tried to do to cheer things up—the tablecloth with a bright-yellow background and green peppers disappeared into the void of the room, as did the bright-orange curtains that I hung. The walls were watery white, the doors ivory colored but barely, as if dyed with an Easter egg kit.

In a small sitting room off the formal living room where hard, resisting chairs drew a square, I hung maps of New Orleans and black-and-white pictures of the destroyed Yellow House on one wall. On the opposite wall, I taped up images of child soldiers, a map of Burundi, and photographs of refugees torn from a Ryszard Kapuściński article. Sometimes I would sit in this room and look to my left and look to my right, at the walls that showed where I used to be and where I was at present, and think about how those two things felt like exactly the same thing.

Without language, I had little control over the narrative and thus became whatever others made me. A man in a bar called me Tutsi after approaching and speaking to me in Kirundi, which happened at least once a day. "Je suis américaine," I was always saying. Another man, another day, called me "Tutsi from the hills," who, a friend explained, were disliked even by ordinary Tutsi. A small boy on the street yelled, "Muzungu," which meant white person, in my direction. Another day, I was Ethiopian. A Belgian woman thought I was Tanzanian or Rwandan: "Tutsi definitely," she said, "but not Burundian. It's the style of your hair." I was Tutsi even to the elderly mother of Alexis Sinduhije, whom I had still not met. "But I am not Tutsi," I told her. "I cannot even speak to you in your own language." She advised me through a translator that I was Burundian; it was just that I had forgotten my language. "That is all," the translator told me. "You have been gone too long."

I was being claimed as Tutsi because of my height, the praline color of my skin, and the sharpness of my nose. Samantha Power had not mentioned this detail of her time in Burundi, how one would be designated and claimed, because she is white. She would not have been privy to conversations about who to turn to if and when the war resurged, as I was. These discussions were a matter of routine, like talking about the weather. When the war comes, "Vous êtes Tutsi, not American," a local doctor told me one night when we were sitting at Cyrille's bar. "Mais, I am American," I said. He explained that under the duress of war, there would be no time to explain and no time to dig up a passport. In so many words, he was saying, I needed to shore up my Tutsi alliances. I kept saying, "Quel horrible." "C'est grave," he agreed, but still true, he said. When I described this conversation to Laurent-Martin he said, "My mother is Tutsi. My father is Hutu. Who will I kill?"

How uncomfortable, people claiming me in this way, when I did not know what having been born Burundian actually meant. I had never been claimed this hard even in my native place. In New Orleans taximen still asked me, "Where you from?" Or they said, "You not from here, are you," no doubt picking up on behavior acquired from my having lived in other places. I always huffed at the insinuation that I was from somewhere else. It is the return not the going away that matters, I always wanted to say. That painful snapping back into place.

At nights, alone in my compound, I wrote thirty-page letters to friends who rarely ever wrote back, or if they did, the letters no longer arrived. My letters from Burundi were one long desire—for my family, for home, for direction: "I wish to see my niece Amelia—and to be talking to the Harlem people in the street," I wrote in one. "I want to write about home, but who doesn't?"

I wrote to my mother: "Dear Mom, I feel like talking to you." Asking at the end: "What ever happened with Road Home?" Mom sent a page-long reply on notepaper with flower borders that left little space for writing. Her letter answered none of my questions, ending instead with scripture penned in her oversize script: "Love the Lord with all your heart. Lean not on your own understanding. In all your ways acknowledge him and he will direct your path."

"Wherever one is in the world," I wrote to a friend, "life begins to go like normal. All the color turns to gray, all the surprise normalizes, and then one can see through. Somehow this goes back to loneliness, about the places on earth where we find ourselves and where we feel at home and where we feel roped in and where we feel lost. Feeling lost in the French Quarter of New Orleans is just like feeling lost here. I've got on my walls photos of the Yellow House breaking apart. I've got to go back to that raggedy falling-down thing and talk about my father. My father, the raggedy falling-down thing of my imagination."

During the three-hour siestas and on weekends I mostly sat inside, reading books and writing letters. I treated my books like people, complaining about which ones I brought with me: "Mavis Gallant was a mistake," I wrote in a letter. "So was Henry James. Mark Twain was a brilliant idea." I read more hours than I worked at the radio station—Gayl Jones's *Corregidora* (for the fifth time), Elizabeth Hardwick's *Sleepless Nights*, and James Baldwin's *Evidence of Things Not Seen*. My letters were full of quotations from these books that said what I could not: "My memory stammers: but my soul is a witness," Baldwin wrote. And from Rilke's *Notebooks of Malte Laurids Briggs*: "I don't want to write any more letters. What's the use of telling someone that I am changing? If I am changing, I am no longer who I was; and if I am someone else, it's obvious that I have no acquaintances. And I can't possibly write to strangers."

"Well, he's right," I wrote to a friend. "But me, I can't stop talking to paper. Kisses, darling."

My hard work and insistence on my own ability to drive had won me the right to a borrowed car from RPA and in this stick shift, I found further escapes from my Bujumburan escape, to UNHCR refugee camps on the Congolese border and in Tanzania, where families hung clotheslines between their white tents with blue tarps for roofs, rust-colored rocks gathered in piles at the bottom to hold the tarp during rains. Everywhere I went, kids in plastic sandals or knee-high rain boots kicked soccer balls in the dailiness of life. During these visits I learned about the United Nations' Guiding Principles on Internal Displacement, wherein people forced to flee their communities due to natural disaster—"internally displaced persons"—have the human right to return. I'd by then read a *New York Times* article about Edward Blakely—executive director of New Orleans Office of Recovery Management, described as "the rescuer from afar"—denouncing the right of New Orleanians who he demeaned as "buffoons" to return. "If we get some people here, those 100 million new Americans, they're going to come here without the same attitudes of the locals," Blakely said. "I think, if we create the right signals, they're going to come here, and they're going to say, 'Who are these buffoons?'"

On weekends, I made repeat trips to a lush village called Banga, which sat at the very top of a hill with a view of Burundi's rolling mountains. Its fertile land was dotted with six small huts not more than two hundred square feet where Catholic nuns rented rooms for two dollars a night. The nuns—who reminded me of the ones at Sisters of the Holy Family on Chef Menteur where Mom worked—laughed to see me driving up, a woman driving, especially up country, being a rare sight. But there I came leaning hard on the horn the entire time, as was the custom, to warn pedestrians and bicyclists, herds of cows or goats led by children. Many of the streets in Bujumbura looked like Times Square or Bourbon Street. If you didn't stick your neck out when driving in Burundi you would wait forever. Inside the hut, surrounded by banana trees, I banged more letters out on an Olivetti typewriter I bought in a dusty Bujumbura shop called Typomeca, after my laptop died.

In Banga, the rain was predictable, seeming to arrive at 5 p.m. daily, in a great rush, at which point the electricity would go out and I would light the plain white candles that were a staple of my life, sticking them upright in their own wax, while the rain beat up the tin roof. After, all the sounds seemed sharper. The cows' moos, the trumpeter hornbills' calls, my own feet shuffling across the floor.

Back in Bujumbura, I asked Laurent if he knew anyone who died "in the storm" when I meant to say massacre. Laurent understood my point, as the wounded often do, and did not correct me. "Everyone in Burundi knows someone who died," he said. "If they needed to, they could give detailed reports on how exactly they died." I understood. A sadness descended on us both.

"One important reason to travel the world is so you know how to speak about things," I wrote in a notebook. "So that there exists in one's mind a system of comparison so that one can realize, finally, and most importantly, that it is true: no one thing exists unto itself and that is finally, I suppose, why I came here."

Five months into my life in Burundi, by summer's end, ambushes and banditry had intensified. There were grenade attacks. Tensions lingered between the FNL and the president's party. Laughable police checks suddenly appeared along roads blocked only with a piece of blue string that a car could easily drive over. The United States embassy held security meetings for the Americans where nothing useful was relayed: security measures concerning us, they said, were still secure the way they were secure before. I knew what they were saying. If war were to break out again, as it threatened daily, we Americans would be the first to get airlifted out of there.

I brought a machete found in the backyard into my bedroom. Consuelette found it under the mattress while making the bed one day and took it back outside.

I mourned the small things that had risen to be great, the five boxes of books shipped media mail from New York that never arrived. I tried to recall which books were lost and figure out where they might be stalled. When these lost children finally arrived, I became ecstatic, as if a best friend had come to visit.

I seemed sad to some. One day in the office I said, "Je suis déprimée"— I am depressed—to one of the journalists, who laughed. "Déprimée," I said again. He repeated the word out loud and said, "No, you are not déprimée. You must have said the wrong word." Embarrassed by my feeling, I said, "Yes, tu as raison, you are right, I have the wrong word."

Friends urged me to return home.

I said the moment you want to leave is probably when you should try hard to stay. It sounded nice, it was a good idea, but I had no idea what it actually meant. Still I stayed. Mostly because I felt I had no other place to go.

A curfew was declared so that the army could "hunt down the enemies of peace." One night, returning home, I was followed by a truckload of armed men. They waited as I waited to enter the gate to my house. My watchman was asleep inside; I waited a long time, blowing and blowing the horn, not knowing what would happen next. Eventually, the gate opened and I went in. That night, I put my mattress on the floor and slept there thinking that an attack was imminent.

When Alexis Sinduhije finally arrived in Burundi six months after I had I was ready to leave. With his appearance, however, the pace of the city, and certainly of my work, seemed quickened, as if he had given everything heart. He seemed always to be running to and fro. Wherever he sat, a meeting formed around him. I found him invigorating. He scolded me for acting too Burundian—saying yes when I meant no, laughing instead of protesting. "When they act Burundian," he said, "you must act American." Alexis made every gathering part school lesson, part political rally, part strategy session. "I am fighting for ideals, not Hutu not Tutsi, because I believe that justice is about humanity," he would say.

His big news was that he had returned from exile in Europe, despite the Burundian government's threats, having decided he would run for president, finding that the power of radio was not enough. He had formed a political party called MSD, Mouvement pour la Solidarité et la Démocratie. Emmanuel, he told me, was now head of RPA. Emmanuel had a short thumb, was hypercontrolling, and stared at my breasts the entire time I spoke about anything.

Alexis was in Bujumbura for short bursts, when he was not campaigning up-country. His house, where I first lived, was now heavily secured. One day a man with whom he was building his political party was kidnapped and later returned. Alexis kept on until an assassination attempt forced him to flee to Europe again.

My loneliness bored holes in me, especially on weekend afternoons, Sundays in particular, when no one, not even the housekeeper, came. "I tried talking in a letter to sarah d today about James and Alvin and started crying at the Olivetti: it seemed to last for ages, my heartache, but then when I reread the letter it was only one graf or so of talk—the very little I actually gave at the moment felt like an awful lot," I wrote in a notebook.

The letters were no longer sufficient company. I watched war movies on the computer, lusting for the food; even the sticky rice in those films looked delicious. I ate to fill a gluttonous hole: mukeke, local fish from Lake Tanyanika; and ndagala, tiny fish with the eyes still in them that you ate whole. Beans and rice. Spinach and rice. I sought the perfect avocado, having never in my life tasted such delicious alligator pears, as my mother calls them. In this way I gained twenty-five pounds. Enough to make my clothes fit badly. The Burundian women noted this, saying: "You are fatter than when you came," which was meant as a compliment.

I woke often with a start, from dreaming and thinking I had heard, say, a man's voice or someone walking just outside my window.

Had I? I considered the possibilities only to arrive back at the beginning: there is nothing I could do regardless—and so usually I read myself back to sleep until it happened all over again. In this way I had sleepless, restless, damaging nights.

I woke ravenous; I was never full.

I lost faith in the radio station, in the idea that I could ever "help" Burundi. I felt for the country, how its natives thought it was the greatest place on earth, but how it was almost always passed over for funding and attention, which generally went to Rwanda.

What cheered me up at the end of my stay was securing for the station a small grant from Canada for the new radio programs. But money moved around in funny ways, it seemed, to support Alexis's presidency or his new ventures. He cared about the station, but he was using it and us, too, rearranging our lives and duties to support his presidential aspirations. It had become another thing we laughed about in bars at night—Alexis's running for president when he could not show up at meetings on time.

Everything was life and death; if you didn't laugh you could die inside, too.

Many things had shifted over the course of my life in Burundi: I understood more French, was freer going around speaking it badly. I even learned some Kirundi. I loved the sound of it, how when you said no it was oya and when you said yes it was ego, which sounded like *heeeeeey-go.*

More of this story would only sound the same. By Christmas, I knew it was time to leave. And two strange things happened. The first was that I swallowed a piece of goat meat too fast. The huge lump of meat with some bone still in it scarred my throat going down. I thought I would die in Burundi standing upright at a dinner party. I had been too happy to see and eat meat, after so much beans and rice. The story of my demise would have been dark comedy: she didn't chew the tough meat; she choked standing up. Somehow, I willed the meat down. Afterward, though, I couldn't swallow my own spit without severe pain. After days of this, Laurent drove me to a private doctor in a hospital where Burundians who couldn't pay their medical bills had been chained inside, forbidden from leaving. This doctor performed an endoscopy on me without anesthesia. The first several tries, I fought the tubing going down my throat as if it were an oversize person lying on top of me. I thought nothing of having this procedure done in this way until I was back in the States and seeing a doctor who expressed horror at hearing this story.

And then, days after: Evening time. I was sitting on my sun porch, reading. A dog barked beyond the gates. Inside, on the CD player, Billie Holiday was singing about how some man was her thrill when I was stung by the Nairobi fly, a bug drawn to the halogen lights above where I sat. Somehow the bug lost its footing and fell down onto me. If stunned—and shooing it off your skin counts—it emits a toxic acid that scars. For my remaining days in Burundi, I wore the bug's long, thick-blistered kiss on one side of my neck like a dangling earring. It was full of pus and hard to look at. People stared anyway. Everyone who saw the mark cringed and said how unlucky I was for that rare occurrence to have happened to me. I took these two events as signs.

I had not had a meaningful conversation with any of my siblings during the entirety of my life in Burundi. Their stories were frozen in what I last knew, which made me feel that my family—my connective tissue—was lost to me. I had ripped myself away. What I sought in Burundi was understanding from people who, I reasoned, ought to already know how to resolve the loss and migrations I was reacting to. But this could never be true: the people who knew, *my family*, were still in the place where I left them. My time in Burundi had helped me to place New Orleans in a more global context as part of the oft-neglected global South where basic human rights of safety and security, health care and decent housing, go unmet. But the distance only clarified; it could not induce forgetting. My traveling to Burundi was my trying the elasticity of the rubber band, pulling it all the way to the point where it should have broken, but did not. The band snapped violently back, and I found myself in the bowels of the city I left searching for. I took a job in Ray Nagin's city hall, in New Orleans, on a street named Perdido, which in Spanish means lost.

# VIII

## *Perdido*

*January–August 2008*
*Burundi–New Orleans*

*H*ow had this come to be? It began in Burundi, on New Year's Eve. I celebrated my twenty-eighth birthday in the backyard of my compound, seated at a long table, candles stuck in their own wax, blocked from the night breeze by empty wine bottles. Around me sat the foreign family I had made. A writer friend from New York had flown in. My first and only visitor, she sat close to me, our faces shiny from humidity, lips wine bruised, laughing and singing aloud, using bottles as mics. Drunk.

In the Archipel nightclub afterward, we sweated into 2008, danced as if for our lives, butts low down, arms contracting like giant happy wings, our whole bodies involved, when in the middle of a Congolese song the DJ yelled, "HAPPY NEW YEAR."

HAPPY NEW YEAR!

No one stopped dancing; 2007 became 2008. I wondered about my mother in St. Rose for whom the new year was still seven hours away. I hadn't been able to call her for days because Bujumbura had been without electricity for days. That night I knew I would not finish another year under Archipel's strobe lights, that I was going back to America, from where I had displaced myself, and possibly to New Orleans, which is the same as saying I was going back to my position and grounding in the family.

Just before Christmas, I had begun a series of phone conversations with Ceeon Quiett, the director of communications for Mayor Ray Nagin in New Orleans. "Come work with us," she implored, "to rebuild this wonderful city." From the table in the office of my compound where I sat talking to her, I watched Gortien, my latest watchman (the last of four), sweep the same spot over and over on the sidewalk just outside the window. There was a breeze but the marigold curtain at the window was too heavy; it did not stir. I have a lot to offer, I told Ceeon, but no political experience. "Your experience in Burundi is major," she had said. I talked about the "exhausting context" that was Burundi, which was how the NGO workers described it. I worried that if I stayed in Burundi too long, I'd never be able to reenter anyplace else. My American friends who were in Burundi were career expats, which I did not want to be. Gregoire seemed swept into the country's vortex, extending and extending his stay until his return to his family in Germany seemed a distant dream. Foreignness, I had discovered, could become a geography and a job, as could the perpetual search for a haven. I no longer believed in havens. Also, I had traveled all the way to Burundi for people and a place I would never know. Why on earth wouldn't I go home? "I decided to return here because I was afraid to," James Baldwin had written in 1961. This mantra hung at eye level on my bathroom mirror.

Ceeon explained that she, too, was a New Orleans native who had left home for better work opportunities only to return for the city hall job. This moment, she was telling me, was "an opportunity to do something." She explained how she built a communications department that was well run and progressive. We would, she assured me, get things done. Recovery funds that up until then had been stymied in Louisiana's bureaucracy had finally arrived and were ready to be spent. As senior writer, I would tell the story of the city's unlikely recovery, would "start grabbing and shaping the mayor's tone" was how she put it.

Would I come home? she wanted to know.

I could collect *evidence* about how the city was run from inside it, the journalist part of me reasoned. This seemed likely then, as do all untested ideas.

The notion of evidence had taken on great importance to me during my time in Burundi. If I couldn't find the paperwork, the written background to support an idea, it was hard for me to believe in it. This was, I can see now, a facile response to all that had been erased. I was still writing everything down, as I had learned to do during high school in the Yellow House, especially the rote detail, as if by doing so, I was making things real, findable, fighting disappearance.

When I was finally able to reach my mother by Skype to tell her that I had accepted an interview with Ray Nagin, her voice went from cheer to disbelief.

*You did?* She was not happy.

When I returned to New Orleans from Burundi, I did so with the intention of living there for a long while. It would mark the first time I lived and worked in the city for a continuous stretch as an adult. In January 2008, I interviewed for the speechwriting job in the mayor's office on Perdido Street. I knew vaguely the direction of city hall, having entered it once before in the early nineties when Mom and I visited the tax assessor's office. I recall our not being able to find the entrance. How once we were inside, the air was cold, the floor sky-blue marble, the elevator cranky. I had a weak bladder from always holding everything in for too long and the bathroom was hard to find. Once we found it, it required a key. I peed myself. For this reason and for a long time, I associated city hall with locked doors that should have been open—bureaucracy's essence. The discomfort of the wetness I carried around that day made the memory stick. And the fact that the tax assessor was not in. After all of that. Mom and I turned around, headed back to the parking garage, and drove the seven miles over the interstate to the Yellow House, feeling that the trip and my public humiliation had been in vain.

For the mayoral interview more than a decade later, I was staying in Le Pavillon Hotel on Poydras Street downtown, a white, majestic building with archangels the size of ancient Roman pillars out front. On the complimentary water bottles in the room, Napoleon Bonaparte is quoted as saying, "Imagination governs the world." Some marketing person added: "With a history stretching back to the Gilded Age and impeccable French decor throughout, Le Pavillon Hotel of New Orleans piques the imagination in a way the emperor himself would applaud."

One night during my three-day stay in Le Pavillon, which was built in 1907 and whose website describes it as the kind of place where guests can instantly "conjure up the days of genteel luxury, romantic evenings, and glittering nights," someone fired what sounded like four gunshots outside my door while I sat in bed watching HBO. For a moment, I felt confused about where I was, having just returned from Burundi. But I was no longer there. No, this was the fifth floor of a luxury hotel in New Orleans. I dropped down to the floor where I tried to squeeze myself underneath the bed. From there, I reached my hand up to the telephone on the bedside table and dialed 0 for the front desk operator, who said: "It's being handled, all under control ma'am" and hung up. I stayed on the floor looking toward the crack underneath the door as the sound of chaos broke out. First someone was cursing and then the sound was of police officers' walkie-talkie noises. When I opened the door many minutes later, a man and his daughter were sprinting toward the exit doors, a moss-green plastic suitcase in the father's hand. I slept.

In the morning, I noticed the glass next to the elevators had been shattered, but other than that there was no sign of violence to the facility itself. There was also no news of what might have happened in the local papers or on the television. When I mentioned the commotion to the manager at the front desk, she tried shushing me and then offered a "continental breakfast on the house"—which I declined.

I met with Nagin on the second floor of city hall. It was plush, with bright-red carpeting and dark wood furniture. On the wall of the waiting room were black-and-white photographs: brass bands, local musicians, and second lines; the St. Louis Cathedral wrapped in fog. When it was time, I entered through a half door as if stepping onto a witness stand. This was the passageway to the mayor's office.

When I was born, New Orleans had a black mayor, Sidney Barthelemy, second in a long line that would end with Ray Nagin. Ernest "Dutch" Morial, my mother's favorite, the eventual namesake of my elementary school, came first, before Barthelemy and Marc Morial, Dutch's son. Each of these men served two terms for a total of twenty-four years. I was that old when Nagin was first elected, had graduated by then from the University of North Texas. Black men running the city was my norm. These mayors were light skinned with recognizable family names linked to black Creole heritage. It was tradition for everyone in our household—and in the city—to follow the elections of these mayors closely and with verve, to speak about the men in intimate terms, as if they were applying to become a member of the family. My mother, who voted along person over party lines, always liked that Nagin was a businessman who ran Cox Cable successfully. *He should know how to do something,* she judged by the quality of our cable news programming, betraying how little faith she had in city politics.

And here he was, standing before me, C. Ray Nagin in a suit with a shiny red tie. His trademark shaved head. I had seen him on television but still wasn't prepared for how it glistened. He was a politician; he eyed me as if we had already met. He was a beautiful man, I thought, with an easy way.

Nagin had been reelected for a second term in May 2006 when two-thirds of New Orleanians were still displaced and pop-up voting booths were everywhere in the state. Some of the displaced voted absentee, others were bused in to vote then bused back to their exile. It was a historic election—the victor would determine the course of the recovering city—with an unprecedented twenty-two initial candidates. Nagin, out-fund-raised and politically marred—much of his business and establishment base had turned against him after he declared New Orleans "Chocolate City"—was the underdog in a place whose founding narrative is essentially a comeback story. When I was growing up, people were wearing paper bags over their heads at Saints football games (that's how sad a team the Saints were), but the crowds still showed up. Nagin had survived the Water. He could say, I stayed. I was here. His not leaving meant: I am one of you. That was a Purple Heart in a city where outsiderness is never quite trusted. Before the storm, New Orleans had the highest proportion of native-born residents of an American city—seventy-seven percent in 2000, which meant that only a small fraction of New Orleanians ever left for elsewhere. This was why the mass displacement meant so much. And why those, like me, who had left and returned had to prove their nativeness all over again.

It was a conversation instead of a job interview. There was little of the interrogation I had prepared for.

"Are you sure you're ready to return to the Deep South?" Nagin had asked.

Because I had not known what the question meant—we were only just beginning down the road together—and because I had not yet learned that everything ever said in politics had an ulterior meaning, I answered too literally. I set out to please the man.

"Yes!" I said.

"Why come and work for a vilified, hated administration?" he was asking now, a large television, the sound muted, playing world news behind us.

Nagin knew how to be a local mayor, I had theorized, watching his performance from afar, but he had no experience as a national one. When Katrina cast him into the world's spotlight, I reasoned, he began to play to the media. "They know every now and then I'm gonna say something wild," he said once. This was what local journalists called Rayspeak. He was also, like most everyone working in city hall, some of whom were still living in formaldehyde-laced trailers, personally affected by and trying to recover from the Water.

But the speech that recast him as "vilified" was delivered on Martin Luther King Jr. Day in February 2006 when he vowed that New Orleans would remain a black city. In a city that appreciates the indirect over the straight way, Nagin's having said this was a distinct drawing of a line. "It's time for us to rebuild a New Orleans, the one that should be a chocolate New Orleans," he had said. "And I don't care what people are saying uptown or wherever they are. This city will be a chocolate city at the end of the day." Uptown was code for white. White is code for power.

Nagin still won reelection a month later, not because the white base he charmed four years earlier voted him in, but because of those displaced blacks who were bused in to vote. The idea of a chocolate city is, to me, the least interesting part of that MLK Day speech, which Nagin posited as a conversation between himself and Dr. King in which Nagin described to King all the nonresponse to New Orleans post-Katrina. In the speech, King answers Nagin back in some variation of the phrase "I wouldn't like that." The speech devolves into a scolding of black New Orleanians who Nagin blames for out-of-control crime rates: "We as a people need to fix ourselves first," King reportedly told Nagin in this imaginary conversation they had. "The lack of love is killing us," Nagin also imagines King saying. Nagin called up a finger-wagging, do-better-for-yourself-or-else version of King.

I was arriving at city hall halfway through Nagin's final term, at the moment of reveal: how much "recovery" would actually be achieved now that the money that had been tied up in what Nagin called "governmental constipation" had finally arrived?

Nagin was concerned about his legacy, said he needed me to make "more of a connect-the-dots narrative, understanding what was behind all the past decisions." He spoke about the demolition of the housing projects as a thing that would "change the map of New Orleans." The year 2008, he had pronounced some months before, would be the "Tipping Point." "New Orleans is about to explode," he had promised the city council. I would document this burgeoning, he explained.

He had run for mayor, he told me, because he wanted to create a city where young people did not have to leave home to make a promising life the way that I had. He said he had been thinking about the future of his own two sons and their high school friends. "What kind of New Orleans would they inherit?" he wanted to know. It was a rhetorical question, but in my head I was seeking an answer. The sound of Nagin's voice jolted me back.

"Welcome home," Nagin had said. "Have fun, and welcome to the team if you take the job."

I stuck around for a few days after the meeting for the reopening of the police department's headquarters. The police had been working out of trailers for two and a half years since the storm, but now there was a ribbon cutting and a speech.

I appeared on the scene and did not know what to do. Ceeon was too busy running around; I found myself eating red beans and rice underneath a tent with the city administrator and the police chief, Warren Riley, who turned to me and said, "You have a different look, a different style. Where you from?"

"I'm from here," I said.

"You don't have a New Orleans accent," he said. I have heard this many times. Normally I say: "Give me enough to drink and I will have one" or "Get me around my brothers and I will have one." But I will not have one, no matter who you get me around. To Riley's remark I instead said, "I grew up in New Orleans East."

He asked the question most New Orleanians ask first in order to place a person: "What high school did you go to?"

"Word of Faith," I said, "off I-Ten service road." I had given this response a million times. This was always the point when the conversation stuttered. Often, when I tell fellow natives that I am from New Orleans East they will say, "Oh baby, don't tell nobody that." And I laugh with them at my outsiderness.

In New Orleans, what high school you went to tells other people what neighborhood you are from. What neighborhood you are from lends

or takes away status. Being from a high school like St. Aug and Warren
Easton with their famed marching bands is a privileged thing, cultural
cachet, firmly placing you in the city's narrative of itself. Word of Faith
had no marching band, had no band at all.

Later, after I am working in city hall, I will edit bios of city council
members for legislative trips to Washington, DC, that open with the high
school the councilperson graduated from, as if anyone outside New Orleans
would know or care, as if high school were the most important accom-
plishment ever.

Riley, still trying to place me, asked about my people. "What's your
last name?" he wanted to know. To his mind, Broom indicated nothing
about my origins. My mother's name, Soule, was much more alluring in
the narrative sense. I knew this instinctively during childhood when I
told Mom that I would take her maiden name, call myself Sarah M. Soule.
I liked the sound of it (see how it looks written down), loved what it
would have said of me. To be called Sarah Monique Soule. My mother
yanked me out of my reverie, said, *Girl, you can't take on a person's maiden
name. That's my name!*

I took the job. I was the senior writer, hired to "creatively tell the story
of the City's recovery after Hurricane Katrina," according to my offer
letter. An at-will employee, I could be released from my duties at any time
without explanation. I was to be the "author and final editor of all communications and marketing materials." The 2008 State of the City address
was in May, four months after my start date. I was to lead the writing of
that, working closely with the mayor, whom I was to call Mr. Mayor at
all times. The State of the City address was a goalpost; in the months
leading up to it I would collect "proof" of the progress made for Mr.
Mayor's yearly report.

But first, I flew back to New York and retrieved my things from
storage before driving them the twenty-three hours to New Orleans in a
U-Haul truck. We—Manboo, Carl, Eddie, and I—unloaded them into a

pink camelback house near Carrollton Avenue in Hollygrove where Lil Wayne comes from. It was February. This camelback was the cheapest house I could find in a market where most rentals were $1,300 and $1,400 a month, four times what they were pre-Water, not much less than the rent I paid in Manhattan. Fifty-five percent of New Orleanians rented before the Water. My sister Karen was one of them, renting a three-bedroom house for $350 a month. It would have been impossible for the same people who rented before to afford the city now. This was partly why my displaced family stayed gone—Valeria and Karen and Troy and Michael were, three years later, settling into lives in Alabama, Texas, and California with no intention of returning.

The Carrollton area held many of the city's contradictions. On Oak Street, which I could see from the porch of my rented house, there was the fanciest snowball stand I had ever seen, which accepted credit cards with a minimum five-dollar purchase. Next door to that was a shoe repair shop whose owner was in town two weeks on, two weeks off so that he could travel to Texas where his displaced family lived. At night, in my neighborhood, it was difficult to find parking because of everyone who had traveled to Oak Street for dinner at Jacques-Imo's, which served alligator and andouille sausage cheesecake as an appetizer. Michael worked as a chef at Jacques-Imo's for six years before the Water. He helped build the menu, became part of the place's appeal and expansion, and wanted to return to help Jacques-Imo's reopen, but the owner wouldn't help him (financially) relocate back to the city that Michael, more than all of us, has forever loved.

After I settle into the rhythms of my city hall job, I will return home exhausted most nights and drive around for fifteen minutes (at least) in search of parking, and I will think of how easy it would have been in the world before now to have a meal in Jacques-Imo's swamp-theme dining room, at a small table in the back. How I know Michael would have appeared in his black-and-white-checkered balloon pants and plastic clogs, call me baby girl, plant a massive wet kiss on my cheek, and give a side hug. How I wouldn't have to order, Michael would send plate after plate of my favorite things. Every night after the "exhausting context" of my city hall job, when I drive past Jacques-Imo's to my rented pink camelback, I will wish this same wish (that Michael was just around the corner) and every night it will not come true.

To either side of my camelback were dilapidated houses that had not been fixed since the storm, but where people still lived. My neighbors across the street were three generations living in a three-bedroom house with five or six children and another on the way.

After I moved in, Mom and Auntie Elaine arrived at the camelback with their sewing machines to dress the windows with Burundian fabrics. Outside, Carl and Eddie sat on the porch cursing passersby with their eyes. "You gotta let these dudes know you got people," Carl had said. "Show them you not living here alone." Even though I was.

I painted the kitchen the same Mardi Gras yellow I had painted my Harlem kitchen and busied myself with dressing the camelback shotgun. A house always insists on being kept. Mostly, I had to find shelves where my books could live.

During these settling-in days, I observed Nagin as much as I possibly could.

I was to serve as his mouthpiece, I kept telling myself. I needed to know his rhythms of speech. This was my job. In despairing moments I reframed it: I was to inhabit Nagin's voice to the exclusion of my own. I would not speak—just as I had not spoken in my own voice in Burundi. All of these things were true.

I watched for him: there was Nagin on the front page of the *Times-Picayune* at a gun show in the Superdome, grinning big and pointing an M-16 rifle directly at Police Chief Riley at a time when the city's crime rate was out of control. My mother looked at the image and said, *How dumb can you be and still breathe!* The next day, the newspaper ran an apology, admitting the photograph was a cheap shot, capturing a "split second as the gun was being lowered," but the damage was already done.

I watched Ray Nagin's weekly appearance on WWL Channel 4's morning show with hosts Sally Ann Roberts and Eric Paulson, a segment that earned him the title "Sugar Ray" Nagin from a local opinion writer.

Here's what happened: The three of them sat in front of a fake cityscape featuring a row of shotgun houses. The mayor began well, speaking of blight and the good neighbor program, which was under criticism because it wasn't working. But then talk turned to recent public information requests for his calendar. "My disappointment is with the way some in the media are handling me personally," he said. "I'm upset with this station. . . . This has gone beyond the point of reasonableness."

"Why would anyone be after you personally?" one of the newscasters asked.

"If you supported someone else, get over it," Nagin said. "I've alienated some people who have significant influence in this community and they are relentlessly trying to destroy me."

Sally Ann's newscaster demeanor turned motherly, what was public became private, on air. Sally Ann's face grew full of concern. "People who care about you may be worried because of your emotional state. I've never seen you this emotional."

Complaints go with the job, both hosts were saying. "You've always laughed it off, kept your composure. How are you planning to deal with your position of power?"

But the mayor was stuck on the possibility that someone could hurt his family. "Somebody approach me wrong. I'm going to coldcock them." he said. Paulsen asked would he ever pick up another gun. "In a different capacity, maybe," Nagin said.

"Can you act appropriately in the emotional state you're in right now?"

They no longer spoke directly to each other.

"How much more accessible can I be?" the mayor asked the camera.

"Be well," Sally Ann said to Nagin, who would no longer show up for his weekly recovery updates on WWL, appearing on its competitor,

WDSU, instead. I watched this scene cross-legged from my art deco bed on the second floor of the pink camelback house.

In the New Orleans I returned to in January 2008, the following things were true: The city's homeless population had doubled from 6,000 pre-Water to 12,000 post. Just a month before I arrived, in December, the city had cleared a homeless camp of more than 250 people who had set up tents in Duncan Plaza, a park visible from city hall's windows. Every day there were protests, the voices of chanting marchers clear inside my office: "Hey Ray what do you say? We need housing today."

There still remained a camp of homeless people, impossible to miss, who had set up tents under the interstate bridge on Claiborne Avenue. Mr. Mayor complained publicly that one of the homeless men living there had given him the middle finger when he passed by in his black car one day. The city under the bridge wasn't good for optics, which is to say tourism, he complained. That there was—and to some extent has always been—a homeless camp underneath the bridge is not surprising. The interstate bridge, erected in 1968 to provide access to New Orleans East and beyond, ran above part of what was once a thriving black community, above what was once more than 150 homes, over what was once the black shopping district with tailors and clothing stores, five-and-dime stores, restaurants. Joseph, Elaine, and Ivory shopped there as children. My mother shopped there when she had children. The neutral ground where the homeless lived in 2008 was lined back then with more than two hundred great oaks—the longest continuous line of oaks to be found anywhere in America—all of them bulldozed to make way for the concrete bridge. MOVE OVER, TREES, read the headline in the *Vieux Carré Courier,* which could afford to be flippant. The French Quarter avoided a similar expressway that would have wiped out the neighborhood, but the city's political and business elite put up a winning fight; for the bridge on Claiborne, there was a battle, too, but black people—underresourced and overextended—had bigger wars to win, like basic civil rights. The bridge won.

The overpass on Claiborne Avenue is where my brother Carl sets up shop every Lundi Gras, where he cordons off the same triangular spot of grass with yellow police tape and babysits it overnight so that on Mardi Gras day the entire family—which includes me and my siblings, but also all of Carl's friends who are our family by extension—can show up to eat boiled crawfish and see the Zulu parade pass by, where we can get up close to the Black Indians, pose in photographs flanked by their feathers, say, "You look real pretty today."

In the city that I returned to in 2008, more than 100,000 people—one-third of the population—were still displaced. A woman whose home was destroyed during Katrina described her return to New Orleans two years later as "like . . . walking into a strange country. It's just totally different. It just feels like you're in outer space."

In that city, 109 bodies had yet to be identified. A stone monument to those who had perished in the Water was talked about but had yet to be erected.

For those who had returned, basic services such as trash pickup and water drainage were still scarce. Mounds of debris remained. Thirty-eight thousand people, including Manboo, still lived in toxic formaldehyde-ridden trailers.

In New Orleans East, the marshes burned. Their smoke made visibility on the bridge near to zero. Cars crashed. I mean major pileups with ten, eleven cars. The city issued "boil water" alerts. The hospital where I was born, Methodist, stayed shuttered; there was no hospital in the East. Seventy-five percent of water drainage stations were operating below capacity; streets flooded at minor rains.

But citizen activism throughout the city was at an all-time high. Residents could not afford laissez-faire. They were forced to know. It was a city full of autodidacts, learned in real estate, construction, insurance, and city politics. Protests sprang up everywhere, people putting their bodies on the line—protesting the school district, protesting affordable housing shortages, protesting FEMA's Road Home Program. In my life in New Orleans before the Water, I could not recall a single protest ever.

∞

Before I could begin work at city hall, there was antiquated-seeming paperwork to fill out. On the question of race my choices were: "American Indian (red), Caucasian (white), Malaysian (brown), Mongolian (yellow), or Negroid (black)."

I was handed a BlackBerry phone and the keys to a black SUV with a white City of New Orleans emblem, which would soon feel like a scarlet letter, painted on the driver's-side door. At stop signs, random drivers shot venomous looks. I started driving in the far-left lane at all times so that the insignia faced the neutral ground. Whenever I drove the city car to Manboo's house on Franklin Avenue, he yelled, "Look what our tax dollars are paying for," from the porch as I was pulling up.

On my first day of work, Ceeon introduced me around as "our writer," and what this mostly meant was that I wrote the mayor's dailies— speeches delivered to visiting groups in town for conferences, at the Nike outlet store opening, or to His Highness, the Emir of Qatar. These speeches, I soon learned, always began with the city's claim to greatness and creativity. "Welcome to New Orleans," they would begin. "Home to Louis Armstrong and Mahalia Jackson and Lil Wayne, for those of you into hip-hop." We had a rotating constellation of musically gifted natives (Wynton Marsalis, Sidney Bechet, and Aaron Neville were favorites) to plug in, depending on the crowd and their mood. Mr. Mayor spoke in short sentences with a lot of lift. He liked to describe things as "awesome." Often in his talking points, I wrote sentences with exclamation points behind them, sentences like: "Now that's commitment!" I was breaking the rule I'd learned in journalism school about having only three exclamation points to use over a lifetime. The speeches always reminded that by virtue of New Orleans still existing, much had been achieved.

In these speeches I wrote, the city was collectively referred to as "One New Orleans"; the work post-Katrina was the "Bricks and Mortar of Recovery" and the story of progress, "The Arc of Recovery"; what Mr.

Mayor was doing was "Reinventing the Crescent City." These were our go-to phrases.

When the mayor did not read from the talking points and winged it instead, which was all of the time I worked there except twice, I wrote responses to the media, slapping them for criticizing the offhanded things he improvised.

The first time I was called to do this was on the occasion of Eve Ensler's V-Day Celebration, which was honoring displaced women by bringing them back to the Superdome, infamous as the shelter of last resort where the roof blew off in the middle of the hurricane. Ensler was putting on her play *Swimming Upstream*. In the press conference before the event, Nagin became emotional, saying he knew how much New Orleans women had suffered post-storm. They needed time to heal, he had said. He was glad Eve Ensler had chosen to return to the city, of which he was, in his words, a "vagina-friendly mayor."

The moment he said it I began composing notes for a response in my head.

Local columnist Chris Rose wrote, "Unpredictable would be if our Mayor said something that was inspirational, that indicated just a hint of gravitas one would expect of the man who was elected to lead the rebuilding of this great city. The point here is not vaginas," he went on to write. "Vaginas are good things."

The furthest I got in writing the response were notes: "Columnist's focus is off, piece is base and cheap. It's entirely appropriate that mayor mentions that we are vagina friendly. Note the ways this is true." Before I could respond, another crisis had come up. The St. Bernard housing projects were being demolished. Community members were enraged that these architecturally sound buildings were bulldozed before there were affordable housing alternatives. Protesters with HOUSING IS A HUMAN RIGHT signs were crashing metal gates and throwing themselves in front of bulldozers on the day the demolition was to begin. These were the real issues, but I saw these things only peripherally. I was mostly chained to my desk responding to media requests or news stories that painted Mr. Mayor in a negative light.

From my first day, the communications department was besieged by records requests from the local media. I spent a lot of time not planning the State of the City speech or figuring out how to communicate about the recovery but working as a liaison between the law office and communications department. The press wanted credit card records, employee car and gas fill-up records, cell phone bills for every employee, and Mr. Mayor's calendar.

In my first staff meeting with Mr. Mayor, he expressed displeasure at the work I had been doing, but indirectly, never looking at me or in my direction, saying only that he would go easy on the new person.

The communications department stayed in reactive mode. Those of us appointed by Nagin to serve his administration were collectively referred to as "Nagin's City Hall" in news stories. The mayor suffered almost daily name-calling. Often, he fed into it. At a press conference before a trip to China someone asked if he'd been briefed on Chinese customs so that he could avoid his typical faux pas. He still made a stereotypical joke about rickshaws. He lived within the image made for him. It was easier, I think. Alone with him, in meetings, I praised the view of him that he kept hidden from the public. He was a voracious reader, an intellectual, as I experienced him. I suggested he write a book that presented this thoughtful side.

In community meetings, the mayor affected charm and distance at the same time, sometimes smacking gum, which made him seem lackadaisical in front of community members who showed up with real problems. One man complained about lack of drainage on his street, how the water had "no place to go. We're afraid of the next rain," he said. There were the uprooted young people now living with grandparents and ignoring community norms by having parties with DJs in the front yards. "Now why can't they do that in the back?" one person asked. Some houses, people complained, were abandoned and unattended after owners "sold to the Road Home." Nagin could turn flip with those who disagreed with his version of recovery: "Man, you've got some issues," he said to one man. Or: "My bullshit meter is at zero. No tolerance for it."

By now, the Road Home Program was generally agreed to be a massive failure. Homeowners had three options: stay at the damaged address and rebuild the home (most lucrative), sell the home to Louisiana and buy a new house in the state, or sell the property to the state for unrestricted money that could be spent however and walk away (least lucrative). My mother was leaning toward the first option, which would have meant more federal money but also would have required she live on a ghost street. Most of us children, except for Carl, tried to dissuade her from rebuilding on Wilson. "Who wants to live on a dead street?" I had said. Finally, Mom settled on option two, which meant she would find another house in New Orleans, but Road Home undervalued the homes in its calculations, especially in less-valued neighborhoods like New Orleans East, by making grant estimations based on a house's pre-storm value rather than what it would cost to rebuild. In areas across the Ninth Ward, including in New Orleans East, this meant that rebuilding costs almost always exceeded grants by an amount that made it impossible to rebuild and therefore impossible to return home. This was the case for many black families who were trying to get back.

Now that I worked in city hall, I tried to expedite Mom's Road Home application, spending my lunch breaks at the desk of a woman in the tax assessor's office, trying to gather information needed by Road Home attorneys assigned to Mom's case. I discovered that tax bills had been accumulating on the Yellow House during the eighties and into the nineties—beginning the year after my father, Simon Broom, died and continuing through the years when Mom was paying for my private school.

Mom kept telling Auntie Elaine, with whom she was living in a small room in Grandmother's house, that she would soon be moving into her new house. Road Home, she kept saying, would come through any day now. This bothered Auntie because it made her feel my mother was impatient with her lot in the world, which she was. Mom spoke of the people in St. Rose as if they were different and set apart. *I never was no country person. It won't be long. I'll be out of here soon. I don't want to leave this earth without a house to my name.* "Mom, stop being dramatic," I would say. Not understanding. Not then.

My mother came to Cambronne Street often, having driven the narrow River Road the fifteen miles from Grandmother's house in St. Rose to my pink camelback. When she came we mostly spoke about her ho-hum life in St. Rose and I gave whatever small updates I had on her Road Home file. *I don't want to leave this earth without a house to my name,* she would say again.

But the lawyers assigned to her case by Road Home kept losing papers. A few times, the law firm that was contracted out to handle our case suddenly and without explanation was replaced. When my father died, it was discovered that the house had been put in his name, which meant all of us children had to transfer our stake in the Yellow House to my mother before she could legally sell it to Road Home for the grant money. After all the labor it took to submit these signed Acts of Donation, the lawyers still lost the files. Each sibling would have to resend the form and then the lawyers would discover something wrong with it. It was a bungling loop. Road to Nowhere, I had taken to calling it.

Always another paper lost. My mother never called the legal documents by their convoluted names; those were impossible to remember. When she and I spoke, our conversations were full of elisions and vagueness. *Did they send that paper those people said they needed for the thing?*

What paper? I was always asking. What thing?

Her language, I noticed, had become more imprecise. *Those people on the news said that thing had hit whatchamacallit.*

Which people? What?

I wanted to talk about the Yellow House one day in the Mardi Gras yellow kitchen on Cambronne Street, was asking my mother how she felt now that she was living outside it.

*Just let that house die like the storm,* she said to me in the clearest of terms.

By April, I had begun writing the State of the City speech. There was also the accompanying event to produce. We chose the Port of New Orleans Cruise Terminal for symbolic reasons. The port was once the economic engine of the city, before tourism. The media intensity—not about the speech but about gaining access to the mayor's calendar, which was a public record—was revving up. Around this time, I was recorded without knowing it, one day in the office when reporter Lee Zurik from WWL, Channel 4, came around looking for the mayor. The office was empty. Everyone was somewhere else, except for me. Which seems suspicious now. I heard a knock on the door and kept it propped partly open with my foot. "He's not here," I had said without affect. Zurik went down a list of names of people whom he wanted to see, none of whom were there. "She's not here," I said. "He's not here."

In the broadcast, which appeared on the nightly news, that benign interaction was cast as part of a smoke screen the reporter claimed to have uncovered. It was a funny-looking thing because the hidden camera stayed seated with the reporter who was looking up at me. "Smoke screen," the television announced in huge dark letters. My brother Eddie called, said he was glad my hair wasn't standing up. The news appearance elevated me to minor local celebrity status for a few days. People recognized me in the city hall elevator. "Hey, you the woman from the news," strangers were saying. That Sunday at the second line: "Hey, you Ms. Smoke Cloud," one dancing man said. I was there with Eddie, whose feet hurt before we even made it to the parade. Eddie could be down on the city—I knew this—and though much of what he said was true, I felt like dancing, not hearing him analyze the dysfunction. "New Orleans is a mentality," he started. "We locked up," he went on. Eddie was just warming up. It was midday, hot as hell. The parade moved from South Rocheblave to Toledano Street, made a left on South Claiborne where the great oaks used to live, then took a right at Louisiana Avenue. I was walk-dancing, twisting my hips.

"From the day you were born," Eddie kept on, "the same shit been happening. People get dressed up every Friday to go out, but they have dead-end-ass jobs. But from Friday through Sunday it's popping." A man buck-jumped alongside us, performed a split three times. I whooped.

We turned left at LaSalle, then left onto Washington, and then onto South Saratoga Street.

I was caught up in the music, dancing right behind the tuba player where I like to be. One man said, "Go 'head now in that purple dress," and I went. Rolling. Eddie was shuffling about in his bad mood. "People spending all this money, you're dyeing your shoes. Come Monday you go clean up the hotel. Where is the logic there?"

The parade stopped at the Purple Rain Bar for drinks and I loaded up on Jack Daniels to drown out Eddie who was now narrating our family history as we went. We continued onto Oretha Castle Haley, which was called Dryades when Grandmother lived there, then to Philip Street where Sarah McCutcheon used to live, then back to Dryades and to Jackson Avenue where Aunt TeTe used to live. As long as we were moving, I did not feel my feet.

No State of the City speech can claim to have one author. Every person on the political team needs to believe they have had their say, but several things about this speech were mine. For one, New Orleans East factored in it heavily. And in the opening lines, when Mr. Mayor greeted those New Orleanians still displaced, he greeted "those still in Texas, Alabama, California, and elsewhere," which was exactly where my siblings were.

Writing the State of the City required that I get out of the office and see recovery for myself, which I loved to do. The first place I went was New Orleans East, but not the Yellow House or anywhere near Wilson Avenue. A colleague and I drove farther east, beyond my now abandoned high school, Word of Faith, toward Michoud where Carl worked. I was looking for someone who came back to the East, rebuilt against the odds. Driving east, I noted the amount of trash. "Sanitation needs to get out here," I wrote in my notebook. Apartment complexes everywhere were still in ruins. It looked like the day after the Water, minus the flooding. One apartment building was devastated by fire; the front facade of the complex had been burned open to the street, making it a creepy life-size dollhouse with peach-colored waterlines. We found Adam Summerall outside a salmon-colored house with a trailer in the driveway. When we approached, I noticed a Bluetooth in his ear. "Oh I was just calling y'all," he said. "Y'all" meant "the City." His street flooded, he reported, after five minutes of rain. "A neighborhood with good drainage, man, that's a dream," he said.

Adam was the first person back on his street, which still looked deserted. He told us how, last week, a body was burned in a car near to his house, an ideal location because there were no police patrols. We were from the City, had the insignia on the driver's-side door, but I knew that there was little I could do to improve Adam Summerall's life.

I wrote Adam Summerall's story into Mr. Mayor's speech, but Adam Summerall disappeared. He had given me a number that day, but when I called, it didn't work. I drove back alone and left notes for him on the trailer parked in the driveway on the ghost street where he lived, inviting him to the speech, where he would be acknowledged, but it was clear that he wanted no part in the version of the recovery story we were trying to tell.

We were measuring recovery by spoonfuls, it seemed, counting every new building, no matter how small the repair. The Mahalia Jackson Theatre was under renovation, one of the larger projects. We were erecting giant billboards around the city, sometimes in front of minor street repairs. "Planted nearly 6,000 trees; repaired 113,117 potholes; replaced 14,646 street signs," we bragged in the State of the City booklet.

The night of the State of the City speech was charged. The Mississippi River was visible through a wall of windows. The optics were right. Local celebrities like the actor Wendell Pierce were there in support of Mr. Mayor, who I watched while standing in the back of the hall where I steadied myself for his improv.

"Thank you for meeting me at the river," Mr. Mayor began, his head shiny like his gold tie. He read every single word without a single change, using his hands to deliver it with passion. The speech was the city's origin story, its comeback tale: "From this city's founding, there was much to overcome: mosquitoes, yellow fever, hurricanes, tornadoes, and floods. In spite of having more than our share of swampland and being built below sea level, we have consistently beat the odds, as we are doing today."

The river was the metaphor: "It keeps moving . . . it does not always stay the same. Over time, it has changed course." In the section about neighborhoods and housing, Mr. Mayor bragged about the demolition of over eight thousand houses. I thought of my Yellow House, of other people's gone houses, the stories they contained.

The one time I thought about going to where the house used to be, I wanted to bring a coworker with me to visit Carl, whose love for me appeared to grow whenever I brought a beautiful woman around. I had been bringing attractive women around for my brothers to appreciate looking at all of my life. When I described the short end of Wilson where the Yellow House used to be to this coworker she said, "Oh yeah, I know that scary little street." I changed my mind. We did not go.

It was odd to be in New Orleans and not to visit the street where I grew up. Odder still that at a friend's urging I had begun writing letters to the house, which was only fifteen minutes away from the rented pink camelback. "Yellow House," I wrote. "Sarah Dohrmann suggested I write to you. You who I do not know but can envision, more than that, can feel. I am unsure of how to go home. This exercise seems silly, but that is a cop-out; there is so much to say. Up until recently, we spoke of you often, called you the old house, and Carl still goes there to you to drink beer with his buddies as if you are still there. It is obvious that you are gone and yet you are not. Our psyches keep you. You are ravenous and gluttonous."

Nagin's speech ended with a flourish—a broadly sketched vision for New Orleans ten years down the line. A city with great neighborhoods, good schools, high-paying jobs, where the river was a destination with a state-of-the-art amphitheater overlooking the water and a Canal Street that was bright and bustling.

The end of the speech was my favorite part to write. It rested on the myth of New Orleans's exceptionalism, but that was also the rousing part: "Remember that from the unlikeliest stretch of swampland rose the likeliest of cities. . . . We drained the swamplands and built a city with distinctive architecture . . . and when the city flooded, we built up again, drawing on our past, but focused always on the future.

"After Katrina," Nagin said, his voice booming, "when some said we shouldn't rebuild below sea level and were calling us refugees and KAPS [Katrina-affected persons] instead of our real names, they didn't know where we'd come from. They didn't know what we knew. They never lived or played here. They didn't have skin in the game. They didn't have our genes.

"This is our city, from the Mississippi to Lake Pontchartrain, from New Orleans East to Algiers. We can't get distracted now. We can't stop now."

The day after the State of the City speech marked day one of hurricane season. It was June 1. We were all gloating. The speech went well; Mr. Mayor said every word; even the media backed off. Now that the big speech was over, where was the new goal line? More and more I began to feel that I was on the wrong side of the fence, selling a recovery that wasn't exactly happening for real people, not for my mom or for Michael, Karen, Valeria, or Adam Summerall.

After the big speech, my dailies included a line of warning about storm preparations—just in case. We launched Mr. Mayor's TV show *One New Orleans* to capitalize on the goodwill generated by the State of the City. Somehow, and I still don't know how this came to be, I became the host, which got me out of the office and allowed me to focus on natives who were doing things inside the communities where they lived. I was back in journalist mode, interviewing people I found personally interesting: Carol BeBelle who ran a community center on Oretha Castle Haley; Mr. Syl who ran the Backstreet Indian Museum in the Seventh Ward. At the end of each of these interviews I usually forgot to say the show's sign-off: "Don't *forget* to rethink, renew, and revive *your* One New Orleans." It was as corny as it sounds.

When I was not filming the television show, I was fighting with Ceeon over my salary, which was far lower than what she quoted when I was in Burundi. This salary issue was only one of the things that led me to look elsewhere for work. Clearly, no answers were to be found in city hall. It was concerned only with protecting itself; that is the nature of politics. The story we were most focused on telling was Ray Nagin's. The recovery wasn't happening, for many reasons: Nagin didn't have the relationships to push things through in a tangled political web of Louisiana and DC; the city's anticorruption safeguards were actually adding layers to processes and thus slowing recovery; but also, Nagin—his perceived ineptness—became the story in a way that the city's residents never did.

The job was so emotionally draining that some days I sat at my desk and felt the entire right side of my face go slack. I would think, "Have I just stroked out?" but not move to do something about it. What I felt in those moments was the absence of feeling. Meanwhile, towering signs were being raised on wooden stilts in front of buildings: OUR RECOVERY IN PROGRESS.

My days passed like this, without real significance, without real achievement. I kept writing the mayor's dailies and sometimes reading the papers to see if any of the words I had written had shown up. They rarely did.

In August, a mere six months after I had arrived, I fled my job and left New Orleans. I was embarrassed to have lasted only half a year in city hall, but I was happy to go. By leaving, I reclaimed my voice. The circle felt complete, somehow, even though little had changed. Carl was still displaced. So was my mother. Others of my siblings were angry, couldn't imagine returning to the broken city. By the time I left, even though I worked in city hall and had been described by my coworkers as indefatigable, I had not moved one inch closer to getting Mom's Road Home application finalized. That would not come for another seven years.

# MOVEMENT IV

## *Do You Know What It Means? Investigations*

*the thing I came for:*
*the wreck and not the story of the wreck*
*the thing itself and not the myth*

Adrienne Rich


*A place belongs forever to whoever claims it hardest,*
*remembers it most obsessively, wrenches it from itself, shapes*
*it, renders it, loves it so radically that he remakes it in his own*
*image.*

Joan Didion


*His journey is a pilgrimage; it is a journey into the interior of*
*the self as much as a travelogue, a vision quest that concludes*
*in insight. But there is no conclusion. The journey itself is*
*home.*

Sam Hamill

# I

## *Sojourner*

*W*hen I returned home to New Orleans for a second try at making a full-time life there, it was winter 2011, six years post-Water. In the days after Perdido, I moved back into the exact same Harlem apartment on 119th Street that I had left, three doors down from Lynette, as if it were base, the neutral ground of my adult life. Post–city hall, I nurtured an interest in the nonprofit world, in the matter of saving other people's lives or easing them, however slight. I was, I think now, paying penance for my unfruitful, wrong-side-of-the-fence stint in city hall. In those intervening years, I had fallen in love with a man with whom I built dreams of marriage. I still could not, however, fully imagine a house of my own. I believed then, and to some degree still believe now, that even at their best, houses were perpetually in a state of entropy. It was just gravity doing its work. But together, this man and I fantasized and planned for our own created family and its accompanying house (built to our specifications, from the ground up), where we might live out our days together.

But this relationship of mine imploded brutally and without warning; I still cannot pinpoint what caused this denouement. For all of the violence I felt, it was the quietest of endings, a sudden slipping away. It had the now-you-see-it, now-you-don't quality of a house disappearing suddenly from the landscape, of a father there one day, gone the next.

But the man I had intended to marry was still alive. He had not died; the force of his exit only made it feel so. I grieved the loss of him as I would the dead, submitting myself to the emergency room thinking I was having a heart attack when I was having a panic attack. Had no appetite, for the first time ever. Wandered Harlem streets as if set loose. No map. No compass. No desire. A friend saw me once, in this state, on Lenox Avenue and said, "I'm taking you for a double-meat hamburger." I cried in the middle of sentences that tried to explain my ache—in restaurants, in the theater, in the back of taxis, at dance parties, in work meetings. Whenever I felt, I felt sad.

I fed the gaping hole (that bare plot of fetid land) in my emotional world with a big executive director job I had taken in 2009. I was running a global nonprofit with more than three hundred employees, a free health clinic situated in Burundi's mountains with offices in New York City. It was the kind of job where the following could happen: On my fifth day in the role, one of our drivers, Claude, was ambushed on his way up the mountain to deliver medical supplies and staff to the clinic. Claude, who I had met and liked, was shot in the head and died. The other five people in the car pretended they were dead and thus escaped. When I arrived to Bujumbura days after this tragedy, I was retrieved from the airport in the same pickup truck Claude was driving when he was murdered, the bullet hole still in the front windshield. His blood had been scrubbed away.

I find it impossible now, in the retelling, to know exactly how I decided to move back to New Orleans that winter. My misery then was so great. It is hard, too, to talk about returning to a place you have not psychically left. Undoubtedly, it had something to do with the intensity of my work in Burundi and the dissolution of those personal dreams, the combination of which made me long to return to the place where my mother lived. Though I suspect there is an ancient reason for this, moving back to New Orleans and successfully living there had been a goal of mine ever since leaving.

"Paying attention to being alive" was how poet Jack Gilbert described what I wanted to do for a year in New Orleans. Where before, I reasoned, I had lived my familial life by rote, beneath the carapace of clan, now I would be present, physically at least, more than I had since that original departure to Texas, in 1997, fourteen years before, when I was not yet eighteen and riding to college in Eddie's pickup truck squeezed in between Carl and Michael.

But that was not all. I wanted to work full-time at being what I had never wholly allowed myself to be: a writer. I would observe my family and my city, spend time in the city's archives and with my mother's old papers, collecting my family's stories as a journalist might. Carrying a red tape recorder, I would document almost every word, and these stories would become the book you are reading now.

In that New York fall of 2011, my boxes sat all around me in the Harlem apartment, like cardboard spectators, their labels addressed and predestined: Sarah Broom care of Ivory Mae Broom, St. Rose, Louisiana. I quit my executive job and had nice savings and a small book advance. This was not a Good-Bye to All That moment; I understood nothing beyond this solitary fact: I was going.

The books traveled ahead of me; they arrived before. I took the long way back as if seeking literal grounding in the people who confirmed and composed crucial parts of my identity, flying from New York to Vacaville, California, where Karen and her family still lived. Troy and Herman were still there, too.

My mother cheered on this journey of mine, as if by making these stops I would reconnect the fraying family edges, advising me by phone on how I might achieve this lasting dream: *When we talk and if something doesn't go in a straight line, y'all want to stop. Y'all patience wear out. Like y'all already got it planned in your mind, how the story gonna go. Everyone tells stories, but have we listened to Troy's stories? We have to be quiet and invite someone not so up front to say something. Everybody needs to be listened to. My main thing is legacy. After I'm gone I want everyone to love each other and understand each other.*

What I mostly took away from these conversations was how my mother had begun using the phrase "after I'm gone." As in: *Maybe that Road Home will come through after I'm gone.*

Melvin and Brittany, Karen's children, adults now, retrieved me from Sacramento's airport. That Melvin was now a grown man driving his own car surprised me. I watched the speedometer from the passenger side, aware that doing so lost me cool Auntie points. How settled in they seemed: Brittany studying biology at the University of California–Merced. Melvin, still deliberate and shy, but married and in the air force. Karen worked in social services for the state. Troy was still unloading boxes at Walmart. Herman had found his calling as a used car salesman, a job he, with his bluster, seemed designed for. Unlike me, not one of the displaced had it in their mind to ever resume life in New Orleans.

During the day, Byron and I shopped to find a used car in which I would drive to visit others of my siblings in Arizona (Darryl) and San Antonio (Michael). Early on, when the journey still held the romance inherent to all beginnings, I thought I would visit the southern contingent of my scattered family, too—Deborah in Atlanta; Simon Jr. in North Carolina; and Valeria in Ozark, Alabama—but this would not be so.

In Vacaville, I wore my red muumuu for the first four days. Byron encouraged me to sleep without an alarm. Whenever I woke, I sat in a roller chair in Byron's garage and spun across the concrete floor while he worked underneath a car. I told him about my heartache, the same story on repeat with different points of emphasis. At the perfect right moment, Byron would speak up to defend me, which made the world seem kinder than I felt it to be. Often, when Byron and I were together like this, we'd call our mom and put her on speakerphone. *Byron is my baby boy*, she would always say to him at the near end of our call. *And you are my baby girl.*

I stayed for two weeks.

The morning of my departure from Vacaville, I woke to find Byron already loading my things into the car. As I drove off, I watched him through the rearview, standing as in his Marine picture, hands in his pockets. Water collected in my eyes and I let out an audible huff, not wanting to go but knowing I could not stay.

I hit the highway. Driving alone, I recalled the lessons bestowed by my brothers. How to follow the flow of traffic while speeding, checking the rearview at all times, taking cues from eighteen-wheelers who have the long view. By night, I was pulling up to Darryl's handsome two-story house. His four sons burst through the screen door and surrounded me in the car. Before I could step out, they were grabbing suitcases and rolling them inside. Darryl was at a Bible group, they let me know, but he had made red beans and rice, which I dutifully ate. I had not seen my brother in six years, since Grandmother's funeral. I couldn't call up the last conversation I'd had with him. I'd met his sons only once, when they were babies. After dinner, I searched for traces of Darryl in the house, *his house*, spotting an old sweatshirt hanging in the laundry room, "Darryl's Construction Company" on the front. The boys followed me around and stared, trying to decide who I was to them. Darryl had a younger daughter, Sarai Monique, my namesake. When my mother told me that Darryl had named a daughter after me, it rearranged my presumptions about my relationship to Darryl, which were, I realized, suspended in the moment when he hid underneath my bed in the Yellow House.

I was asleep when Sarai and Darryl arrived, but Sarai burst into the room and shook me awake. She had shoulder-length braids and wore black, plastic-rimmed eyeglasses too wide for an eight-year-old face, especially when they slid down her nose and she let them stay there, looking at you over the frame. Darryl appeared in the doorway. Chewing gum. I watched his face. He was heavier than I remembered, which I took as a sign of his being drug-free, a sign of overall good health. I watched his scar, the bullet graze beneath his left eye. It looked like a star. It was him. I grabbed and hugged Darryl two or three times. Like I hadn't in my life before. Was glad to see him and nervous, too. He left the room and returned with an embarrassing photograph of me from high school. He looked at the image and then looked at me. "You still look the same, baby," he said. My eyes shifted to notice his sneakers. To change the emotional tenor, I gave him the most humorous update possible on our siblings in California.

Somewhere in the house, the kids fought over the TV remote. Inside the bedroom, Darryl was telling me that he was proud of me. I had left home and stayed gone even though, he joked, I was going back now "for some crazy-ass reason." I searched for buried messages in his face, which was not unlike the face of Michael. He had Michael and Eddie and Carl's thick hands, Mom's eyes. I had his cheekbones. I was noticing of all these things, it seemed, for the very first time.

After Darryl kissed me good night, I hid my purse and my car keys. It was an old habit. In the hallway, I heard him say, "OK, group, shut it down." The house went quiet, as if a light switch had been flipped.

Darryl's house of five children made me think of the Yellow House. During the night, I dreamt of it for the first time in five years. I was at the locked front door attempting to bang it down. Bam-bam-bam was the sound I made, but it didn't yield. In the dream, the weight of the door hurt my hand too much to keep going. The next morning I woke exhausted and wrote the following in my notebook: How to resurrect a house with words?

By the time I made it to Michael in San Antonio, three weeks had passed since I left New York and I was already desperate for the journey to end, though in a way it had only just begun. My mother advised against rushing it, but still I did, abandoning plans to visit Deborah, Valeria, and Simon, who were disappointed and let me know it. My visit with Michael was shortest of all, especially once he decided he would accompany me to New Orleans. Like back in high school, I dropped Michael off at his restaurant job at the Hilton Palacio de Rio in the afternoon. I retrieved him at midnight, the car loaded with our things. For the first three of the eight-hour drive to Louisiana, Michael talked for entertainment. Then he slept. I drove the entire eight hours, my fury at sleeping Michael gaining by the mile, to the sound track of his snoring, fighting my own exhaustion by rolling the windows all the way down and pretending I was Bob Marley's backup singer.

We entered Louisiana as the sun came up, the car silent, racing to St. Rose and our seventy-one-year-old mother, to Grandmother's house.

# II

## *Saint Rose*

Grandmother's house. It can only ever be called that. Mom still lived there with her only sister, the only person I have ever called Auntie, in a small room, not more than three hundred square feet, with a row of windows facing the backyard, where she and Auntie Elaine spent most of their time, sitting among the azaleas and jasmine and gardenias their mother, Lolo, had planted, the flowers and the house having survived her. The backyard is where Michael and I, when we finally arrived, found Mom in a chair, reading.

This subdivision, Preston Hollow, contains two streets: Mockingbird Lane, the street I know, and Turtle Creek. After the Water, the old-timers and the newcomers, as locals call them, live here together. The newcomers are mostly the displaced whose psyches or houses or livelihoods or families—sometimes all four—were destroyed by the Water. They live with grandparents or cousins, aunties or uncles, who have been in this neighborhood forever.

The old-timers gather in back of their houses for parties, the newcomers in the front yard. Old-timers speak when they pass you by—whether on foot or by car. They tolerate all manner of odd behavior. A good example: One day Eddie and I are sitting outside Grandmother's house when a neighbor enters her gold Jaguar, drives directly across the street to another neighbor's house, exits Jaguar, activates car alarm so that it beeps as she approaches the neighbor's door with a small bag. After she hands the bag over, able-bodied woman reenters gold Jaguar and backs the ten feet into her own driveway. "Is that not the most retarded thing you've ever seen?" Eddie said. When the woman exited the car and headed to her front door, we waved, as is the custom in Preston Hollow—for some.

The new people tolerate no quirks of personality; they have no code, old-timers complain. The couple renting next door to Grandmother's house are in the junk business. Their junk commerce butts up against Grandmother's flowers. It is uninteresting trash—fake leather office chairs, yellowing refrigerator doors, washing machines, sometimes a dead car. These junk-business neighbors resist police citations, community pleas, threats by grown men like my brothers, angry stares, and gossip.

In Preston Hollow now, the elderly are justifiably scared into self-imposed house arrest by frequent home and car robberies and flying bullets.

But this is where my mother lives now, the first house I entered days after being born.

In the backyard, Mom picks at me as if I am her baby chimpanzee. I am skinny, as small as I've ever been, weighing 155 pounds, which looks like 110 pounds on my five-foot-eleven frame. I earned this size by flinging my body through the air, running. The grief, too. Mom doesn't care. She turns me around, pointing out areas where I should fatten up. *These arms are way too little.* She wraps her thumb and pointer finger around my wrist. *You need a lil meat. Even dogs like some meat on a bone.*

You were always tiny, until recently, I say.

*I was never no skinny minny. I was proportioned. I didn't have bones and thing sticking up.*

Only much later do I realize that my size reminds her of my father's size just before he died. *He looked to be wasting away,* she told me once, even though he kept saying, as I had, that he was fine. She thinks I am wasting away, too.

*You gonna run yourself into oblivion*, she says about my exercise habit. And then: *How do you think I look?* I tell her I think she looks beautiful, as always. She thinks she lost weight. I tell her I don't quite see that. We sit together in the yard, our backs to the ugly corrugated fence erected to block Preston Hollow residents' view of a fancier subdivision built over the park where we played as children. I scan the yard: MINDY is spray painted in black on the side of the storage shed. Tiger, one of Carl's dogs, had died the year before, and now Mindy was dead, too, after a pit bull belonging to a newcomer came into the backyard and attacked her. Carl, who had by now moved back to New Orleans East, went to court over this. "I don't want no money," he said to the judge. "Just my dog back. That dog then made it all the way through Katrina. Just to die like this?"

After a time, sitting and talking and catching up, Mom and I go inside to her bedroom where she has stored the remains of the Yellow House—things salvaged by Carl for her after the Water, but before the demolition. Behind the tall dresser where Grandmother made her prayer altar stands the still life of vase and flowers that Michael painted on velvet and that always hung by our living room door, on the perch. Underneath Mom's mattress are the designed women Lynette made. On the linoleum floor, patterned to look like marble, beneath the bed frame, fragments of beloved possessions collect: the marble top belonging to the table that once sat in our living room; the legs from the side tables that were hell to polish. *I was thinking maybe your uncle might be able to glue them back on.*

I sit cross-legged on the bed. The room has very little floor space and Mom is shuffling around it. All of the furniture in this room has been in this house forever. The bed frame, the two dressers, the mirror. These are Grandmother's beautiful, lasting objects.

Mom and I are close in the way that makes possible sitting comfortably together in small spaces, losing time. This is partly because of all we have in common. Mom is the youngest girl and so am I. She was born to a phantom father whom she never knew, and so was I. We get agitated in the same ways, too, when we haven't had enough time alone, what Mom calls my acting *ugly* or my *Monique self.* But right now, we are in our element. Mom is bent over and digging in the closet that is too small for her entire body to enter. Out she comes with a silver metal box full of papers. We close her bedroom door, as if the box were a secret. Mom sits on the bed, unfolds the yellowed papers, some of them in ziplock bags, the low-hanging ceiling fan whirring like a miswired helicopter blade above us.

*Turn that fan off please.*

I jump to do it.

Mom unravels our report cards and the tassel I wore at high school graduation from Word of Faith Academy. The navy-blue satin honors sash, still in plastic, had been eaten through by rats during the time it lived in the Yellow House. There is a pile of death certificates folded in threes and falling apart, belonging to Mom's father, Lionel Soule; Edward Webb Sr.; Simon Broom Sr.; and her mother, Lolo. There are stacks of receipts, one for a gold chain Byron bought in 1988 that she still has; birth certificates; programs from school events; and old letters that I sent Mom from college in Texas. Mom reads aloud from one: "You have got to teach me to cook because everyone here wants to know if I can cook gumbo, and I feel so bad when I have to tell them no." We laugh at the old me.

She finds Dad's discharge papers. I rub his right index-finger print with my thumb. "Oh my God," I say. "He has Carl's handwriting exactly."

Mom examines each of these items first, as a docent would, before passing them on to me. I look at them hard, trying to locate the special detail, photographing some of them with my phone. When my examination moves too slowly, Mom flits the next paper at me. *Here, here, here, here, girl. Take this.* As if the paper is evidence burning her hands. *Papers tell so many stories,* she says, watching me look.

# III

---

## *Saint Peter*

*T*he next morning Mom and I drove the thirty minutes from St. Rose to the French Quarter. My leased apartment, where I would live out the year, sat on the busiest, most photographed, written about, *used* corner in all of New Orleans, where all of the city's ideas about itself converged and sometimes clashed. And where, from my narrow balcony three stories above it all, I could watch it happen.

That balcony overhangs St. Peter Street, but the entrance to the apartment was around the corner, behind a massive green metal door on Royal Street, which the city directory published in 1941, the year my mother was born, described as a street that "once seen, can never be forgotten, for there is no other street quite like it in America, replete as it is with picturesque characters, real and imaginary, and ancient buildings with an aura of romance still clinging to them." In 1941 and in the many years following, black people—picturesque or not—would not be fully welcomed on this street or in any of its famed antique and curio shops unless they were passing through on their way to work.

This apartment of mine in the LaBranche Building, named for sugar planter Jean Baptiste LaBranche, is famous not for the owner or for the structure itself but for its "striking cast iron balcony railings," as one seventies-era book describes them, with "beautifully symmetrical oak leaves and acorns" likely hammered out by slaves. Built in 1835, this "brawny sentinel" of a building was flanked on all sides by historicized icons of the city, places that when taken together form what historian J. Mark Souther calls "a collage of familiar images." These images, he writes, lend to the visitor feelings of "exoticism and timelessness." These symbols appear on advertisements and postcards and coffee mugs, along with such taglines as: "It's New Orleans. You're different here." Or my favorite: "We're a European city on a Po-Boy budget."

At the end of my block, where St. Peter and Chartres Streets merge, stands the Cabildo, the construction of which began in 1795, directed by Andres Almonaster y Roxas. The Cabildo—City Hall during Spanish rule, and site of the Louisiana Purchase ceremonies, in 1803—is a museum now. The St. Louis Cathedral, just next door, is the church that voodoo priestess Marie Laveau attended and where more than a dozen bishops, church leaders, and other citizens are buried underneath the floor. Just outside its doors sits Jackson Square with the statue of Andrew Jackson tipping his hat on a whinnying horse, which I looked out upon every day as a teenage employee of CC's Coffee House. Jackson Square was formerly Place d'Armes, site of military barracks under the Spanish and French. And the city's first prison.

These streets—fifteen parallel, seven intersecting, seventy-eight square blocks, less than a mile walking from Canal Street to Esplanade, three minutes slow driving—contain the most powerful narrative of any story, the city's origin tale. This less than one square mile is the city's main economic driver; its greatest asset and investment; its highly funded attempt at presenting to the world a mythology that touts the city's outsiderness, distinctiveness, diversity, progressiveness, and, ironically, its lackadaisical approach to hardship. When you come from a mythologized place, as I do, who are you in that story?

From my balcony, I could look over to the Moonwalk, the promenade that runs along the Mississippi River. Some days I jogged along its banks, past homeless people wrapped in sleeping bags. Just across from this balcony is an apartment that overcharges rent because Tennessee Williams lived there briefly and, some say, wrote half of *A Streetcar Named Desire* under its eaves. Every day when the tour guides passed by that apartment with their paying customers in mule-drawn carriages, they told the story of how, in 2006, during the Tennessee Williams Festival screaming contest when Stanleys compete to yell "Stella" best and loudest, the winner that year yelled "FEMA!" instead. It was a story that I never tired of hearing.

Behind my apartment, in Pirates Alley, is the house where William Faulkner briefly lived, now a bookstore called Faulkner House. Nothing in this district is without an accompanying story, and there is no shortage of supporting evidence—anecdotal or otherwise. Much of this material is housed in the Historic New Orleans Collection, a few blocks from my flat, where it is possible to find the history of any French Quarter property, going back to the city's founding, in about the time it takes me to type this sentence.

This history was, I suppose, partly why I chose to live in this neighborhood. I wanted to know what it would be like to live in the French Quarter. I wanted to stay in what I thought might be the city's liveliest neighborhood, where I could sit on my balcony for entertainment, walk to the gym and the grocery store, run along the levee. Rarely use the car.

Those were the easily explained reasons. For all of my life, the French Quarter was the place where I and many of my siblings worked, a place for rushing through, and certainly not a place where we might live and sleep the night. In the 1920s, when my grandmother was growing up and living in the city, the area was described as "the area of New Orleans over which the wraiths of valorous men and beautiful women still hover." But what was the mystique really about? And how had one square mile come to stand in for an entire city? In the 1960s when

Joseph, Elaine, and Ivory were young adults, Elaine Armour wrote to the *Times-Picayune* after an article called "If You Live IN New Orleans, You Are a Tourist Guide" appeared. Elaine Armour couldn't understand how to get her guests to the "MUSTS," the places in the French Quarter where the article insisted all visitors go. "Perhaps you are not aware," Armour reminded readers, "that 1. Negroes are not housed in Vieux Carré hotels. 2. Negroes are not served in Vieux Carré restaurants or coffee shops. 3. Negroes are not served in Vieux Carré night spots." She went on, "Negroes (who happen to be citizens of New Orleans) DO have visitors from time to time. . . . Might I remind you that they eat, sleep, purchase, vote and pay taxes just like every other kind of citizen in New Orleans."

In my growing-up years, those of us who traveled from the East, that abandoned suburban experiment, into these streets for work were the supporting players, the labor, the oil that fired the furnace, the engine that made the wheel turn, the key that opened the door. I have a deep connection to this city's soil. It grew me. I love much of its rhythm, its ritual as lived by the citizens who make this place. This is the place to which I belong, but much of what is great and praised about the city comes at the expense of its native black people, who are, more often than not, underemployed, underpaid, sometimes suffocated by the mythology that hides the city's dysfunction and hopelessness. If the city were concentric circles, the farther out from the French Quarter you went—from the original city, it could be reasoned—the less tended to you would be. Those of us living in New Orleans East often felt we were on the outer ring.

Thus it could be said that my reaching to understand the French Quarter was a yearning for centrality, a leading role, so to speak, in the story of New Orleans, which is to say, the story of America.

On move-in day, Mom and I entered my new building through the green metal door on Royal Street, after having pushed through a crowd of

smiling clapping people with drinks in their hands, gathered around a
clarinetist with long braids whom I felt I had known all of my life. The
woman's name, I would later learn, was Doreen.

The green door's handle was like a lever of memory. I recalled the
walk home from my barista job at CC's Coffee House, wearing that stained
uniform, how I passed this very door when I took the scenic route home
along the backside of the St. Louis Cathedral toward Canal Street, where
I waited underneath the three-sided bus stop that left all of us who were
carless exposed to the rain. Even then, the green door always had a FOR
RENT sign with illegible contact information written in black marker. Never
in those passings did I imagine that I would ever be privy to what lay
behind its gate.

I remembered a time long before that when I was a child on a field
trip from Jefferson Davis Elementary School to the French Quarter to
visit "history." The yellow bus bumped down Gentilly Boulevard, avoiding the High Rise bridge, and sped down Esplanade Avenue, the same
route I would take, in later years, to drive Michael to work. How, on that
elementary school trip, we parked at the edge of the Quarter, on the rocks
by the train tracks and old wharves, entering the less than a square mile
of history through the French Market and onto Royal Street. The French
Quarter, we were told back then, when I was in fourth grade, contained
our origin story. It was the place where our ancestors—African, German,
French, Haitian, Canadian—we were taught, had converged in this bowl-
shaped spot below sea level along the river. It was, our teacher said, the
impossible and unfathomable point from which we had all spread—across
Canal Street to the Garden District uptown, across Rampart to back of
town, farther away from the river and closer to Lake Pontchartrain. In
the more recent past, we learned, we spread across the man-made bridges
and the man-made Industrial Canal, down Chef Menteur Highway, which
is how we came to be sitting in Jefferson Davis at broken wooden desks,
in a trailer for a classroom, hot and irritated.

∝

Inside the green door, Mom and I faced a long narrow brick alleyway. Dimly lit, it led to four different doors. At our feet, water drained down gullies on either side. The door leading to where I would live was the first black door on the right. Entering it led to a sunny courtyard. Above us, reaching several floors up, were balconies belonging to former slave quarters. That was what the real estate agent said. Those quarters, I would soon find out, were tiny detached rooms that tourists would pay a lot of money for the experience of sleeping the night in.

Mom and I abandoned my luggage at the base of the stairs and climbed three flights up the curving wooden staircase. At the top we were again faced with choices. There were two doors: one to my apartment, a five-hundred-square-foot, two-room pied-à-terre; and another to its accompanying slave quarters. Both spaces belonged—temporarily, at least—to me.

In the apartment, the outside sounds were inside, and this would be my life. From the bedroom, I heard every single word Doreen the clarinetist sang: "Baby, won't you please come home. I'll do your cooking. I'll pay your bills. I know I done you wrong." I heard the crowds cheering her on. I thought about how my life would be loud like this every day for a long while. Mom pulled aside the floor-to-ceiling lace curtains that had been scalded threadbare by the sun to reveal windows so tall we opened them up and walked straight through onto the unshaded balcony that faced Tennessee Williams's onetime apartment.

As was the family custom, Michael, Carl, and Eddie were summoned to help lug my suitcases and boxes up the three flights of stairs. Michael and Eddie arrived first; Carl was a long time coming. We knew not to call and harass him or ask his whereabouts. Pushiness with Carl could get you the dial tone. When Carl finally called, he said he was on Esplanade Avenue, parking. "Walk straight down Royal," I told him. I called him back to describe the green door, but by the time I made it downstairs and through the numerous doors to outside, he had already passed me by. I walked toward Canal Street where Carl had headed, seeking his head above the crowds. I spotted him in a blue-and-white-checkered shirt walking back toward me. He was disoriented, his eyes unfocused. For a short time, I watched Carl be lost without him seeing me. He looked uncertain, his head turning left and right, like someone in a foreign land. Being watched without knowing it is such vulnerability. After a while, I called out: "Carl! I'm here!"

I led my big brother who was now forty-eight years old through the green door and through the black door into the courtyard. I locked us inside together. Carl said the maze of doors was a safety hazard. "Too much maneuvering," he figured. "Too many blind spots and corners." Of all the places in the city to live, he least trusted the Quarter, didn't find its busyness interesting or intriguing or key to anything—as I did, then.

We climbed the wooden stairs; our feet made loud sounds together. Upstairs, I showed him the small apartment where I would live and the detached room. "You can always come to stay," I said. "Anh hah," Carl said back.

I ran out to buy a rotisserie chicken from the store across the street. Mom served the meal on china she'd unpacked from one of my boxes. Eddie didn't move very much but sat outside on the balcony, his back to Royal Street, looking toward the Mississippi. He was unimpressed by the so-called skyscraper building, the French Quarter's first four-story building, erected in 1811. "It looks like it belongs in the third world," he said of its pink-and-green, peeling facade, which I thought lent it romance. "You can really enjoy yourself out here," Eddie said. "I mean, you're not gonna come from Idaho and not see the French Quarter. That would be a total waste of a trip." I'm thankful that Eddie's not threatening to "get too deep." He's too tired for that, having come here after work at the oil plant. "If I was you," Eddie said, "I'd have a small gun. Almost all your brothers had guns growing up. If you were a New Orleanian then, you had a gun. It was like putting on a belt." But that was once upon a time, when the sight of a gun led to fistfights instead of shootouts. Carl had a more ingenious idea. He suggested that from time to time I don the Michael Myers mask he would wear on Halloween night so criminals would think I was insane and leave me alone. He bragged about how the mask's hair was "one hundred percent real." It looked it; when he put the mask on to demonstrate, he was terrifying. Carl reasoned that if I wandered onto the balcony a few times wearing this mask, whoever had a thought to hurt me would be too scared to attempt it. We all laughed, but Carl was serious.

Crime in the city was no more out of control than it had always been. What had changed was the brazenness with which crimes were being committed in the formerly sacrosanct French Quarter. "The French Quarter used to be off-limits; it was an unspoken rule. You did not go there with that shit," said Eddie. But the city wasn't that big. That the criminals would target the French Quarter was only a matter of time. They knew, too, that the people with the most money were from out of town. Boys were riding through the streets on bicycles snatching bags as they went. Days before I moved in, a man forced his way into a house on Dumaine Street at one in the afternoon; the owner hit him on the head with a statue and the robber fled, but many more victims were less fortunate. On Dauphine Street, a doctor was found dead in a pool of blood. The newspaper article described the man as "out of his element" in the French Quarter. On Halloween night, there would be a shootout on Bourbon Street—thirty-two bullets, hundreds of police standing a few feet away. Warnings to tourists now hung from placards on fern-covered balconies: CAUTION. WALK IN LARGE GROUPS.

Michael leaned over the balcony, smoking and talking nonstop about how he was trying to get back to New Orleans to live closer to his pregnant daughter in New Orleans East. His shoulders were more noticeably uneven, the scoliosis advancing his lopsidedness. The metal rod placed in his back when he was a teenager was still in there: "Feel it, Mo, feel it," he told me one day. When I failed to find it, he grew annoyed: "Girl, you can't feel that thing?" I seemed unable to tell the difference between metal and skin. "Oh I see, I feel it," I eventually lied.

The next day, Michael said, he would start looking for restaurant jobs in the Quarter. Carl participated in the conversation by saying, "Yeah,

Mike, yeah, yeah" from inside the apartment. From time to time, he stooped and poked his head out onto the balcony. His refusal to bring his body all the way out was how I discovered that Carl was afraid of heights. I laughed and joked and drew attention to this, as baby sisters are allowed to do. How could it be, I railed on, a man who survived days on top of a roof, a man who is routinely launched thirty feet into the air to change a lightbulb at work, how is this man afraid of heights!

This visit to St. Peter Street would be Carl and Eddie's first and last. "Not everybody meant to be in them Quarters," Carl would say all the times I pleaded with him to visit.

By the time Doreen broke the band down at 8 p.m. everyone had left except for Mom and Michael, who were staying the night. Mom set up her sewing machine and made a shower curtain out of bright yellow Burundian fabric. Even though I would live there for only a year, I dressed the place as if it were forever. The apartment was furnished, but I had brought my own linens, books, and art to set around or hang from the brick walls. I scrubbed every surface of the place with Sure Clean. Over her reading glasses, Mom watched me go, go, go, go, go.

It was after midnight when Mom finally slept in my bedroom and Michael behind a fortress of boxes, his sharpened knife set close, on the love seat in the living room instead of on the bed in the slave quarters because according to him, the lock on my apartment door was shabby, and there had been strange people in the building earlier—the property manager and her brother, a white-haired, nervous-looking man with a mop bucket. I surveyed the apartment alone. The two rooms and sliver of balcony in the main apartment could not be considered great. But the additional room that overlooked the more private interior courtyard gave the place heft. That small room had been remade so that the walls were partly yellow stucco with splotches of exposed brick. The full-size bed swallowed the space, forcing me to navigate sideways around it to get to the tiny toilet room next to the recessed shower. These openings in the room—minor cutouts—offered the illusion that there were places within the room to go. Only after you'd stepped inside and closed the door behind you, as I would do hundreds of times over the course of the year when I welcomed Airbnb guests, could you see the entire room—the lime-green settee against the wall and the small closet that contained cleaning supplies, but also a mysterious black hole leading to nowhere, a former chimney? Often, while cleaning, I'd open the closet and turn my head upward to peer into its vast nowhere. How far above, I wondered, did it reach?

To indicate my settling in, I composed a container garden on the balcony facing St. Peter. Hung bougainvillea plants with bright-orange and neon-pink flowers from the ornate railing. My mother donated a hibiscus plant from Grandmother's yard and Michael, a jasmine vine that knotted around the wrought iron. I bought a Meyer lemon tree that would never make fruit.

I made my rituals, waking in the morning dark, the sliver of time between the last party and the early morning shift, which seemed the only time to catch quiet on the street, which was the same as in the apartment. At this early hour, I sat on the balcony with coffee and the *Times-Picayune* enjoying whatever breeze blew in off the Mississippi. As the day rolled in, I watched pole dancers dressed as purple bunnies, just off their Bourbon Street work shifts, getting into their cars, and the petite stooped woman in all white I'd met one morning on the sidewalk who has, for thirty years, worked in the powder room of Brennan's restaurant where she said she makes her "good tourist tip." The metal doors of the delivery trucks rolled up and banged down. Water poured down off balcony plants onto the streets and the heads of cursing people walking down below.

From inside the apartment, I marked and planned my days. I wanted to remember, to revisit the places I had only glanced at. I wanted to collect the story of me and of my father, Simon; to research the story of my mother's last name; to find out what happened to my childhood friends and what the land that once held the Yellow House was before. I wanted, I wrote in my notebook, not to avert my eyes.

After Michael replaced the lock on the apartment door, he took up residence in the slave quarters for a week while he searched for restaurant jobs. For lunch, he made impromptu dishes with whatever was in the tiny fridge—delicious granola-crusted chicken with yogurt one day; charred sweet potato another. When he left the apartment for the job hunt, I relished my aloneness. Once, he knocked at the newly secured door and even though I heard him from the bedroom where I sat alone reading, I did not move to let him in.

When I was truly alone, after Michael returned to Texas having not found acceptable work, I wished for him to be back.

I met my neighbor Joseph—the only immediate neighbor I would meet in the course of the year—the day he began spraying my thirsty plants from his balcony in the building next door to mine. Joseph's apartment was the apartment where the angry LaBranche widow and mistress lived. I learned this from the Haunted New Orleans walking tours that began nightly at dusk; crowds gathered underneath my balcony where guides dressed in Goth told and retold the story of how Joseph's building was haunted by LaBranche's widow and his former mistress, who was pissed about having been chained to a wall by Widow LaBranche and starved to death. Guides said her ghost made residents nervous and jumpy—not by throwing things, but by turning you so crazy you'd do it yourself.

Joseph and I spoke through the balcony grates.

"Brother Joseph," he said, introducing himself. He wore a tan fedora.

"Sarah."

"You here for six months?"

"A year," I said.

"Long time."

Mine was an apartment for transients, he said, for people who do not plant flowers. The people who lived here before me danced in

Bourbon Street clubs; the balcony was for suntans. I assumed Joseph was from New Orleans, judging from looks—midsixties likely, light skinned with one strip of curly hair beginning in the middle of his head and running down the back like a runway—but Joseph was also a transplant, having lived in New Orleans for three years. Home was a brick mansion in Crown Heights, Brooklyn, where his two adult daughters lived. He ran an art gallery a few doors down from us that promoted local artists in a way that other galleries on Royal Street did not. That gallery had another courtyard, lush with fountains and oversize foliage, Buddhas sitting among the palms.

Joseph was the kind to prophesy over Saints games, calling the score in advance. Often, he was right. When it rained, he walked down the street with what he called a parasol but was actually a patio umbrella, massive with a thick wooden pole. When Joseph strutted down the street stomping in his cowboy boots and holding the green-and-white parasol, everyone made space.

On the day we met, he told me of his likely departure from his apartment, imminent because his landlord wanted to sell the building even though he had tenants with leases. "He don't know I ain't no Southern Negro," Joseph said. "You want to go to court, I'll take your ass to court all night long. Oh, you don't want to mess with no Northern Negro.

"Yes, sir, no sir," he mocked, changing his voice to female and afraid.

Joseph elocuted as if always onstage. His lips pushed out to form a canopy above the bottom half of his mouth when he made important points. I spent most of our talks on the balcony mesmerized by how his mouth moved. When his stories meandered—he specialized in tangents—I hurried him to the point. He hated this tendency of mine.

"Jesus Christ, darling," he would say. "Will you find some patience?"

Besides Brother Joseph, the only other person I knew in the Quarter was Manboo's brother Henry who passed through the streets to work maintenance at the Bourbon Orleans Hotel, which in the 1800s was the Sisters of the Holy Family convent and St. Mary's Academy, the city's first secondary school for black girls. In 1965, it moved to its current location on Chef Menteur Highway in the East, which is how Michael and Eddie came to attend their boys' school, St. Paul's Academy, and how my mother came to retire from the Lafon nursing home, where St. Mary's sisters lived in their old age. I saw Henry, whose job required that he hose down the hotel's sidewalk, only when I was walking to my car. "Monique," he called. When I heard him, I'd run to hug him. If not, he'd run after me, which he complained caused him to "dirty up his black uniform."

"I been calling your name, girl, you didn't hear me saying, Monique, Monique, Monique?" I was not accustomed to anyone in those streets calling me by my familiar name.

If I were to scream from my third-floor apartment, my voice would not stand a chance against Doreen the clarinetist and her band playing on the street in front of Rouse's grocery store, below. In the libraries where I undertook many of my investigations, I found pictures of Doreen playing on the exact same corner in the early eighties when I was in kindergarten. On certain days, Doreen's youngest daughter appeared, wearing All Star sneakers, to play the drums. Joseph, who has stories on everyone, said Doreen's sidewalk concerts put all of her children through college.

Doreen's music had become the soundtrack to my days. On Sundays her set began at 11 a.m. "Lord, Lord, Lord, Lord, sho been good to me" always came first, followed by "Wade in the Water." "Over in the Glory-land" preceded "Just a Closer Walk with Thee," a crowd favorite. If Joseph felt moved enough during the time we were sitting on our balconies talking through grates, he would pretend to speak in tongues and go the three floors down to tip Doreen's white bucket on the sidewalk.

Except for me, the five-apartment building where I lived was empty most of the time. People owned these places, but visited only from time to time—say, for big football games when suddenly I would hear doors slamming and find the evidence in the morning, vomit and beer cans alongside the trash cans in the courtyard.

# IV

## *McCoy*

𝒜 lmost daily, I abandoned my French Quarter apartment to drive to Carl in New Orleans East, where he could reliably be found. I'd take Orleans Street to Rampart Street and Rampart to the interstate. Ten minutes later, I'd have hit the apex of the High Rise and from there cruise down Chef Menteur to where Carl sat his watch.

If Carl was not at the Yellow House I knew to find him on McCoy Street. McCoy is the kind of street where murderers think to dump the bodies. Where Lien Nguyen, a forty-year-old Vietnamese store owner and father of three, was driven, tied up, and shot in the face. News reports said Nguyen's body was discovered in the "grassy area along the road," which was described as "remote," an eastern New Orleans "no-man's-land" where things and people go to disappear. But this was the street where Carl lived now. In the police photograph that ran in the newspaper, behind the metal fence sat Carl's small house.

Neither location is imminently findable, unless you know the geography of the East. No one happens upon the short end of Wilson or Old Gentilly Road, nor do they simply find themselves on McCoy Street.

If the French Quarter is mythologized as new-world sophistication, New Orleans East is the encroaching wilderness. The East is less dressed up; it's where the city's dysfunctions are laid bare. And wild things do happen there: canebrake rattlesnakes, one of the most poisonous in North America, are routinely discovered slithering around neighborhoods or in the abandoned Jazzland theme park, sometimes measuring over five feet long, which gains them the name "monster."

The East, in general, especially post-Water, provided good cover for snakes and for people. The large majority of its streetlights had not yet been restored, and this is why men have led cops on wild-goose chases through the East's marshlands, and why an escaped prisoner from Orleans Parish Prison hid out in the rafters of the abandoned Versailles Arms apartment complex. This is partly why Carl loves living there—because the only people who can find him are the people he already knows. Living where Carl does requires Maroon-like levels of self-sufficiency and independence. There are, of course, more populous areas of the East, neighborhoods with associations and monthly meetings, neighborhoods where city services are provided regularly, like those subdivisions closer to the brand-new Walmart on Bullard, whose opening was the biggest news the East has had in years—but where Carl lives is not one of them.

The East's minuscule lighting budget prompted its city council representative, Jon Johnson, best known as the operator of subpar Burger King franchises, to complain in a council meeting that eastern neighborhoods were so dark at night that coyotes were running through them. I tried, in the course of my investigations, to ask about the coyotes, to discuss the East's past, present, and future with Jon Johnson, calling his office in city hall, but for months he put me off. It was hard, as it turned out, to find anyone who was willing to speak in any official capacity about the area where I grew up.

After five months of phone calls to Jon Johnson's office, I read in the newspaper that he had pleaded guilty to federal conspiracy charges for fabricated invoices related to the rebuilding of his East New Orleans home.

If Carl was not on Wilson, babysitting ruins, I'd take Chef Menteur to Read Road to Old Gentilly Road, the same Old Road on which Carl taught me to drive. What you mostly see now though, driving down the Old Road, are eighteen-wheelers speeding recklessly or cars with their emergency flashers on, cars that are breaking or have already broken down, cars whose drivers wave their left hand from the window for you to pass—go, go, go—but carefully because the road is pocked and lopsided, and it is one shared lane. Whenever I crept down this road in my car I fretted over the seemingly inevitable flat tire.

Businesses on the Old Road included Colt Scrap Tire Center and Metro Disposal and Topiary Sculptures by Ulness. The Gentilly Landfill and JMA Trucking, Acme Brick, Southwest Freight, and Richard's Disposal. The corner of Old Gentilly Road and Michoud Avenue, closer to NASA, is where you went to get lucky at the Palace Casino.

The dead are relegated to the Old Road, too. Alvin, my best child-hood friend from Wilson, is buried on it, in Resthaven cemetery. One day when I was driving to reach Carl, I stopped in on a whim to visit Alvin. It was overcast when I drove underneath the cemetery's white archway. Seeing that cemetery was like recalling an old dream. I had not stepped foot in there since Alvin was buried twelve years earlier. No groundskeeper was present the day of my impromptu visit or any other day, I later found out, for six years, ever since the Water. The small white house where a grave tender would have been was deserted. Inside, water-logged books containing handwritten names of the dead were overturned everywhere. A few of them sat opened, looked rifled through. Other people had been trying to find their lost ones, too. On foot, I roamed the flat plain of the cemetery reading tombstones in search of Alvin's burial plot. I could barely remember where we had all come that rainy day, but I thought I knew the general vicinity, behind and to the left of a stone mausoleum. Searching alone in the great big graveyard made me jittery. Slightly paranoid. I heard every flap of every bird's wing. A black car pulled in. I watched it. A man stepped out and knelt down by a grave.

I called Rachelle, Alvin's sister, to ask his whereabouts in the ground. "He don't have no headstone, Mo," she said. I had believed with absolute certainty that he did, but how would I have actually known since we do not stick around to see our dead deposited into the ground? Nor do we stick around when headstones are erected. The machines do that.

Rachelle suggested I ask the grave tender. I didn't tell her that there was no tender, his post having been abandoned. The man who had pulled in earlier came over to me, said he was visiting his mother. He gave me a number to call for information. I wrote it down. For months afterward, I called Resthaven's main office, leaving the same voice message that was never returned. "Looking for the location of an Alvin Javis, J-A-V-I-S," I would say. "In Resthaven Cemetery. Please call me back. Thank you."

At my feet lay stuffed animals someone had placed on a child's tombstone. The wind had picked up and now flowers that would never decompose, no matter how much time passed, blew from grave to grave.

I left to find Carl on McCoy Street, less than a minute away. One of two short streets off the Old Road, the rare residential section amid industry, McCoy loops around to draw a horseshoe, running parallel at its bend to the Louisville and Nashville tracks—the same train that passed behind the Yellow House—linking up with Darby Street where fifteen years before I was born, my mother lived briefly with her first husband, Webb, and his mother.

Carl called this place where he lived his "lil room" or sometimes "chicken shack" or "my studio apartment" when he was trying to be funny. It wasn't his full-time residence, more like a getaway. He mostly slept nights in the poorly named Chateau d'Orleans apartments on Chef Menteur Highway with his girlfriend, Lisa, with whom he had a son. We called this boy, who was barely one year old when I moved into the French Quarter, Mr. Carl for how grown he acted. Carl's possessions lived among these three places: Grandmother's house, the lil room, and Chateau d'Orleans.

Besides Carl on McCoy Street were two shotgun houses. When the women who lived next door to him pulled out of the drive, they raced down the short street. Carl waved as they flew. Across the street sat a house with boarded-up windows and no front door, suspended in green marshland, like a houseboat.

At night, the one streetlight illuminated a metal box enclosed in wire fencing that belonged to the electric company. Otherwise, McCoy Street at night was completely dark, full of croaking frog sounds coming from the direction of the houseboat.

Carl's house was white wood plank, a tiny house long before the fad. Beside his front door, a single exposed blue bulb dangled. The one room inside held a small kitchen and bathroom with a shower. The blinds in the front window have been irreparably damaged from Carl bending them into peepholes.

Carl seemed to rearrange the furniture weekly, a king-size cream-colored four-poster bed and a kidney-shaped love seat. On my visits, I drank flavored vodka (even though I most loved bourbon) out of a blue Las Vegas cup that someone gave to Carl and he has regifted to me, with blinking lights that power on whenever I take a sip.

There was also a bullet hole in Carl's wall, a small circle above his bed, to the right of the window that held the air-conditioning unit, just beneath a Raiders flag. A man on Darby Street tried to shoot another man but missed. I found the headline in the newspaper one morning while sitting on my French Quarter balcony: NEW ORLEANS POLICE INVESTIGATING . . . MALE SHOT IN SHOULDER . . . 4200 BLOCK OF DARBY.

When my mother tried to ask Carl about the dead Vietnamese man deposited on his street he became heated and enraged. "I don't know about no damn killing," he said and then hung up on her.

This prompted Mom to want to visit Carl. I drove her there one day. Inside the car, Mom tapped her finger on the window toward the spot of land where Webb's mother, Mrs. Mildred, used to live. The men who stood around outside did not know that she was trying to recall the world before them.

*This is worse than Wilson,* Mom said of McCoy. Her voice dropped to a mumble, her dissatisfied, thinking tone. We pulled up to Carl's lil room, which was directly behind where Mrs. Mildred's house used to be.

*That door keep somebody out of here?* Mom asked Carl once we were all seated inside on the kidney sofa.

"Anh hanh," Carl said.

*They got lights back here at night?*

"Yeah. They just got some new lights up on that post," Carl lied.

*Carl, you ain't got no full-sized refrigerator and no microwave?*

"Unh unh. Nah, cuz I don't really be in here."

*You better get you a lil microwave.*

"I don't need that."

*This is what you call one room, huh?*

"Chicken shack with no chicken," Carl said.

*At least it's kind of clean.*
"Oh yeah, it's clean."
*They got a lock in that bathroom?*
I asked Mom if she needed to use it, trying to redirect.

*No, I was gone clean up a lil bit.*
"Oh no, it's clean in there," Carl said, seeing where she was headed.
"Y'all go," he told us. "Y'all go bout your business. I don't want y'all to get caught in all this rain, it's about to storm. Y'all go head on, beat that rain out of here."

*You ain't got nobody hiding in the bathroom, huh?*
"I'm saying, it's about to storm."
*You don't have no place to take a bath, wash off?*
"Got a shower in there," he said as we walked out the door.
Back in the car, Mom did not attribute Carl's eagerness to see us leave to her interrogation. *He probably had some gal coming over.*
On the drive back, she remade Carl's place without lifting a finger. *He can get a little table and put in there. . . . He act like he don't know how to make things home. Put a little curtain up at the window.*
We stopped on the short end of Wilson and walked up and down the empty lot where the Yellow House used to be. Mom sought out whatever grew, found half-dead flowers that Carl had brought and abandoned. We took the plants with us. It felt good, leaving with something from our land in our hands. Mom planted them in Grandmother's backyard where, in no time, they flourished.

# V

## Photo Op

"*Be* a tourist in your own hometown!" reads the ad posted on the blue-painted door of the shop on Royal Street that sells expensive French linens. The advertisement is a visual mishmash of cartoonish delights and local iconography: streetcar, swaying oak trees, riverboat, streetlamp, French Quarter town house with ferns hanging from its upper balcony, the St. Louis Cathedral, people leaping and running wild, arms up, gyrating. The sign prompts: Go to touristathome.com.

But I have already been that, I thought, a tourist in my native place. It would bore to list all of the times we visited this one square mile for special occasions: Karen and me standing in front of the Café du Monde sign, dressed in our best sweaters and jeans, hair recently pressed. Mom and me with Lynette and Michael posed on a bench with St. Louis Cathedral as backdrop. That time Lynette and her boyfriend visited from New York City, how her boyfriend bought an alligator head from a trinket shop on Royal Street, not ten steps from where I now lived. The pictures confirmed that we came from an interesting place and thus were naturally interesting people. Now, I rented these experiences for ninety-nine dollars a night to strangers on Airbnb to whom I pitched a "super charming room . . . historic . . . LaBranche . . . famous building . . . one of greatest corners . . . location," I wrote in the apartment description, "is DAZ-ZLING." And also, I was careful to include: "super safe," even though it was not.

I left a stack of brochures by the bed. Often, guests asked for advice on where to eat and where to hear music. Never once did they ask about New Orleans East, where I grew up. "That's why I always say New Orleans will survive without the East," Eddie said when I told him this. "They don't even know it exists. What does New Orleans East have to hang its hat on?" Arguments some residents of New Orleans East would make in future years when neighborhood leaders threatened secession under a new name: East New Orleans.

At first my mother visited often. She liked the lemony smell of the street-cleaning soap in the morning. *I'm seventy-one,* she announced from the balcony the day after I moved in. *And this is the first time I'm sleeping in the French Quarter.* She turned to me. *What does living here do for you?* I talked about how living here helped me examine my braided, contradictory ideas about the city. Then said, I don't know yet; I'm trying to know the answer.

Mom's visits reminded me of how I was in the apartment at first, noticing every sound. From the bed where we were sleeping, Mom would lift her head and look around the dark room, say, *They are really partying. Is that a parade going on?* It was. When I first moved in, I used to jump up and run from wherever I was to look at the parades passing down below, but over time I learned to know and distinguish the sounds even with the windows closed, could tell whether it was a hired wedding band or an actual second line with tried-and-true New Orleans musicians.

My mother's delight was recognizable. I understood it. It was the same delight I had on my first trip to Paris, but here she was in her own hometown.

In the mornings, Mom sat at one end of the narrow balcony facing Royal Street and I at the other, facing the Mississippi. She polished her nails and drank coffee at the same time, hiding her body behind the lemon tree, peering around its branches to watch me. Sometimes when we were playing out our morning ritual together, she stuck out her tongue at me and giggled, grabbing every simple pleasure. *Look at how they clean the streets every day. Look like it's so different, a whole different set of rules. Other neighborhoods they don't give a damn about the streets, but here you have different galleries and things, right in the neighborhood.*

Together, Mom and I explored. We went to house museums and followed the audio tours and to the New Orleans Museum of Art where Mom read every placard; we spent entire days at music festivals—Satchmo and French Quarter and Jazz—and walked to exhaustion. In these explorations I could, for the time an adventure takes, make Mom forget her uprootedness, which she likened to my own. *I never thought you would become a nomad,* she said to me one day. Which hurt. How, I wondered, was a person with a year lease still, in her eyes, a nomad? Looking back, I think she meant that I seemed untethered, had no place where I was required to be.

Carl's calls always jolted us out of our adventures. "Y'all heard from that Road Home yet?" Carl would say. "Mom needs to get out from Grandmother's house, get back to her own house, get back to that East. Mo, why don't you help Mama call them people?" But I was calling. The new attorneys assigned to Mom's case kept changing. The lawyers had, once again, lost some of our paperwork, which we were in the process of re-collecting from siblings scattered everywhere, rephotocopying, renotarizing, re-priority mailing for eleven different people.

Even seven years after it launched, Road Home was, for most applicants, a dead end, a procedural loop, bungled and exhausting, built to tire you out and make you throw up your hands. Nothing moved forward no matter what we did. No amount of effort seemed enough to unpause Mom's life. In the summer of 2011, a discrimination case against the state for racist practices was settled. Black people were more likely than whites to receive Road Home grants based on premarket values lower than the actual cost to repair their houses. One person received a grant for $1,400 when the cost of rebuilding was $150,000.

Those fortunate enough to escape the injustice of Road Home were often faced with crooked contractors who had a glut of construction work. This was my cousin Pam's story. Child of my father's brother, Pam was caught up in years of litigation over her birthright, a small cottage uptown. Her mother, Ms. Lavinia, intended for Pam to inherit the house where she grew up, which had been in the family for fifty years. When contractors began renovating Ms. Lavinia's house, post-Water, she was ninety-one years old. When she died, seven years later at ninety-eight, the house was still uninhabitable.

On her deathbed in her daughter's spare room, Ms. Lavinia wanted to know whether her house was ready.

"Not yet. They are still getting it together," Pam told her.

"OK. As long as they get it right," Ms. Lavinia said back. In fact the house was already finished, but the house that the contractors rebuilt in place of Ms. Lavinia's destroyed home would not pass muster on a movie set. It could not even pretend to be a house. You knew this just from looking at the outside where only one side of each of the front windows had a shutter affixed, because the windows weren't measured properly. The structural engineer took one look at the foundation and declared the home uninhabitable, suggesting Pam "return this piece of trash to whoever made it and get your money back." That simple advice was unfeasible, a losing battle that Pam, to this day, still mourns.

"I can relate to what Carl is going through," she said. "Because we would go by the house even though we hated seeing that monstrosity of a structure there, would go by just in hopes that we would experience some sense of justice and then we realized, 'Hell, ain't no justice, Mom is gone.'" Would this be my mother's fate, too?

∞

Not yet Thanksgiving and already Doreen was singing Christmas carols. "Come on, it's lovely weather for a sleigh ride together with you." It was still scorching outside. As if reading my thoughts, someone on the street below yelled, "A Christmas song never hurt nobody."

At this time of year, Living History characters, people dressed as historical figures in the costume of the past, roamed French Quarter streets playing free people of color, Marie Laveau, and the war general, Andrew Jackson. This year, there was also the pirate Jean Lafitte and Madame Josie Arlington, who ran a Storyville brothel. These characters stopped and had discussions with random people on the street, whoever had a vague interest, their past mores clashing against the present: "Where is the bottom of your dress?" the Madame, who I had passed countless times on the way to the gym, asked me. I was wearing black leggings and a sweater that reached my waist. Feet away, an actor playing a free man of color held forth in a brown three-piece suit and halting staccato to a growing crowd. A tourist wearing shorts, flip-flops, and a Hawaiian T-shirt interrupted to say how he couldn't believe that there were free people of color who were not slaves before the Civil War. "BEEEE-LIEVE," the man who played the eighteenth-century free man implored. I wanted to dawdle, hear what else the free man of color would add to the story, but I was rushing to get to St. Rose.

This was normally the time of year when Mom began decorating Grandmother's house for the holidays, but she wasn't in the mood. Sitting at the table in St. Rose with Uncle Joe and Auntie Elaine, she had broken down at the mention of Grandmother. *I'm sorry for ruining the mood. I just don't feel like my normal self. Where is Ivory?* she wanted to know.

I pulled up a chair next to her and rubbed her back, which I had never done before. She laid her head on my shoulder for an instant but quickly raised up and grabbed the side of my head as if to right the natural order of things. This moment reminded me of how so much of her life was still a shambles.

We kids had recently pooled money to fix up Grandmother's house, to replace floors and knock down a wall in the living room to create more space, but Mom took this to mean that she would live out the rest of her life in her mother's house. At Grandmother's house, instead of Christmas decoration, dust blew everywhere while the contractors worked. Nothing was in its place, not even the live Christmas tree that had been moved to the garage for the renovation. Mom's blood pressure skyrocketed. I accompanied her to the doctor for a stress test and an EKG. The doctor thought Mom might have a leaky heart valve, but it was really low-thrumming anxiety. When the doctor asked her family history, Mom told him her father had died of a broken heart.

For the longest time, Mom couldn't hear out of one ear, but none of us knew it. We discovered this after the Water when several of us noticed how her eyes bored into us when we spoke. She was reading lips. We bought her a hearing aid in 2011, and Mom was still getting used to hearing well. *When I got my hearing aid I really heard my own voice for the first time in a long time. My voice is not a distinguished voice. And the world just sounds too loud.*

I spent New Year's Eve, my thirty-second birthday, alone. The year before, I'd spent it riding a camel in Cairo, but I did not long for that distance or for adventure of any kind. I craved togetherness. My siblings said they didn't come to where I lived because the parking was bad. They said they didn't come because they didn't like crowds or because they didn't want their cars towed, as happened to my cousin Pam when she came over to help me with my container garden. When I visited Manboo, Carl's best friend and Henry's brother, on Franklin Avenue, to complain about Carl not coming over, he gave me the truth: "Carl don't like the Quarters. Hell, we live here!" When I asked Manboo to stop by, he pointed to his neighborhood, full of abandoned houses. "It's quiet around here," he said. "Them Quarters not safe."

My mother, having recently decided that she would no longer drive after dusk or on highways or in rain or in fog, refused to meet me on my birthday because of a thick mist. I drove alone to Jean Lafitte National Historical Park and spent the day there, the only person on a tour led by a park ranger obsessed with pirates, their booty, and an alligator named Trash Can for where he tended to hang out.

After this solo journey, I tried Carl, but his phone only rang. In the apartment, I slept my birthday away while the street made its noise. Only after 2011 had become 2012 did I sit groggily on the balcony and see the HAPPY BIRTHDAY balloon Joseph had left. This cheered me. I was not totally alone. Spotting me dazed on the balcony, Brother Joseph started up complaining about the "Mickey Mouse fireworks" that made a show on the river. I was glad for the sound of his voice. He talked me into meeting him on the sidewalk. I appeared on Royal Street in a black catsuit with pointed shoulders. Joseph, more than twice my new age and a total gentleman, wore long coattails under a short blazer. Wearing something long that hung down on New Year's Day was part of his spirituality, he said. He had explanations for every single thing.

Walking the streets, Brother Joseph and I ran into Goldie the Bourbon Street Cowboy who said it was his first night back on the job. Everything on him was spray-painted gold, including his sideburns, which had the texture of Astroturf. He wore gold beads around his neck and a cowboy hat. On his feet were gold-painted orthopedic shoes. He and Brother Joseph praised how God had brought Goldie through surgery to remove four bones from his leg. Even with the missing bones, haranguing pain, and a slight limp, Goldie reported, New Year's Eve was not a bad "money night." "It wasn't a three-hundred-dollar night," he said. "But it was OK." I asked what he did, whether he was one of the men who stood frozen still for a tourist tip.

"Nah," Goldie said. "I walks around. I'm a photo op."

In Joseph's Royal Street art gallery that night, grown men stooped before his water fountain as if bending to something extraterrestrial. "All the way from Europe for pictures of bubbles," Joseph said. The magic? Joy dishwashing liquid, ninety-nine cents on sale. Sometimes Joseph, in his slapdash style, put in too much and the bubbles overgrew the fountain, making ever-widening concentric foam rings that burst their fragile stickiness on someone's sandaled foot. The bubbles drew customers in a way the local art hanging everywhere did not. "Someone told me I could find bubbles here," a person with a camera said one too many times, which led Joseph—needing to make money somehow—to charge people for the privilege of photographing bubbles. The summer I lived there, bubbles blowing through French Quarter streets was a thing. Whenever there was an event in the Quarter, and there was always an event—manufactured or real, just time going by was one—the neighbor in the building opposite mine launched her bubble machine, pointing it in the direction of the river. Down below, people traipsing through the streets took photographs of the thin, iridescent circles. "Is today a special occasion?" asked a man on the sidewalk. A few of the bubbles landed on the thorny limbs of my dying bougainvillea plant and popped. One time a bubble floated inside the apartment where I sat at the desk planning my investigations, the clear bubble aiming for the spot between my eyes. I stood up and backed away.

Sometimes, when I was watering my plants on the balcony, someone down below would snap a photograph of me with a zoom lens. I fixed my pose for the camera's eye, becoming for it whomever. Believing, even against my will, that to be photographed is to be present, alive, confirmed. "You never know how you look until you get your picture took," my mother says my father, Simon Broom, was always saying.

I imagine the stories that might get told about that image of me on the balcony: Here is a Creole woman watering her flowers. Or here is the descendent of an old New Orleans family, free people of color. Or else, here is a wrought iron New Orleans balcony, the lens meant to catch the object, having nothing whatsoever to do with me.

The historicized past is everywhere I walk in my daily rituals—to get to the store or to the gym on Rampart Street or to my car to visit with Carl. Historical markers are everywhere you look—underfoot and on buildings. The Vieux Carré Commission was sanctioned in 1921 by the city to "protect, preserve, and maintain the distinct architectural, historic character, and zoning integrity" of the French Quarter. It is nearly impossible to legally demolish an entire building. The official, preapproved paint colors for buildings, colors with names like Paris Green, Cornflower Blue, Sunwashed Gold, and Sea Green, are coded. The more important houses in the Quarter, according to the commission's Guidelines for Exterior Painting, have purple and blue tones; the least significant, orange and brown. Those in the middle have pink, green, and yellow. This attention to detail, keeping the French Quarter trapped in a calcified past, requires money and wherewithal, of course, that other parts of the city, languishing and decaying, do not have.

Meanwhile, the present does whatever the hell it wants to do. Almost everything here, in terms of cultural appropriation and feel-goodness, can be bought or sold for the right amount. Actual parades were banned from the French Quarter in 1973, but an impromptu-seeming second line parade costs between $500 and $1,500, not including police and permit costs. The French Quarter's tourism site makes it plain: "You don't have to be dead and/or famous to get a second line parade. You don't even have to live here. Organizing a second line is not hard, though it requires a few hundred dollars and some advance planning." For the right amount, Jazzman Entertainment will give you a second line for your bachelorette party. Want to buy a Mardi Gras parade on your day off from the education conference? The right number gets you a float pulled by a pickup truck down French Quarter streets from which drunken people throw beads and hit random passersby in the head. Seeing these bought carnivals in the streets makes me curse.

The present, commingled with this prettified past, can sometimes feel unsightly, even crass. The Black Indian wearing a dirty purple suit, posing on the edge of my block for photographs with a Home Depot tip bucket hidden behind his feathers, feels like a transgression. The Black Indians are generally seen only twice a year—on St. Joseph's Day in March and on Mardi Gras morning when they appear to show off the costumes they have made with their own hands, sewing and gluing down beads for 365 days in a row. But now, you can be photographed with a man dressing up as one for a dollar, at your command.

The mythology of New Orleans—that it is always the place for a good time; that its citizens are the happiest people alive, willing to smile, dance, cook, and entertain for you; that it is a progressive city open to whimsy and change—can sometimes suffocate the people who live and suffer under the place's burden, burying them within layers and layers of signifiers, making it impossible to truly get at what is dysfunctional about the city. Or those layers get oversimplified as in *Treme*, the HBO show, which never achieved the depth of *The Wire*, precisely because writer-producer David Simon's love for New Orleans crippled his ability to break down the city's dysfunction. The story he ultimately told was, on the whole, romanticized, more concerned with trotting out all of the city's tropes (Hubig's pies, WWOZ, street musicians, Black Indians!) than with actually examining the ongoing corruption, a failing criminal justice and health system, poverty, education, and lack of economic possibilities that create for the average local the life-and-death nature of life lived in the city. A city where being held up while getting out of your car is the norm, where many children graduate from school without knowing how to spell, where neglected communities exist everywhere, sometimes a stone's throw from overabundance.

This is also why, when, in 2017, the local nonprofit the Data Center published a census story about how 92,348 black people—about a quarter of the city's total population—had yet to return to the city after the Water, the image that accompanied the story's social-media post was a Black Indian in full regalia, yet another romanticization of the displaced, who even if they were not Black Indians should be able to return home. Even the great writers succumb to this magicalizing of the city, as the otherwise searing (on the subject of Sacramento) Joan Didion does in her notes for *South and West*, writing sentences like "In New Orleans they have mastered the art of the motionless," which does little to explain why it takes so long to get things done—Road Home, for instance.

In conversations with friends, I have described New Orleans as a city of feeling. It has taken me a long time to understand what I meant when I said that. Sometimes, people's response to my being from New Orleans is a sound—moans, gasps of re-memory—which generally precedes their own story (usually characterized as wonderful, singular, sometimes magical) of the city. In these instances, they imagine Garden District, Marigny, and French Quarter charm while I picture New Orleans East. Most often, when you ask people what they love about New Orleans, they describe the way the city makes them feel—to the exclusion of all else. Feelings are hard to localize, to intellectualize, and thus to critique. One's relationship to the city of feeling is personal and private, and both states are to be protected at all costs, which makes criticizing New Orleans difficult.

Why do I sometimes feel that I do not have the right to the story of the city I come from? Why, when I want to get down to it, just say the damned thing, do the thoughts pool and ring out in a loop in my head a childish chorus of "Oh, oh, oh, don't tell on your place." Telling on. Like giving it all away. Giving *what* all away?

Often, the focus of criticism becomes not the dysfunction itself, but rather the person who speaks against the city of feeling, against New Orleans. To criticize New Orleans is to put one's authenticity at stake. But I resist the notion that if you have left the city for better things, if the city is not testing you, if your life is not in danger, you ought to stay quiet.

Who has the rights to the story of a place? Are these rights earned, bought, fought and died for? Or are they given? Are they automatic, like an assumption? Self-renewing? Are these rights a token of citizenship belonging to those who stay in the place or to those who leave and come back to it? Does the act of leaving relinquish one's rights to the story of a place? Who stays gone? Who can afford to return?

# VI

## Investigations

$\mathcal{W}$hen I wanted to know the story of the French Quarter apartment where I lived, I checked into the Williams Research Center in the Historic New Orleans Collection on Chartres Street where the entire lineage of every address in the French Quarter is organized digitally.

In the time it took for me to type in my address, I discovered its history going back to 1795. "A lot forming the corner of Royal and St. Peter with an irregular depth." I learned that it was originally owned by a free woman of color, Marianne Brion—"(f.w.c.)" the papers read per the law—and a portion was transferred to another free woman of color, Adelayda Pitri. Marianne Dubreuil dite Brion was daughter to Nanette, a former slave who was sold along with her four children to a French-woman and her husband. Nanette received manumission "because of the loyalty and constancy they have served me and my husband," the records show. Under Spanish rule, free people of color could receive property from whites. This is likely how Marianne inherited the property.

I discovered that Cecile Dubreuil, another one of Nanette's daughters, began accumulating property soon after she was freed in 1769, buying several buildings on Royal Street. In 1795, in New Orleans, there were only three free people of color who owned more than five slaves. They were all women. One was Marianne Dubreuil dite Brion, who owned the apartment I rented and also owned seven slaves.

That same afternoon I learned these facts I visited a used bookstore on Orleans Street in search of books about New Orleans East. The owner told me there were none. The East, he said, was too young for history. But this was faulty logic. We are all born into histories, worlds existing before us. The same is true of places. No place is without history.

What is true is that few things have been written about the East, except for sentence- or sometimes paragraph-long descriptions in books about New Orleans that describe the area as "rakish" or "barren" or "distant, charmless." Nothing had, at the moment I asked, been written about the lives of the people who lived there. The East was not too young for history; it was just that in the official story of New Orleans, its stories and people were relegated to the sidelines, deemed not to matter as much, the place not having earned—through demographics or economic success —a spot on the cartographer's nearsighted map: a situation not dissimilar to the exclusion of Native American tribal lands from early maps of the Americas.

To find the history of the Yellow House, I had to search original deeds, chains of titles, successions. I stalked the Conveyance Office, the Office of Vital Records, the Real Estate and Records Office in city hall, the Notarial Archives, and libraries. The search was full of cross-referencing and confusion.

I arrived many mornings at the main branch of the New Orleans Public Library in the business district, just across from city hall, and waited in line for the doors to open. If you didn't know better, you'd think the city was full of people eager to read, but actually the line was full of homeless people who had slept outdoors and were trying to get to the bathrooms. This sight prompted a letter in the local newspaper: "The atmosphere outside the library is so off-putting . . . unkempt people sitting or lying on the steps or wandering about aimlessly. Inside the library was just as unsettling . . . large numbers of people with their heads down on the tables. . . . Perhaps some police presence is needed to ensure the safety of library visitors and to improve the view for tourists." So this is what the homeless and health care problem all boiled down to for this one citizen: striving to always be a good photo op.

Once inside the library, I rode the packed elevator to the Louisiana Division on the third floor and trained my eyes on the sign that spelled out the rules. Disallowed behaviors, it let us know, included: "Stalking patrons; using or exchanging drugs; bathing; shaving or washing clothes in bathroom sinks."

"No bad smells," it read. "No oblivious transmission of germs or excessive coughing. No washing up in the bathroom sink. No preaching or forcing your ideas on others. No shopping carts and no weapons." Most of these things still happened anyway. These conditions were, as the library's slogan said, "Speaking Volumes."

On the third floor, I shared tables with the mentally unstable who sometimes had conversations aloud and sometimes read quietly just as I was reading. The library staff spent much of the time policing, which made it hard to get research assistance.

I spent a day at the City Planning Commission Office in city hall. If it hadn't been for my time in the mayor's office, I would not have known such a place existed. But this was the office responsible for creating zoning policy, and this zoning policy was responsible for how neighborhoods looked and how people lived there. Lenient policy led to McCoy Street and Metro Disposal Garbage Collection Service being within sight of each other, to the Yellow House being across from a junk business.

I met with a kind, timid man, so new to city planning that he still believed the textbook theories. His diction was academic, as when he said, speaking of zoning classifications: "After six months if they are inactive they resort to the baseline zoning district." I nodded, but for most of our discussion had no idea what he meant. He had the knowledge but not the bedside manner. I wanted to know how it came to be that houses abutted trailer parks, then junk lots and tow centers after the trailer parks had gone. I asked him how the street came to be, but I suppose I meant the question in a more existential way: how *we*, my family, came to be there. The man didn't know. During our half-hour conversation, his inability to answer my questions upset him so much that he kept berating himself: "I just failed planning school," he said more than once. He had not yet learned to say, "I don't know." Not his fault, really. My questions did not belong there in the City Planning Commission Offices, for they were, at base, unanswerable.

In a presentation to the Louisiana legislature in 1981 when I was two years old, Barton D. Higgs, New Orleans East Inc.'s president, addressed some aspect of the question I was now trying to resolve. "With careful planning, you maximize value by avoiding conflict. You don't, for instance, put a factory next to a school or in the midst of an elegant neighborhood without expecting to lower the fair market value of the surrounding property," he said.

In the "Planning for Living" section of one brochure, the ideals of good city planning were laid out: "The home . . . is the point from which the family unit takes form and branches out in various fields of endeavor. . . . The objective of planning is to provide for these normal functions and to promote the greatest convenience, safety, and general well-being in a pleasant and attractive setting."

But here in the city planning office, on the matter of trailers the kind man said, "Every trailer park I've seen has been in areas off the way." He was trying to sort it out. "Trailer parks are different because they are transient. Hmmm. The majority are in industrial-type areas."

I tried to paint for him a picture of what I meant, what had driven me to his office. I kept saying trailer parks and houses and junk lots and train tracks and zoning. "I'm trying to figure out how a residential neighborhood became an industrial one," I said.

"I'm trying to build up an image," the man said.

I said again, "New Orleans East, just off Chef Menteur."

"I actually had that in my mind!" he called out, seeming pleased with himself, as if he had passed a pop quiz.

He seemed to know what to do after that. Together we read the map of the city. I asked about our specific address. He gave me abbreviations that I looked up alone later: IZD (interim zoning district), HI (heavy industrial), LI (light industrial), CZO (comprehensive zoning ordinance), RD2 (single family), RD3 (rural development), MCS numbers, base maps, quadrants. Wanting me out of his office, he instructed me on what I might do for myself, schooling me on the nature of documents I might find and request from yet another office, the clerk of council, "for a nominal fee."

When we were nearing the end of our talk, which mostly consisted of him looking at the square where the house used to be and calling out numbers I could further investigate, a woman appeared in the office and pulled rank on him simply by holding her voice steady. It was a loud voice. Whereas he hesitated, she spoke boldly. Whereas he responded to the emotional tenor of my questions, she spoke like someone doing a routine. I put to her many of the same questions I had already asked.

She explained that unattended houses in light industrial zones reverted back to the zoning classification light industrial, but users, as she called residents, could fight to get the zoning classification changed back to residential, or people living in the houses near one another could team up and rally to regain residential status. She spoke of fighting and advocating and teaming up. I asked for the definition of a residential area.

She stayed silent, waiting for me to reframe this.

If you have three houses can you argue that the block is residential?

"That might be more complicated," she said.

I suddenly felt baffled in a way I had not felt in a very long time, like a grieving person unable to reconcile a loss. I had not shown photos of the short end of Wilson, but they both knew the area. These employees, I felt, had bigger fish to fry than what I was coming into their office with.

Ms. Octavia's house in the light industrial district on Wilson is what city planners would call a legal nonconforming use of space. It was, legally and literally speaking, an exception.

I finally said, "But what if only one person lives on the street?"

She did not entertain the possibility, letting it be known that we were wrapping up. "In this case it's different. You're trying to protect the users from all the surrounding development."

*We*, the houses, were the exception, it was clear. Not the trailer parks. I repeated it back to myself: We lived on an industrial-zoned street where the houses were the exceptions.

The woman left saying, "We don't have the liberty of going around and examining things the way we think makes sense."

# VII

---

## *Phantoms*

*T*hree weeks into the New Year, Carl called from New Orleans East to tell me that the marshes were burning. He said they had smoke instead of sun in the sky. "They got us afraid to breathe out here," he said. As he spoke, I watched Doreen and her band set up below. It was as if he were calling from another city.

I had read a newspaper story several mornings before about a man killed at Mondo restaurant in the Lakeview neighborhood. He was shot seven times, in broad daylight, by the grandfather of his only child, outside the restaurant where he had gone to retrieve his paycheck. The dead man's mother had accompanied him there; she had also watched him die. I tore out the newspaper image of this man lying facedown, his dread-locks splayed on the sidewalk like a star, and put it in a file folder. I didn't think about it again until Carl called to talk about the smoke and said, "You know our cousin was killed out here."

Our cousin, Antonio "Tony" Miller, was the man in the newspaper article. He was the only son of my father's niece. I retrieved Carl one morning from the East, and we drove the hour to Phoenix, Louisiana, where I met Tony for the first time in his casket. It was a terrible introduction. Tony was handsome, with wide shoulders. His dreadlocks had been gathered in a pile at the top of his head. His crossed hands were small and delicate. His lips looked as if they had been spray-painted silver. He had a heart-shaped tattoo drawn in thin lines near his wrist. He was twenty-one years old and the sixteenth person murdered in the first three weeks of 2012.

Months before, a one-year-old had been killed by a bullet meant for someone else. By summertime, a five-year-old would be shot at a birthday party. Around the same time, Mom would call and say a boy was shot five times while sitting in his car on Mockingbird Lane. The newspaper headlines shouted CITY RATTLED BY A SURGE IN GUN VIOLENCE, and the THOU SHALT NOT KILL signs of my teenage years in the nineties, though smaller now, sprouted along the neutral ground.

Mayor Mitch Landrieu, who was always threatening murderers with words at press conferences, said that New Orleans had long been "a violent town" and resolved to stamp out the city's "culture of death." A big part of the problem, Landrieu said, was a lack of conflict-resolution skills among young people. But that seemed, to me, the very least of it. What about the debilitating inadequacies of the educational system and the paltry job market? An economy based on selling as many elements as possible of New Orleans culture via tourism as opposed to actual industry? Unemployment was at seven percent, and twenty-six percent of those who did work were in the hotel and food-service industry, which was the lowest paid of all professions. Health services were still crippled, and mental health services for people with post-traumatic stress disorder, what my cousin Pam called "Katrina crazy," were virtually nonexistent.

In order to curb the soaring murder rate, Mayor Landrieu launched midnight basketball games and instituted curfews in the tourist-heavy French Quarter and Marigny, restricting those under eighteen years old from being in or near those vicinities after 8 p.m. "Save a tourist and bury a native," a local columnist wrote in response.

When none of these ploys worked, community members pleaded with God. PRAYER MOVEMENT GEARS UP IN EFFORT TO HEAL NEW ORLEANS, one headline said. The story described two women driving around and laying hands on the streets, pleading the "blood of Jesus" for protection.

Tony's funeral reminded me of Alvin's funeral more than a decade before. The young men wore the same hard faces that broke into pained grimaces when they saw the dead body, just like we did as young mourners for Alvin, but instead of wearing white T-shirts with pictures of the dead, they wore bright-red matching Dickies jumpsuits with Tony smiling on their sleeves and on their backs.

At the burial, after the crowd had mostly gone, the grave tender, dressed in green coveralls, drove a tractor with the tomb's lid suspended by two metal chains. It dangled in the air like a low-flying jet. For many minutes, the sole sound was of those chains grating as the lid was lowered over the tomb. I stood facing this with several of the pallbearers, who were all young men in red jumpsuits each wearing a single white glove. After the lid was on, one of the pallbearers threw his white glove to the ground and stormed off, lifting up his sunglasses, wiping his eyes, sniffling. The grave tender worked at the speed of someone late for his next appointment, removing the Astroturf that had been laid down around the coffin to make a decent presentation, folding each piece like a cherished carpet, and then finally sealing the tomb permanently with cement. By then, the other witnesses to Tony's burial had left the scene and I stood there alone. I was thinking about how rare it was, our staying to watch Tony lowered into ground, and of how all of my childhood friends were either dead (Alvin) or in prison (James) or, generally speaking, lost to me (Chocolate T, Red). The moment was more wordless than I am now making it.

On the drive home, after dropping Carl, I thought about James, my sister Valeria's son, who was now thirteen years into his prison term; and Alvin, as many years in the ground, and without even a headstone. Because I was used to acting on things in lieu of feeling, I called Resthaven Cemetery's main office even though it was late at night and left another voice mail about wanting to find Alvin's spot in the ground. When I entered the green door leading to the alleyway of my French Quarter apartment, I slammed it shut despite the DO NOT SLAM DOOR sign and leaned all of my body weight against it, as if I had just escaped something.

Back at the apartment, I gathered the latest letter from my nephew James.

To: My Tete—Princess P
From: Your nephew—Blacky Boo J
Reason: Just received your letter and glad to know that you got
   my back [smiley face]
Request: Never to give up on me

James never dated the letters, never mentioned holidays or birthdays or time in general, except the length of his prison term, which was the only time that mattered.

I had tried to professionalize a personal thing, highlighting in neon yellow James's bold black lines, organizing his letters in a file folder labeled "James Jenkins" that included an underlined newspaper article about the possible closing of Avoyelles Correctional Facility in Cottonport, Louisiana, where James had served the first few years of his twenty-year sentence.

I can see now that all that was missing from my rude compartmentalizing of James—who was born a month before me, the two of us sometimes sharing a crib on the living room perch, and who is thus not only my family but also my elder; this man who I knew in infancy, in bottle-sucking years and childhood and teenage years—all that was missing from my organizing of him and our relationship was his prisoner number instead of his name on the file folder.

We are thirty-two years old now, James and I. The six letters I have from him represent for us the entirety of an adult conversation, dispirited and fragmented with no glory, begun when we were twenty. His correspondence has been prejudged, marred with officialdom's faded red warning: "Mail uncensored. Not responsible for contents."

Our correspondence starts and stops. It is always me who stops talking, and it is always me who reinitiates. James never disturbs the silence between us. These fits and starts have mostly been due to one or two lines in James's letters—requests, declarations, questions whose answers seem impossible to muster. I find it painful, for instance, to try to describe for a grown man who has been removed from the landscape what the view outside my window looks like. This particular torment of prison, the blinding of the curious and seeing, an attempted mass burial of the live—James calls prison "going dead"—makes me feel that I have unlawfully survived.

James's handwriting has changed over these thirteen years. Six years ago it was a tight cursive, nearly calligraphic, etched into the paper, but now there is only print, the letters spiritless and grave. The way he addresses me on the envelope changes, too. In the beginning it was Sarah Broom and then all three of my names and then lately just Monique Broom, which implies a familiarity I cannot claim. I do not know what James looks like anymore. I make him a face based on images I have found that are here before me. Photographs of James, placed in random books, fall out at unexpected times. From Cormac McCarthy's *The Road* fell a Polaroid that James's mother, my sister Valeria, had given me of James posing before a fake landscape of clouds forming over high-rise buildings with mountains in the distance. In the photograph, there are thin tattoos like popping veins on James's skin. He is on one knee in front of the confused city/mountainscape that frames him now but will frame another prisoner next—for a fee. I study this image. "Dear James," I am moved to write in a new letter, "who I love." I judge this line of mine. It takes me a long time to know what to say next.

Over my six months back home, I had come to know Carl in a way I had not come to know others of my siblings. It was not that we spoke in a way that I did not speak with the others. Precisely the opposite. Whenever I related too much personal detail, Carl would say, "All right bey, I don't need to know all of that." Carl was a quiet sentinel, but sometimes when

I asked a question he told me a story from the world before. Many of his sentences began with "Mo, remember when." No, I would say. I can't remember, because I wasn't born yet.

I tried once to ask Carl why he visited the Yellow House, hoping for a philosophical take having something to do with the importance of the land. "To cut the grass," he answered.

Carl and I did most of our relating while riding together in the car, either Carl driving me or me driving Carl, sometimes with Mr. Carl dozing in the back seat. Carl drives my automatic with two feet as you would a stick shift—one foot hovers over the brake, the other on the gas. We have made countless trips to St. Rose to visit my mother, our dirty laundry in the trunk for washing.

But of all our journeys, most memorable was Carl's personal tour, on bicycles, of New Orleans East. At the lil room where we met, Carl's bike was all dressed up, with a huge front basket lined in green tape that glowed at night. The wheels were lit, too; there were bulbs between the spokes that flashed when you pressed a button. "That's my baby," Carl said of the big-bodied bike with chrome wheels. At the very back, attached to the rear wheel, was a solid-red flag atop a skinny red-and-white pole rising nearly five feet.

At NASA Carl had found me an old blue cruiser that he said was mine to keep forever. Before we took off, Carl weighed down his vest pockets with sand as a way of getting exercise as we went. We started off down Old Gentilly Road, in the direction of the Yellow House, going the way my father did when he worked at NASA, but the closer we came to the Yellow House, the more fallen trees and dumped trash blocked our way.

Carl and I walked our bikes down the Louisville and Nashville tracks. This was the back way to the place we knew.

Finally, we crossed outside the tracks and pedaled onto the short end of Wilson, flying past the Yellow House as if we'd never seen it before, racing to beat the light, across Chef Menteur Highway and onto the long side of Wilson. We slowed our bikes to pedal past what used to be Ratville apartments near where the Ebony Barn was, away from where the Grove used to be. Toward where Jefferson Davis was. This silent tour took us in the direction of Livingston Middle School, which, to my surprise, was gone. The new school was now in trailers, the architecturally sound buildings in which I passed my middle school days having been torn down before they could age.

After stopping to look, Carl and I biked to the apartment complex where Michael lived when he was a young man. Carl rarely turned back to look at me, but a few times I raced up ahead to ride alongside him. Carl wanted to ride farther out, through Lake Forest where the Plaza used to be and into Bullard where Word of Faith used to be and where the new Walmart was, but I vetoed this. Everything we passed "used to be" something else. What, in this landscape marred by Water and neglect, had recovered?

On the bike ride home, Carl took a different route from the way we'd come, which required we cross Chef Menteur Highway again, but rather than go the back way on the Old Road, we headed eastward on Chef Menteur Highway. For a long stretch there was no sidewalk and certainly no bike lane. I thought of the ghost bikes propped up against light poles all over the city to memorialize cyclists killed by cars. Carl and I were in the far-right lane of Chef Menteur with nowhere to go. He was ahead of me and not turning back to see. I imagined Karen trying to cross Chef Menteur with Carl when she was in third grade, how she was hit and dragged down this road. I thought how I'd better not think too much and I'd better not fall. An RTA bus drove behind me now; it seemed to be gaining speed. I stood up to pedal faster, and the oversize cruiser wobbled from side to side as I powered on. "Whatever you do, Mo, you can never panic," Carl had told me that time he relayed his Katrina story. But Carl was out of sight now; he had turned right. The bus changed lanes and passed me by. When I finally caught up to Carl, I was cursing under my breath and mad on my face. Carl waited without any outward appearance of fret. We rode in silence back down the Old Road. When we arrived at McCoy Street and the bike ride was over, I was still shaken up by the raging Chef Menteur, pedaling for my life on the boogie-mannish highway of my childhood. I puzzled over this the entire drive home, fixating on the same question: why, I wondered, didn't Carl ever look back?

The next day I took my mother to visit her half brother, Joseph Soule. I had only just heard the name Joe Soule for the first time in my life, after he came up in a recent conversation with Mom. She told me this: Joe Soule was Lionel Soule's firstborn. His mother was a woman named Cora Jones, who had come from Raceland. I learned that this Uncle Joe, who also knew my father (they shared the same birth date and were in the navy together), lived uptown, minutes from the pink camelback where I lived during my city hall job, in the house he inherited from Lionel Soule in 1977, which happened to be the same year that Joe Soule took his three half siblings—Joseph, Elaine, and Ivory—to court in order to gain sole possession of his father's house. Joe Soule had the "big lawyers," Auntie Elaine remembered him saying. They didn't need to worry about anything, he had promised.

He would handle their father's bequests and they would divide ownership of the property. Elaine and Ivory signed over to him their power of attorney. "Hoodwinked," Uncle Joe Gant says now. Next thing they knew, they were being served with subpoenas, which neither Auntie nor Mom remembers holding, but the papers exist to prove it. Because they didn't respond to the request to appear in court—my mother had eleven children at the time— Joe Soule was granted sole ownership of the Willow Street address in the case of *Joseph Soule v. Joseph Gant et al.*

We were driving down Carrollton Avenue on our way to Audubon Park for a walk when Mom said out of the blue: *I was trying to see. We might be somewhere around Joe house.* Mom wanted to dwell not on who he used to be but who he might be now. We crisscrossed the street to jog Mom's sight memory. She was directing the car from the passenger side, telling me where to go, but she had been to her father's address only once, sometime after his funeral in 1977, and even then she'd stayed outside the house, on the sidewalk.

I stopped the car in the middle of the street. *Excuse me,* Mom called to two men sitting on a porch. *Y'all know where Joe Soule live?*

They had not heard of him. After more slow driving, a man appeared at Mom's passenger-side window and pointed out a blue-and-white cottage sitting close to the sidewalk. *Let me out,* she said.

I parked the car across the street and watched Mom knocking at the door. I could hear her talking, but she was not waving for me to join her yet. *You know who I am, huh?* I heard her say.

"Well, you look familiar," a man's voice said. "I'm trying to get who you are."

*It's Ivory. I'm Ivory. Your sister.*

Mom waved me out of the car. The tall man stood behind the screen door in a red robe with flannel pajamas hanging out the bottom. He wore socks in slippers. *This is Joseph Soule, my brother.* He was eighty-nine years old now and frail.

*Joseph, that's my baby girl, Monique.*

"How do you do," my uncle Joe Soule said.

∞

We went inside. Mom's first time inside the house of her father, Lionel, the man she hid from, who never came back to try meeting her again, whom she never met. I scanned the room, saw the garbage can holder with a cross inscribed into its wood, the gold mirror hanging from the ceiling by a thick gold chain.

It was like strangers meeting—Mom had not seen Joe Soule in more than twenty years—until we sat at the kitchen table where Joe Soule asked me: "What's your name again?"

*This was a spur-of-the-moment thing, Joe, nothing planned.*

"Sarah," I said.

Joe Soule was a stranger I had just met and Lionel (my grandfather, my mother's father) was a stranger I had never known. That made me an interloper. Joe Soule lit the stove burners for heat. He asked me to make coffee in the two-cup pot. The phone rang in the bedroom and Joe Soule shuffled off to catch it.

*They might think we're here for an ulterior motive if that's his children on the line.* I focus on the coffee. *You got to make sure they got cups and things that are washed.* I nod yes.

Joe Soule returned, seeming reenergized.

"Where are you now living?" he asked Mom.

*Saint Rose. My mama's house.*

Right away, I wanted to tell him the whole story of the Yellow House, argue how his past actions hurt Mom in the present, but I stayed quiet, kept on with the coffee.

Mom looked around the kitchen. The ceiling sloped above our heads, making a boxed-in feeling. It was a dark house, without much natural light. *This is where him and Ms. Bessie, this is where they lived together? Wasn't she killed here?*

In the summer of 1977, Lionel Soule's wife, Bessie Soule, was murdered in what was likely a robbery. She was found lying on her bed, hands and feet bound, mouth gagged with a pair of stockings. She was seventy years old. When Lionel Soule heard about his wife's murder, he said to family members, "Yesterday was the worst day of my life. I cannot bear to think about it," then suffered a heart attack right there on the spot and died, exactly one day after Bessie. *They say he died from a broken heart,* my mother says.

Lionel's quotation above, which appeared in a newspaper article, are the only words my mother can attribute to her father. It is, of course, possible that he was misquoted in the retelling, his words and the timing of his words reimagined for dramatic effect.

His obituary told the story he had lived by, not the reality: "Lionel Soule," it read, "is the beloved husband of Bessie . . . uncle to many . . . Father-in-Christ to Sister Mary Jacinta . . . survived by twenty great nieces and nephews, a host of other relatives and friends." According to the obituary, he and Bessie had no children.

Still. Lolo thought that the three children she and Lionel made should attend their father's funeral. My mother was thirty-six years old when her father died. She'd given birth to eight children and was mother to eleven when she saw her father for the first time, at the double funeral, lying dead next to Bessie, his wife. *I don't even remember the woman's coffin. I must have just been concentrating on him.*

*He was a big man in the Catholic Church,* man of the year in 1962 for his "outstanding qualities," the newspaper announced. But when Lionel Soule's children met with the priest before the funeral service, explaining that they carried his last name and thus belonged to him, the priest said because Lionel had not recognized them when he was alive, he could not take it upon himself to recognize them after he was dead.

"I stood in line," said Uncle Joe Gant, "like I was one of the friends of the family. I was there. But not in no official capacity."

My mom's recounting of this led Joe Soule to revisit, of his own accord, the painful saga that my mother and her siblings have wanted to, but have not been fully able to, forget. "These two lawyers," Joe Soule tried to explain, "after Father died, said they found out I was the closest relative my daddy had living."

At the time, he explained to Mom, he already had a house across the river and wasn't thinking about Lionel Soule, who was never really in his life, either.

"The lawyer said we gonna continue our research but it looks like the property will go to you. Now this is what he told me," Joe Soule said, speaking only to Mom. "He said my daddy had these other childrens on his wife, when he was married, said when I was born to Cora Jones out in Raceland, when I was born—"

*He wasn't married to Lolo,* Mom interrupted.

"Right. They told me he's legally your daddy because of that fact. Now we looking at some illegal children those lawyers told me. They can't be classified as legal."

I watched Mom. She was wearing her all-black workout outfit with bright red lipstick and Nike sneakers. Her hair was slicked into a ponytail. Her hands were folded on the table. She looked closely at her brother's face. Joe Soule, stirred, I think, by her quiet, said he thought Grandmother had their last names changed so that they were no longer Soules.

My mother finally spoke.

*We all rose up as Soules. Even Joseph.*

*We have never not been Soules,* Mom said, from the deepest register of her voice.

She told me to retrieve her purse from the car. When I got back, she opened her tidy wallet and pulled out a photocopy of her birth certificate. This is how I learn that she had, since the Water, carried her "papers" around. If she had to flee again, the evidence of who she was would be on her person.

*Monique, you got your glasses? Read it.*

My voice was unsteady. I kept my head down. "Female child, Ivory Mae Soule, colored, unlawful issue of Lionel Soule, a native of Louisiana, age thirty-nine—" "Unlawful issue," I said again and stopped.

"Who was thirty-nine?" Joe Soule wanted to know.

*Our daddy when I born.*

I read on.

"Occupation, laborer and Amelia Gant, native of Louisiana, twenty-six."

Mom wanted Joe Soule to review the evidence with his own eyes, but he said he didn't need to do all of that. Mom did not push. After some time, they moved on to talk about Joe Soule's ailing health, his thriving children. When it was almost time to go, they discussed my father, Simon Broom. Mom put me into context for Joe Soule: *She didn't know her daddy at all, only what we talking about.*

After the visit, Mom and I rode in silence back to St. Rose where Mom debriefed her siblings, Joseph and Elaine, around the kitchen table. *He said we weren't natural children to our daddy.* "Yeah, you were natural," Joe Gant said. Auntie Elaine, always the fighter of the three, argued for equal ownership of the house, saying, "This house we in right now is for family. We are the owners, the three of us, and that's the way it should be with the house Joe lives in." But my mother was allergic to the idea. *Y'all can have it. I'm not going through that. Let it ride. It should have been done years ago. I don't have a house. I mean I'm sharing this house. And one day I do want . . .*

"Well you do have a house, how you saying you don't have a house?" Auntie cried in a fit of rage.

*My personal, I mean my own, Ivory's house,* my mother said on the verge of tears. *I'm still hoping one day to have my own house, a personal house for Ivory.*

"I'm hoping for your ass," says Uncle Joe in the kindest, most deflating, big-brother way.

A month after that visit to Joe Soule, all of Lionel Soule's children gathered at Grandmother's house. Joseph Soule and Joseph Gant posed for photographs in which it is clear how natural they actually are—the same faces, noses, and coloration. Joe Soule and Joe Gant both have as first names their father's middle name; the same massive hands, which are the last hands on earth you want to fly across your face. They drive the same Ford Explorer. They are each six feet, four inches. The only difference is age—the ten years between them. The case of the Willow

Street house did not come up again, but I continue to think of it as strange irony for Mom who, of all the things she ever desired, wanted to make a new world with Ivory Mae rules. That is what it meant for her to own a house.

And what, I wonder, would owning a house mean for me?

My father is six pictures. There is my father playing the banjo, with Lynette in the frame; my father at a social and pleasure club ball with grandmother Lolo; my mother sitting on my father's lap; my father walking Deborah down the aisle; my father in a leather coat and black fedora, sitting at a bar with Uncle Joe, raising a beer, mouth open, saying something to the picture taker; and my youngish father standing in front of an old Ford, pointing his finger at the camera's eye. Someone wrote "Mine" in red ink on the hood of the car, and beneath the image: "He knows the score—." Did my father, Simon Broom, write this? I wonder.

These photos can be shuffled around, pinned up on my wall in various configurations, held up high in the palm of my hand, and then dropped to the ground, and still they are only six pictures. I met with clarinetist Michael White, who had performed with my father in Doc Paulin's brass band. He told me how, rather than wear the structured, more expensive hats like the rest of the band members, Simon donned a sailor's cap. He told me that many of the band's parades were filmed, that he actually thought I could find my father in motion pictures in the Historic New Orleans Collection archives, mere blocks from my apartment.

The day I went there to search the archives for the visual evidence of my father was memorable. Local musician Lionel Batiste, who we called Uncle Lionel, had died. His funeral was historic because of what Uncle Lionel and his music meant to New Orleans but also for what happened when mourners arrived at Charbonnet Funeral Home: some people walked in, saw Uncle Lionel seeming to lean against a French Quarter streetlamp wearing his customary sunshades, and ran out thinking Uncle Lionel was alive again and walking. The undertakers had made embalming history by presenting the corpse upright, it was reported in the local news, a coup for the funeral home, whose competitors all came by to figure out exactly how it had been done.

But I had skipped the funeral—for the archives. Seeing my father, Simon Broom, in motion would change everything, I kept telling myself (though I couldn't say exactly how). This notion on repeat stirred anxious feelings in me. I felt on the verge of discovery, which was my favorite place to be, and also felt I had a secret. I signed in downstairs and stored my belongings in wood lockers. Up the marble staircase and inside the ornate reading room, I sought out the film I needed from metal cabinets and sat hunched in front of the TV monitor, watching.

Michael White, the clarinetist, told me that because Dad played trombone and because the bands marched in formation, he would have been first in the line of men walking.

How would I know him? I thought to go back to the apartment, retrieve the photographs, jog my memory. Instead, I ran through my mind the six pictures I knew. Part of me was afraid to see him alive. To see him moving would confirm that he was not always dead, as he was in my particular story. In the world of dead parents, logic fails. It is only ever about feeling. When it came to my father, I didn't know the most basic things. Recently, I'd asked Byron, to whom I could pose any question, "What's the difference between a father and a brother?" He tried to explain, but his words fell short. "A father was tougher, more responsible for steering the child . . ." He trailed off. I could tell he didn't really know how to answer, but he couldn't say that. I thought his description of a father was similar to my definition of a brother.

I watched the movies.

Here was a dark woman in a white head wrap and dress wearing nurse's shoes, dancing in front of a row of shotgun houses. She took off her shoes so she could dance right. Other women in golden-hued blouses gathered around her like a protection.

And then there he was. Almost before I was ready for him. Was this my father? A man playing horn, not trombone, but with Carl's rough alligator hands, a yellow flower tied to his instrument. The camera lingered on those hands; my eyes fixed on them. The man with gray in his hair, beat-up dark knuckles, turned to face the other band members. Showing off. My father, I decided, would likely do that. The man's hat was different from the others, a sailor's cap, slightly yellowed instead of clean white, just as Michael White said. He was different, set apart.

I saw the same man in another reel, the man who was my father. Leaving city hall by the front steps, playing in a Martin Luther King Jr. Day parade, wearing a big wool overcoat, one massive hand playing the horn. My father was heavier than the six pictures showed. Cooler.

There was Dad again with the flower on his horn.

Young boys danced in the camera's face. They gave a good show. A woman strutted with pink foam curlers in her hair; one of them was coming loose like the parade, the hair unwinding itself. Serious faces everywhere matched the upright postures, lips sucked in like a fish's gasping.

After looking at all the films, I relocated to a table, pored through binders of stills from the same video collection, and found ten of the man with the flower on his horn. Excitedly, I approached the research staff behind their tall wooden desks. Photocopies of these! I asked. I have found him! The man working at the desk showed no emotion and did exactly as I said. I paid ten dollars for ten photographs and left the building, elated, my father riding along inside a manila folder. I have searched—I thought to myself—and I have found. It was a spiritual feeling, as if an important inner light had been restored. My entire year of investigations—the reason for this return—had been only about this moment, I thought.

I traveled around the city with these black-and-white photocopies in my tote bag, meaning to show them to my brothers, meaning to show them to my mother who said she was excited to see. But many weeks passed before anyone else saw them. When I was at the Yellow House or on McCoy Street with Carl, I always forgot to show him, or I didn't think the time was right, but then my mother came to visit. She was sitting in the living room of my apartment reading Ralph Ellison's *Shadow and Act* when I handed her the folder and turned away to make a salad for lunch. I could hear her thumbing quickly through the photocopies.

Her silence spoke a world.

She was gentle.

*No, daughter, you have not found him. Not yet. But keep looking.*

She looked through again.

*Now, see, this look more like him,* she pointed behind the man with the flower on his horn to a shadow of a man far in back of the procession. *See the way his hairline recede? Your daddy hair looked more like that. That might be him.* But we could barely make out that man's face.

*Your father had very keen features,* my mother said to me.

*He mostly played a sliding trombone.* Not the horn as did the man in the pictures.

*Your father had a very sharp nose. He wore his hair low to the head just like Carl. No gray because he always dyed it black. He was strikingly tall,* my mother said again.

I felt bad for making her conjure up all she loved about my father. The detail could sometimes make you feel too much.

Mom carried on with the *he was this and he was that*, but I no longer heard a word she said.

# VIII

## Dark Night, Wilson

The street mostly changes in the small, cumulative ways of decay. These ways do not easily draw attention. If one pipe bursts beneath the concrete, creating a running puddle, it takes on the look and appearance of every pipe that has ever burst and every puddle that has ever run. There are always cars parked along the street, mostly broken-down vehicles that do not move except for when they do, another hunk of rusted metal deposited in the former one's place. What is noticeable now is how the car shop that used to be the laundromat on the corner has suddenly gone missing. There is only the concrete foundation and a FOR SALE sign. The laundromat was the place where families took refuge after Hurricane Betsy in 1965. When my brothers say, "I learned to swim," they mean they learned to swim to the laundromat that housed the offices of the trailer park that used to be Oak Haven. After the laundromat closed in the eighties, it became a used tire shop where men loitered, the shop sign spray painted on a piece of wood leaning against a great oak.

Michael has just arrived back on the Greyhound bus from San Antonio for a job interview in a hotel restaurant. Out of the mass of shuffling sleepwalkers there he came, wearing shining white sneakers and a black outfit, creases pressed crisp, ironing being for him a meditative practice, executed with sincerity. The rigor that Michael has for pressing his clothes is the rigor my mother has and the rigor of my grandmother before her.

Together we wait for Carl, who has insisted we meet him here, on Wilson. We stand where the front of the house used to be. I examine the table where Carl holds court. Beyond repair now, the wood disfigured from too much rain. Bottles are strewn on the front lawn while others lie neatly in the back of a pickup truck.

A man across the street greets us like he knows the place.

"What that dude name is?" Michael is asking. "Huggy or something like that?"

"They say he burned down the laundromat," I tell Michael, repeating what Carl told me. Calling places by what they originally were, especially when the landscape is marred, is one way to fight erasure.

The man crosses over to us.

"How you doing, my love? My hands kind of dirty, my respect," he says grabbing and bending my hand to kiss it. He disappears back into the house across the street.

"That's Rabbit coming now," Michael says after we have waited for at least an hour.

Carl parks directly in front of the one cedar tree still standing, where he had always parked when there used to be two cedar trees framing the walkway.

"What's up, big boy?" Michael says to Carl.

"What's up, Mo?" Carl says to me.

I say, "What you got in there for me, Carl?"

"Look here," he says lifting up a bottle. "A Long Island ice tea. You got a cup? Shake it up good. That's one good ice tea."

This stuff is potent. Keep away from direct sunlight, the label warns. It is early evening by now, the sun, set.

Carl calls the name of the man across the street so that we can never forget it: "Oh, that's Poochie. Crazy, drunk Poochie."

Poochie lives inside the brick house with the arches that Mr. Will from Mississippi built, the house he finished just days before dying of a massive heart attack. Poochie is squatting on Mr. Will's estate. Before the Water, Poochie lived in a junked-up bus on Old Gentilly Road, before he moved to "the house on the hill," as Carl puts it. He has stored his belongings, a mass of rusted things, along the side of the house, which is pink painted wood, not brick like the front. Was the house pink on the side and brick on the front all along, back when I praised and felt cowed by the house's facade, the dark mystery wrought by those peekaboo arches where I always imagined a satisfied Mr. Will from Mississippi sitting on the porch seeing but not being seen? That was and still is, to some degree, my definition of power.

Poochie has planted an American flag in front of the house where the sidewalk used to be. Now there's just broken-up concrete. The house is still triumphant, in a way, by the fact of its existence and the posturing of its arches in the front. Poochie is proud of the house, it is clear. Ever since Poochie took up residence, the house has gained several myths. Carl's favorite is the anaconda story. "They say they got a snake in there bigger than your tire," he tells me. "Ain't never got him yet." I know this is Carl's story, that he is the originator, because I know how much he loves the film *Anaconda* (parts one, two, and three). He is fascinated with snakes, such as the anaconda in Poochie's house that will, Carl says, one day take him out. That or the Bigfoot also living in there—the Bigfoot's paw is to blame for the large hole in the roof that has never been patched, not since the storm when something flew through it. According to Carl, either the anaconda or the Bigfoot or Poochie's own mouth will take him out. Poochie is another presence tonight. He is meddlesome in a way that disturbs Carl for it contradicts his religious-like belief in minding his own business.

Over the course of the evening, a great many things happen. The mailman passes at 6 p.m., delivering mail to the one rightfully inhabited house on the block where Rachelle lives with her two daughters and delivering to the one business on the block, Crescent City Tow. But it is not so simple a mail drop. Carl and Michael and anyone else formerly belonging to 4121 Wilson can still receive mail even though there is no box and no house. Carl receives mail in Ms. Octavia's mailbox. He and Michael brag about 4121 still being their official address on driver's licenses and in voting records.

In my childhood drawings of the house (a house seemed the only thing I could ever draw), I always made a mailbox with our address, 4121 Wilson, written across it. After the storm, when the house was already demolished but the mailbox was still standing, when the space we grew up in seemed to have been swallowed by the ground, even after the street turned against itself, becoming the junkyard it always tended toward, the postman still delivered circulars to mailboxes with no houses. I know this because I was standing there to witness it with my own two eyes.

Seeing the mail truck head toward Chef, Michael laments the absence of a mailbox belonging to 4121. "Like there used to be," he says.

"We'll dig a hole and put one up," promises Carl.

Michael raises the idea of buying the whole street, "making it a museum or something," which rouses our imaginations. Carl imagines redoing the blue house closer to Chef that once belonged to Ms. Schmidt: "It would be nice to make those doors face that highway," he says. "Some French doors." This way the house would look upon Chef Menteur rather than run parallel to it. I think that's a bad idea but don't say so. "I'm thinking lots of big trees," Michael says. "We could make Uncle Joe be the overseer and make sure everything is done with quality."

That's key, I say.

"We gotta watch the money," Michael says. "We shrewd though, we shrewd. We could put all antiques in there." About the Davises who were our next-door neighbors, to whom much of the empty parcels of land on the street still belonged, he said, "We not trying to push them out. We not trying to push out they heritage. We can tell them we lived on this place, too. We lived here."

Just then a strange cat passes by.

"That's Yellow," Carl says about the gray cat with the bad eye, filmy and colorless. "That cat was here during Katrina. She was stranded in a tree. Do a story on her ass," he tells me. We laugh. Yellow gained her name by living in the Yellow House after the storm, before it was erased. Now she is outside like the rest of us.

Street: Completely dark except for a single lightbulb shining cold white on Rachelle's front door. From time to time, the small orange eye of Carl's cigarette. Lights flashing on Chef Menteur Highway, yellow, red, and greenish tints refracting back on us, changing from caution to stop to go to caution again. The three of us stand around Carl's parked car on one side of the street.

Carl stands near to me. "You cold, Mo?" He is wearing narrow black sunglasses made of hard plastic that slit his face. Sunglasses in the pitch-black night, a form of willful blindness. Who and what does Carl not want to see?

A ten-year-old boy wearing pajamas appears from the direction of Chef. Someone calls the boy Notorious.

Notorious lives in a white house closer to Chef Highway.

"Where do you go to school, Notorious?" I say.

"Nelson," he says.

"Where is that?

"On Bernard." Meaning St. Bernard Avenue, ten minutes west from here on the interstate.

"He catch the school bus," Carl says.

Notorious was looking for a playmate at eight o' clock at night, but Rachelle kept her two daughters in sports or else inside as a form of protection.

How will the children living here now describe the street on which they grew up? What will they have to say, these children growing up on a block with two houses left, in an abandoned, disparaged section of New Orleans where a city councilman claims coyotes reign after dark? What will they say about the world they came from and the world before them? "The East," W. G. Sebald wrote, "stands for lost causes," but I do not accept this dire and grim view, precisely because of the children.

Over the course of this night, Poochie will cross over to us and cross back to where he came from. He will fall in and out of Carl's grace. Strangers will arrive on the dark street claiming to be distant cousins. Another man would appear by foot, introducing himself as "A Little Bit of This, a Little Bit of That." He and Michael worked together at the Sheraton Hotel on Canal Street many years ago. Michael named him that after asking him how he arrived at a recipe; he answered, "A little bit of this, a little bit of that." Now he calls himself the name.

The four of us stand outside where the Yellow House used to be. I have never been out here with Carl this late. We are slapping the shit out of ourselves trying to kill gluttonous mosquitoes.

As the night deepens, so do the sounds. A train passes. Then another. Or is it the same one setting off again? A woman's voice floats through the air. Rachelle calling for one of her girls who has escaped the house? We never find out. Crickets and car engines, someone's radio. But greater than all of these is the sound Poochie makes yelling out from across the street. It's so dark we are only voices, but we know it is Poochie because his sentences begin and end with "Rabbit." As in "Rabbit, that man say . . . Rabbit!"

Carl will sometimes address the voice: "Don't put all that trash back here," he says to Poochie about bottles he has left on the ground that used to hold the Yellow House. "Them Road Home people still coming. We ain't never settled with Road Home." Other times, the voice yells YEE HAW or else the voice mumbles. Most times we do not acknowledge it. It will get quiet, then suddenly we will hear "Rabbit," as if it is Poochie's tic, screaming Carl's nickname out. Michael and I look at each other and laugh about it.

Little Bit says he's just returned to New Orleans from Indianola, Mississippi, which he calls the country.

I say, "It feels like we in the country now."

"Yep," says Michael. "Mosquitoes biting you all on the fucking head."

"Not even much like we in New Orleans," Carl says.

"Indianola, Mississippi, top of the delta, we went up there in three cars, stayed up there for five years," Little Bit says before launching into his entire displacement story, which includes a mean wife, demeaning jobs at the Dollar General, and jail time.

"That's what I went through since Katrina," Little Bit says as an ending. "Where you was at, Rabbit?"

"I was everywhere," Carl says.

Little Bit talks to Michael, but Carl is stuck on the past.

"They had the Yellow House taped off," Carl starts saying. "They had DANGEROUS. DO NOT ENTER. Fucking right. I had a lot of boiling pots still in there that was good. My big pot filt up with water. This was salt water, you gotta realize. It ain't did nothing but really cleant them suckers." Carl went inside the house anyway, laying boards to connect one edge of the temporary stairs our father built that didn't hold to the ledge of the upstairs room where Carl grew up. "I went through Katrina. I wasn't worrying about that son of a bitch collapsing."

He collected T-shirts and hats and things still left hanging in the closet upstairs. He gathered silver boxes with Mom's papers. One day after the Water, he saw Poochie in the street wearing one of his T-shirts. "Bitch, you must have been in that house. You been in that closet?"

"You gotta realize," he says suddenly to me, as if embarrassed, "me and him about the same size."

We stand unmoving against the night. The chairs belonging to the table where Carl entertains are pushed forward like in a restaurant at closing time, their front legs lodged in the soft ground. We huddle around Carl's battered Toyota. I photograph my family in the darkness, snapping photos blindly, seeing nothing through the viewfinder. What appears afterward is lit by the flash: Carl in dark black shades framed against the cedar tree. Cigarette by his side. Zipped up. Beard growing in an oval, edging his face. In another shot, Carl looks toward the highway, sunglasses off, mouth slightly open, elsewhere entirely. The cedar tree massive behind him, its leaves delineated into grains, the sole surviving tree, planted when he was only a baby, casting Carl into miniature.

# IX

## *Cutting Grass*

When Carl finally invited me to cut the grass with him it was deep summertime, hurricane season. Cryptic emergency text messages from city hall pushed through regularly on our cell phones: "Turn around. Do not drown." It was the time of year when, as Carl put it, "that grass be jumping." Jumping so high that Carl arrived on Wilson prepared, still wearing his work outfit: navy pants, white T-shirt, a white towel wrapped around his neck like a cravat, and steel-toe boots with snake guards.

"Are there snakes out here?" I asked.

"Prolly," he said, then began loading the riding mower off the back of his pickup truck.

We were cutting grass for the look of it, making a small blot of pretty in a world of ugly. From high up above where the survey pictures are taken, this would not show. But standing on the ground, *we* knew. And, too, the land could be taken away from us for any and for no reason—American History 101—so we wanted to avoid appearing on the long indecipherable list of blighted properties in the newspaper, an entire page of small dots that were actually names and addresses, so tiny that if you were standing two feet away and throwing a dart the point would not, could not, land on a single name. Also in small print, at the very top of the list, the mumbo jumbo of obfuscation: "If the property is declared blighted, it is eligible for expropriation and if the property is declared a public nuisance, it is eligible for demolition."

Along with Michael, who was in town again for another round of job searching, we were all dressed up as if going to a special place. Lisa, Carl's girlfriend, Mr. Carl's mom, wore a neon-pink visor hat that matched the pink ribbon Lia, her nine-year-old daughter, wore. Lisa's hair changed daily and today it was curly frizz hanging down over her eyes. The hair and the large shades covered most of her face. She looked like someone in hiding.

We sat around Carl's ruined table, drinking and passing Mr. Carl around when where he really wanted to be was on the ground running or held by Carl, both his father's long arms wrapped around the base of Mr. Carl's legs so that Carl's hands touched his own waist, giving the impression that Carl held himself *and* the baby. Mr. Carl, who was almost two, was too grown-acting for a pacifier, but he still sucked one, or else he drank from beer cans when no one was looking. After he had taken sips and we had all hollered in uproar, Michael said, "Now he looking all crazy." A drunken baby. Wobbly and sated. Light skinned with a fresh fade haircut, black Buster Browns, and plaid knee pants bouncing on his mother's knee.

"You never came to our house before, hunh?" I asked Lisa.

She shook her head no.

Michael said, "They got a tree right there, a tree right here. That's the front door. Our living room was right there."

Lisa was straining to try and see.

The sun was out and beaming. Carl was tired today, from work, but that was all he said. His patience was running thin; you could tell that. Nothing on the street moved or seemed changed from the week before, except for the addition of a neon work cone midstreet where a water main had burst.

After some time, Carl boarded the riding mower, which suddenly seemed tiny, especially compared with the ones I saw him riding at work, those "big old monsters," Carl called them. Those times when I needed to retrieve something from him, usually money that he wanted me to give Mom, we made our exchange over a tall barbed wire fence with the sign US PROPERTY NO TRESPASSING, Carl in a neon safety vest, reaching his long arm over, saying nothing more than: "Hey Mo, here you go, drive careful now."

Carl cut a bit and then asked if I was interested in cutting the grass. It was not as simple as I thought. There were abandoned cars and Carl's green boat on the lot. Carl sat at the table near to the curb and yelled directions. "Push that clutch in," he said. The mower stuttered and quit.

"Carl, I don't think it's cutting anything."

"You got that clutch all the way in?"

"Yeah."

"You sure? Push that clutch in. Engage them blades."

The mower started.

Lisa yelled, "Go head cut that grass, Monique."

But then when I was out of earshot, my red recorder, always on, captured her saying, "Oh my God."

And then Carl: "Catch her when she run into that fucking house with that mutherfucker."

Michael said, "That girl don't know how to cut no damn grass." Lisa thought my problem was that I didn't have a hat. Carl said, "She need more than a sun hat." Carl called over to me: "Monique! That thing got reverse, yeah. Cut all that round there." He pointed in the direction of Ms. Octavia's house.

I had lost sight of Carl and Lisa up front, but Michael came to me in the back, wearing his pressed khakis and a white undershirt, to pick up stray pieces of rock and sticks that could have blinded my unguarded eyes, which had not occurred to me then. I was high on the new experience. I felt like a child again, doing something for the very first time, with my guardians nearby if I needed them but not hovering. I wore cutoff jean shorts and flat leopard-skin shoes with gold studs. I wore a polka-dot shirt and gold hoop earrings to cut the grass.

In the back where I was cutting, the view changed: the vista opened up in a way I had never seen. From back here, behind Ms. Octavia's house, all of the lots ran together to make an endless yard, leading me to imagine the time before the houses, back when this was marshland and dense cypress swamps. I thought of the stories we made as children, how we called the ground quicksand, the nature of our world evident. We didn't need scientific fact. We were on sinking ground and knew it as children and still we played. This made me think of Alvin, how just before I'd arrived to cut the grass, Resthaven Cemetery called after many months of silence to give me his location in the ground. "HC3-2 is where you can find him," the woman on the voice message said. It was a cold message, puzzling to my ears. Alvin: HC3-2.

While I was thinking these things, I was not considering the grass. A lot happened while I was dreaming. Michael left for where Carl was up front. I realized I'd missed large patches of grass and circled, trying to catch them, when Michael ran back to me. From where I was in back I could see Rachelle's spilled trash cans lying in the street. I had not yet seen Poochie lying down alongside them.

"Get back in front," Michael said taking control of the mower's steering wheel. "We ain't got no weapons back here."

I was confused. I hurried up front, saw Carl sitting sullenly at the table. He drank from a beer can and spoke in a baby voice to Mr. Carl.

Michael told me the story: Poochie was in the background talking the whole while I was cutting grass. Saying he'd give me money if I would cut his grass, of which there was very little.

"We ain't worrying about cutting over there, we cutting over here," Carl had said.

As long as Poochie stayed on his side of the street, in front of the brick house, Carl didn't mind his talk. It was when he crossed the street to come over to where we were that the difficulties arose.

Animosity had been building for months. Poochie had seemed to want to control the street, positioning himself as watchman. When I came around looking for Carl, Poochie would run over to the car to greet me first. If I rang Rachelle's doorbell, he reported on where she was. Poochie's yelling for me to cut his grass irritated Carl, who said, "I'm cutting over here mutherfucker, you worry bout over there. Don't worry about over here. That's why you ain't got no friends now. That's why you over there by yourself."

Carl approached Poochie, who wandered into Rachelle's yard and was headed in my direction. "Man you don't worry about nothing over here. What the fuck you worrying about over here? Ain't that your property?" Carl said, pointing to the brick house where Poochie squatted.

Poochie said something inaudible.

"What happened?" Carl asked. It was a rhetorical question.

Poochie mumbled.

"Man what the fuck you worrying about my sister for?" Carl had said. "You ought to mind your business. That's your fucking problem."

"Ain't nothing wrong with me," Poochie said.

"What's your problem, bruh?"

"What I'm doing, Rabbit?"

Lisa yelled, "Hey, hey, hey," but by then Carl had already punched Poochie out so that he was rolling on the ground alongside Rachelle's spilled trash cans.

That was when Michael disappeared to the front, then ran back to me. "Get back in the front," he had said. "We ain't got no weapons."

Back at the table, Carl kept talking, explaining in his way. "Every time my sister come over here, he got something smart to say." Michael was our big brother. He talked Carl down, tried to re-steer his thinking and buoy him at the same time. "We want to live our life like we living our life right now. We *allow* him to live here," he said.

"My nerves bad," said Carl.

"My nerves are real bad," said Michael. "Now he den fucked up the whole grass-cutting shit."

"We don't mess with nobody and nobody don't mess with us. Ain't bothering nary mutherfucker out here," Carl said. "Mutherfucker, you ain't got no business in that house. Anyway, you a tragedy, you a homeless mutherfucker."

"He a transient, that's what he is," Michael tried to correct.

"No," said Carl. "He a tragedy. He a hobo."

Here was what it came down to now: the thing Carl was holding on to—overgrown land needing a cut—and Poochie, new to the street, but finally the owner of something, however precarious and fragile. You could see it as coming down to the old and to the new. One person's inability to let go, to see the thing shift. Cutting grass was ritual; it was order. Me and Michael and Carl, we were all on the lot for the same reason, tethered to the place we knew best. The house was the only thing that belonged to all of us. We seemed like the only ones who could still *see*.

Cutting grass could seem so simple an act, so light that Carl's friend Black Reg once made fun of it. "I ain't never cutting no damn grass, not ever, no sirree," he had said, but there was a precision to it. Carl knew this. You had to be OK with being alone, riding, knowing that underneath you the blades were doing their work. It was what Carl did day in and day out at NASA, a lone man in a field of 832 acres. We had all inherited from our mother the tendency, the *need* even, to make the things that belonged to us presentable, but even Carl could not put the house back together again. Instead, he stood watch, a sentinel, letting the space transform and be the place it always was. He was the keeper of memory, like the old man I once met in Cambodia at the killing fields, the man who had been polishing a boat carved with the names of the dead for twenty-five years, since the day after the Khmer Rouge was forced out. And now, Carl, drawing a line around what belonged to us, what was ours. Protecting it from name-calling and from dismemory. As long as we had the

ground, I took it to mean, we were not homeless, which was Carl's definition of tragedy. This is what we entered into when we showed up to keep
him company.

I dismounted the mower.
    All quiet now.
    I looked to Carl.
    "Did I do good?" I wanted to know.
    "For your first time," he said, "you did pretty good."

# AFTER

$\mathcal{E}$leven years after the Water, Road Home finally settled our case. Too much time had passed to claim victory.

Mom was seventy-four, and her only sister, my Auntie Elaine, had died one morning in Grandmother's former bedroom in St. Rose. I had flown home days before with a bad case of pneumonia, was sitting on Mom's bed, eating popcorn, when Mom burst in and extended a hooked finger. *Come now.*

I ran to the next room in time for Auntie's final exhausted sigh. My mother, baby sister of Joseph and Elaine, laid her head on Auntie's right arm, lifted Auntie's slack left hand, rested it atop her own hair, and cried. The hand lay there unmoving; Auntie was gone.

One day, not long after Auntie died, Mom signed away the Yellow House and its land, which she had owned for more than half a century, in a small office—the same one we had visited so many times before. To still my mind, I took photographs with my phone of Mom's oversize signature, the act of her signing, the mounds of paper. We made small talk with the bald man behind the desk who pushed the papers forward. We didn't read the fine print.

Afterward, we ate lunch at Antoine's Restaurant in the French Quarter, on St. Louis Street. Imbibed twenty-five-cent martinis, the two max allowed per person. I took a photograph of Mom holding the menu. She smiled off-key, said she would take the paper menu with her, as a keepsake.

She had a small grant and was free to move on, but she would keep on living in Grandmother's house with the door to Auntie's former room shut. She was afraid to touch the money. As if too high a price had been paid.

The land that once held the Yellow House will be auctioned off to become something else. At lunch that day, I wondered what would happen when Carl found out that the land was no longer ours. Would he still babysit it now that it no longer belonged to us? Did I need him to? Where would he go now, to remember and recount? Where would I? There are always, I have come to know, more questions than answers. I wanted to ask Mom these specific ones, but we laughed instead. About small nothings: the waiter who was flirting with her, the way her hair had drawn up to small knots in the humidity, the sloppy look of the Oysters Bienville. We laughed and made light because, what else? The story of our house was the only thing left.

# ACKNOWLEDGMENTS

First I want to thank my mother, Ivory Mae, whose name I love to say. For your appreciative and kind and loving heart. Your soft hands. For telling me the story and trusting me with it. You, poet, raised twelve individuals who know how to be themselves. May I be so lucky to do that even once. You show me how to be. And you always tell me when I'm wrong. Thank you for always bearing me up.

This book was written in and among many communities—inherited and made:

My brothers and sisters, who help compose me and without whom this story could not exist:

Simon Jr./Deborah/Valeria/Lynette/Karen/Byron/Eddie/Michael/ Darryl/Carl/Troy—eleven (intriguing!) examples of who I could become in the world. Thank you for letting me speak your real names aloud and in public; for telling your stories and forgiving me for telling mine.

When I started writing this book, there were Joseph, Elaine, and Ivory. Now there is just Ivory. Uncle Joe: cake and ice cream man, the best teller of stories. How hurt I am to have suddenly lost you. Auntie Elaine: I wish I had read this book to you when you asked. I'm sorry I was afraid.

My just-like-real brothers and sisters: Manboo, Judy, Muffy, BeBe, Goldy, Pickle, Black Reg, Arsenio, Randy, Rachelle, and Herman Williams, all of the Davis family. Alvin Javis: rest, dear friend.

My greatest friends and most intimate congress: Liz Welch, who has known me from the first line and inspires me to be a better human; Jaynee L. Mitchell, who never lets me forget or get lost; Rachel Uranga, the best question-asker and heart mender I know; Daffodil J. Altan, my sister; and Walton M. Muyumba, who always picks up the phone and delivers profound intellect and humor.

Marie Brown nurtured and prodded and kept and taught me that eldership is a full-time job. Her encouragements and reality checks are largely the reason why this book exists today. Deb Shriver appeared (always fashionably chic) at crucial times and did everything she promised. Dale Djerassi's allyship and friendship nurture me and inspire me to dream beyond. Gratitude to my *Oprah Magazine* family, my first true writing home. J. J. Miller, Nick Leiber, and Tari Ayala lit a path. Pat Towers taught me discretion and nurtured my love of reading aloud during countless midnight galley-reading sessions. Thank you for teaching me to write stronger sentences. Amy Gross gave me the shot and the advice I needed to keep earning more of them. Thanks to Gayle King for her support and early investment of time.

My writing teachers throughout the years: Karen Braziller and her amazing coterie of writers like Daphne Beale and Catherine McKinley. Hettie Jones in whose 92nd Street Y workshop I first began writing formally about my best childhood friend, Alvin; and Joyce Johnson, under whose careful tutelage I continued. Cynthia Gorney, Michael Pollan, and Mark Danner were my writing professors at UC–Berkeley, along with the late Clay Felker who rammed into my head three words I shall never forget: point of view. My work with Gail Sheehy taught me how to organize and put together a book. Amy Hertz gave me my first (and only) book-editing gig, which kept me on the right side of the fence. Abigail Thomas, one of our great writers, invited me into her home and into one of the warmest circles of writers I have known.

My incredible and reality-checking agent Jin Auh at Wylie signed me in 2005 to write this book, then waited six years for the proposal. More than an agent, she's an incredible editor, necessary grounding force and friend. The Grove team who believed: Amy Hundley, Elisabeth Schmitz, Morgan Entrekin, Deb Seager, Justina Batchelor, Sal Destro, Julia Berner-Tobin, and Gretchen Mergenthaler. Designer Alison Forner made iconic cover art. Scott Ellison-Smith, photographer, friend, humanist, edited the photographs. Michael Taeckens, a great human and publicist, took me and my work on.

Judy Stone pored over every single word of this manuscript (sometimes with only one eye working!), and prodded—with clarity and brilliance—until I faced in the right direction. David Remnick took my out-of-the-blue call and accepted my pitch to write something for *The New Yorker*'s Katrina anniversary issue, which gave me an incredible psychic boost and refocused my work. The *Oxford American* feels like home and published early snatches when I was still finding the story.

Research assistant Lisa Brown, then a Tulane undergraduate, transcribed hours and hours of Broom family interviews for a pittance, trusting that one day it would become something. My favorite geographer, Richard Campanella, literally rode alongside me, narrating long eastern-winding drives. He has helped me see and integrate the disparate pieces in ways I otherwise might not have. This book needed all of the books he has written.

So many have watched me grow up in the course of writing this book. Sarah Dohrmann met me in Burundi just like she said she would. Adam Shemper, my southern brother, has accompanied me with compassionate, rigorous inquiry into mind and heart. Bilen Mesfin urged me to apply for a job in Hong Kong and has always been my steady warming light. Poppy Garance Burke, Chee Gates, Randa Chahine, Shea Owens, Christina and Paul Graff, Kim Roth, Maggie Cammer, Louise Braverman and Steven Glickel: thanks for keeping the faith. Other artist friends in the struggle and fight: Jamey Hatley, Robin Beth Schaer, Kiese Laymon who read and read me, Jana Martin, Evo Love and Romaine Gateau, Heidi Julavits, Leo Treitler, Marco Villalobos, Linda Villarosa, Jami Attenberg, and Maurice Carlos Ruffin.

∞

My cousins: Bryant Wesco, Michelle Wesco, Lisa Trask, Edward Wesco, Pamela Broom, and all the others. My more than fifty nieces and nephews who always know the right name to call. Melvin and Brittany Broom who also grew up in the Yellow House and Alexus Broom who spent her early life on the short end of the street—love you all down deep.

For the future: my niece Amelia Miriam Gueye. You'll always be the baby on my hip at the party. I love you. Bella Grace D'Arcangelo in whom I see so much of myself: you reach and inspire me.

I started making scratches and scribbles toward this book shortly after leaving New Orleans for college, more than two decades ago. This book was formally begun at one of my favorite places on earth, the Djerassi Residents Artist Program in Woodside, California; continued at the Mac-Dowell Colony in New Hampshire; UCROSS and Jentel in Wyoming; and I-Park in East Haddam, Connecticut. A year of it was written during a fellowship at the William Steeples Davis House in Orient, New York. Pieces of it were written in New Orleans; Paris (over eight visits); Cambridge, Massachusetts; Raceland, Louisiana; Rome; Milan; Los Angeles; New York City; the Catskill Mountains; London; Kenya; Uganda; Israel; Dominica; Washington, D.C.; Laos; Cambodia; Vietnam; Egypt; Berlin; Istanbul; Burundi; and places I've now forgotten or wanted to forget.

Immense thanks to Courtney Hodell and the Whiting foundation for awarding me the inaugural creative nonfiction grant, which buoyed and spurred me through the final draft of this book.

Visual artists and friends Mary Frank, Joan Snyder, and Myrna Burks invited me into their studios over and over again. For the many spiritual (and spirited!) conversations about process and art and family and grief—over the best bourbon.

And finally,

My One: Diandrea Earnesta Rees, for the most incredible accompaniment of my life. Without you, I would never have finished this book. You, artist, make me know. You are the wish and all I never knew to wish for. I love you. I see you. I admire you fellow f.a.c. Keep busting the sky open. No home absent you.

# Photographs

*A*ll images courtesy of Sarah M. Broom and the Broom family except where indicated.

p. iii: Dedication

(top): Amelia Lolo Gant Williams

(bottom left): Elaine Soule Wesco

(bottom right): Ivory Mae Soule Broom

p.18: A young Amelia Gant, Magnolia Studio.

p. 22: (left): Joseph Gant at junior high school graduation, Magnolia Studio.

p. 22: (middle): Elaine Soule (l), Queen of McDonogh 36, with classmate in 1946.

p. 22: (right): Fourteen year old Ivory Mae Soule in 1956 at eighth grade graduation, Magnolia Studio.

p. 26: Women riding in a parade.

p. 38: Edward Webb and Ivory Mae after their wedding, September 1958.

p. 40: Ivory Mae on Roman Street.

p. 47: A young Simon Broom.

p. 50: Eddie, Michael, and Darryl Webb as young boys on Dryades Street.